Cyber Alert

Cyber Alert

How the World is Under Attack from a New Form of Crime

Peter Warren and Michael Streeter

First published in 2005 by Vision Paperbacks,
a division of Satin Publications Ltd.
101 Southwark Street
London SE1 OJF
UK
info@visionpaperbacks.co.uk
www.visionpaperbacks.co.uk
Publisher: Sheena Dewan

A catalogue record for this book is available from the British Library.

ISBN: 1-904132-62-6
2 4 6 8 10 9 7 5 3 1

Cover and text design by ok?design
Printed and bound in the UK by Mackays of Chatham Ltd,
Chatham, Kent

CONTENTS

ACKNOWLEDGEMENTS

Our thanks first of all to our agent Chelsey Fox for her encourage-
ment and patience, Charlotte Cole at Vision for her guidance and of
course our families for their forbearance.

Many people have been interviewed in the research of this book or
have made information available to us; our deepest thanks to all of
them, including those who, for reasons of confidence and security,
cannot be named here.

Among those we can name we would especially like to thank
Detective Chief Superintendent Len Hynds of the National Hi-Tech
Crime Squad in London; Felicity Bull, the Unit's Corporate
Communications Manager; and the unit team, who agreed to be
interviewed and were so patient with our questions: Inspector Marc
Kirby, Detective Constable Tony Neate, senior analyst Helen
Saunders and Detective Constable Steve Adams.

At the FBI we would particularly like to express our gratitude to
Dave Thomas, John Gillies and Neal Schiff for their tremendous help
and co-operation.

In addition, special thanks to Professor Neil Barrett and Peter
Sommer, who have put up with a lot of questioning over the years
and done so very patiently, and also to John Austen, Mark Morris,
Simon Janes and Simon Davies. A particular thank you to the staff of
the cuttings libraries of the *Daily Express*, *The Sunday Times* and *The
Scotsman*, plus to Philip Swinburne, Edward Venning, Paul
Strassman, Steve Linford, Hans Hubner, Fungus the Bogeyman,
Eugene Schultz, Wendy Woolford, David Lacey, Patrick Tyrrell, Mike

Corcoran, David Pincott, John Regnault, Peter Tippett, Malcolm Skinner, Katherine James, Graeme Pinkney, Kevin Hogan, (in alphabetical order) Dr Andrew Blyth and Dr Andrew Jones, Sandra Quinn, Des Drury, Richard Starnes.

Thanks also to Bob Jones, chairman of Interpol's European Working Party on IT Crime and Technical Manager of the Computer Related Crime Research Centre, Queen Mary, University of London, for his invaluable guidance and assistance; Marc Blanchard and David Emm of Kaspersky Lab for their observations; Mikko Hyppönen of F-Secure; risk consultant Roger Miles for his invaluable insight; and Terry Sullivan for his views on spamming. We also express our gratitude to Helen Martin, editor of Virus Bulletin, for her support and VB's consultant Matthew Ham for giving up so much of his valuable time. Finally, but not least, thanks also to Vladimir A Golubev, Director of Computer Crime Research Center (CCRC) in the Ukraine; Robert Schifreen; Kevin Mitnick; Jaron Lanier; Graeme Newman; Frederic Forsyth; and Andy Mueller-Maguhn.

INTRODUCTION
A New World of Crime

At the time, British Prime Minister Tony Blair and his team of close advisers had plenty to keep them occupied. In early 1999, barely two years into the new government's first term, issues of health, education and crime were looming large, exactly how to handle the problematic subject of the Millennium Bug was causing headaches and United Nations weapons inspectors had just withdrawn from Iraq: in hindsight the start of a slow countdown to war.

However, soon Blair and his security staff had one more pressing issue to deal with.

It happened by chance, during a routine monitor of the complex computer network. The high-tech security team could scarcely believe their eyes, yet here was the proof in front of them. The security apparatus on the computer network registered an intruder alert. Someone had been hacking Downing Street, the heart of British government, and for some time, too. This wasn't some random computer joyride by a 'script kiddie' as young hackers are sometimes disparagingly known. This intruder, whoever it was, knew just what he was doing and knew how to lie undetected for some time.

But now, with lightning speed, the attacker had cut like a laser through the expensive and complex encryption system that was supposed to deter such assaults and homed in on the target. Before anyone had been aware of it the intruder had rapidly downloaded some files and then vanished back into the black hole of cyber space just as quickly as he had arrived.

The security guards who had discovered the intrusion were not sure what astonished them most: the sheer audacity and boldness of a full-frontal attack on a computer in Downing Street; the speed with which it had evidently occurred; the fact that the intruder had escaped detection for so long; or the remarkably easy way in which the attacker had overcome the encryption system. Could this be an inside job?

Within minutes of the discovery a full-scale internal inquiry was launched, though details of the unprecedented security breaches have remained a closely guarded secret until now. Among those involved were, of course, the security services (notably specialist staff at GCHQ from Cheltenham), Downing Street officials and senior staff at Cable & Wireless, who were managing the Downing Street communications network.

Their initial attempts to trace the source of the hack proved unsurprisingly fruitless, the trail running cold when it was found the attacks had been launched from a computer using a mobile phone line. The investigators later found that the cyber assault originated somewhere in the former Soviet Union, probably Russia, though even now details about this remain sparse. The information apparently seen and taken by the intruder was not sensitive, though its loss was hugely embarrassing; and there were still some more red faces to come. During a massive overhaul of security of the supposedly impregnable Whitehall network that followed this incident in early 1999, investigators found that fibre-optic cables linking directly into the secure system had been left sticking out of a hole in the ground on a street.

Yet more experts – including a former hacker – were called in from the world of computer security to run so-called penetration tests to make sure that the Downing Street and Whitehall networks were safe once more.

To this day no one is quite sure what lay behind this mysterious and sophisticated hacking attack.

Some in the close-knit computer security industry have suggested it was linked to a hack attack called Moonlight Maze, an incident that like so many before and since has passed into hacker folklore.

Moonlight Maze was supposedly a massive penetration of the US Department of Defence by Russian hackers whose existence eventually came to light by 1999. Information lines used by the hackers involved the dumping of information at a site in the UK. In a Congressional hearing two years before, the Deputy Secretary of Defense John Hamre had warned of an 'electronic Pearl Harbor' and went on to imply that Russian hackers were stealing vital US information via the internet.

The very existence of Moonlight Maze has attracted massive derision from hackers, who see it as a myth perpetuated by the intelligence community to justify an increase in their already large funding. Yet according to a well-placed British source, the data being moved in Moonlight Maze was both considerable and important. He told us: 'We worked with some of the US technical people to put together a box that imaged the information as it passed through the system, and were surprised to see things like fighter plane and cockpit design passing through.' He says this hacking was sourced back to Russia although, eventually, because of the political implications, it was left for senior diplomats and ministers to handle. Whether the mysterious Number 10 hack was itself linked to the events of Moonlight Maze remains simply conjecture.

Meanwhile, a few years later, a woman named Nancy used a call centre in Texas, which, as usual, recorded certain of her personal details on a computer. There was nothing unusual in this; Nancy had used call centres many times before, and had never had any problems. This time, however, something went wrong, so horribly wrong it was to make her life a misery for the next two years.

Another woman, also called Nancy – we will call her Nancy2 – had hacked into the call centre database and pulled up Nancy1's details. The next step was child's play. Armed with key facts about Nancy1's life, Nancy2 got hold of her social security number and took over the woman's identity. From now on there were two women of the same name with the same digital life.

Up to that point Nancy1, a teacher, had held a faultless credit history and lived a quiet life in a neat suburban house, set on a pretty little lawn in a modest Pennsylvanian town. Now, however, all that was to change. First it was the credit cards and trying to get loans. For the first time in her life Nancy1 was refused a credit card and told she was ineligible for a small home improvement loan she wanted to take out.

Horrified, Nancy1 took it up with the authorities and discovered that she was a credit risk. It seems her alter ego, Nancy2, had been racking up credit card bills and spending money like it was going out of fashion, all using Nancy1's digital identity. The authorities were informed and eventually Nancy2 was arrested and charged with fraud. Nancy1 breathed a sigh of relief forward to getting back her life – and good name – again. But to her horror she realised that once her digital persona had gained a bad reputation, it was almost impossible to remove it.

It seemed that the computers of a Texan car company had her down as a bad debtor and that information was passed onto the credit reference agency Experian. Other disgruntled companies had done the same thing, all thanks to Nancy2's crime spree, and Nancy1 now had a bad credit history with Equifax, TransUnion and another seven other credit agencies across the US.

In an attempt to restore her reputation, Nancy1 got the help of the US' Identity Theft Resource Centre and her credit history was monitored daily by a company called ID Analytics, and some of the damage was repaired.

But there was yet more bad news to come. To make extra money, Nancy2 had sold on Nancy1's credit card details to criminals around the US, causing her records to get confused and corrupted all over the country and meaning that even her cleaned-up credit records could get tainted once more. To make matters even worse, Nancy1 then learnt that her namesake was using the hacked credit card details even while she was awaiting sentence on the original frauds.

Understandably the teacher feels both helpless and furious in the face of such events.

'How can she allowed to keep on interfering with my life like this?' she complains. 'It has completely devastated my life.

'I have begun to realise that as a person I am only as good and only as safe as the digital record that society keeps on me. It's just so scary.'

On the other side of the world, in February 2004, a young British photography student called Matt Glen finally managed to track down the digital camera of his dreams. For months he had been searching for a Canon EOS 10D, a high-spec piece of kit favoured by professionals, at a price that he could afford with his 21st birthday money. Now he had found such a camera on eBay, the hugely popular international auction site.

The current bidding on the auction was £300, a mere fraction of the £1,800 this camera would sell for in a store, though Glen knew that as the auction process came to a conclusion the price would rise rapidly. In the meantime Glen had emailed the seller for full details about the camera and to reassure himself about that person's bona fides. The student was happy to see that the seller had a good online rating from previous satisfied customers and even happier when the person emailed him to say if Glen would bid £900 for the camera he could have it there and then. In fact, as the price rose steadily online, the pair agreed on £1,000; a sizeable sum but just within Glen's reach and still a huge bargain compared with the usual retail price.

It was agreed, at the seller's request, that Glen would send the money via Western Union and that the vendor, who had a London address, would use his passport as identity to collect the money. The process cost Glen another £50, as Western Union checked his own credentials as well as ensuring that the recipient of the money – the seller – would have the correct ID at the correct Western Union office. Eventually on 9 February the money was transferred, and Glen sat back and waited for his camera to arrive.

And waited, and waited. Eventually a week after the money had been sent an email arrived from the man to whom Glen had sent the money. Or rather, a message from the email account used by the man. It turned out that this latest message was from the true owner of the email account and of the eBay account Glen had been dealing with, and 'he' was in fact a 'she' in Australia, who had not been able to get into either account for some time. When she finally did regain entry, she found a number of emails from people such as Glen, who had sent money for goods bought via eBay and who now demanded to know where on earth the products were. The answer to this was now fairly clear; even if the items had ever existed there was no chance they would ever be delivered to Glen or any of the other victims who had handed over money for them. It appeared that the 'seller' had assumed the identity of the innocent Australian woman's email and eBay accounts, had offered for sale high-value goods that were sure to sell quickly, and had then disappeared with the money. Along the way he had managed to create an ID for himself via a fake Italian ID card which he used at the Western Union office; apparently he had used at least one other name, also convincing enough to satisfy the vigilant staff at Western Union, when dealing with another victim.

As Glen, who was now nearly £1,000 poorer as a result of the fraud, recalls, the conman had known how to attract victims. 'He had chosen someone with a really good seller rating as well to encourage trust from buyers like myself and had all the answers I could want,' says Glen. 'The reason I thought it was safe was because he was able to answer all my questions.'

Just a few months before Glen's unfortunate experience, one of Britain's largest and most respected financial organisations itself had cause to wonder at the ingenuity of the criminal mind. At precisely 11.15 on the morning of 25 October 2003, Halifax's popular online banking website at www.halifax-online.co.uk was the victim of a cyber attack[1]. Criminals – ultimately traced to somewhere inside Russia – had set up a fake Halifax website and started emailing the bank's customers to direct them to this 'cuckoo' site. The intention of the conmen was simplicity itself: to persuade customers to reveal their bank account names, numbers and passwords online and then to plunder their accounts of cash. The capturing and reeling in of cyber victims like this is called 'phishing', a typical computer-land inspired variation on the word 'fishing'. Some 400 customers had contacted the bank to query the unexpected emails and the site. Halifax immediately emailed its other customers to warn them about the scam and then took down the site for 36 hours so that it could, in the words of a spokesman, 'crawl all over it' to see what lessons could be learnt.

Fortunately, because of the poor quality of the imitative site and of the basic language used in the emails, customers were too suspicious to hand over details and there were on this occasion no reports of losses. However the bank and other financial institutions now knew for certain one thing; the phishing wars had started.

The examples just given may at first glance seem very different, involving subjects ranging from government to an individual to a company. What they all share, however, is a common characteristic: all involve victims of cyber crime. They therefore serve to highlight one of the most important but often overlooked issues facing civilised society around the world today; how in an increasingly digital world can we protect ourselves from a massive increase in cyber crime? Whether we are in government, a private citizen or part of a corporate body, we are all now vulnerable as never before to a new breed of crime, in some cases to a new breed of criminal.

Crime is of course nothing new. Humankind has suffered and perpetrated crime ever since the first caveman stole a neighbour's log to put on his fire. And doubtless crime will be with us for as long as we live and breathe on this planet. Yet crime today – or at least cyber crime – is significantly different from what has gone before. A young man sitting in front of a modest PC in the Philippines can cause tens of millions of pounds of damage around the world by the relatively simple means of releasing a computer virus onto the internet. Elsewhere an organised gang of cyber criminals in, say, a former Soviet Union state is launching 'phishing' attacks on unsuspecting bank customers around the Western world, stealing their passwords, account numbers and ultimately their money.

Meanwhile out of Africa comes a torrent of emails beseeching recipients for help in releasing vast funds tied up in foreign bank accounts, in return for a share of the proceeds, the only 'catch' being that the victims may have to pay some modest fee upfront or hand over details of their own bank accounts to help in the process. Or a betting firm may find its website under threat from some cyber toughies in another country, who have vowed to put its site out of action – known in the jargon as a denial of service (DoS) – before a big sporting event such as the famous British horse races the Grand National or the Derby unless they are paid off.

What unites these crimes is that they can all be perpetrated from an apparently safe distance, from a different and possibly less rigorous legal system than the one in which the victim lives and the crime takes place. The reach of the skilful criminal has always been long. With the use of computers and the internet that reach can be infinite, indeed literally beyond this world. In one case, discussed later in this book, hackers actually succeeded in moving a satellite in orbit. Never before have so few criminals being able to commit so many crimes at such distance. The remoteness of much of cyber crime is one of its most distinctive features, and one of the reasons it can be so hard to detect and fight.

Though it is not a central theme of this book, there is also a geopolitical edge to this new wave of crime. As the earlier examples show it is increasingly common for criminals to hide behind less robust legal systems and law enforcement agencies in the developing world, to prey on victims in the wealthier digital world of the West. It is yet one more task – in a world already fighting terrorism – for the law enforcement agencies and governments of the developed world to ensure that their counterparts elsewhere are able to deal effectively with cyber criminals who seek to hide from the consequences of their actions.

An issue often debated in the world of computer security is whether cyber crimes are really new crimes at all, or whether they are just 'traditional' crimes wrapped up in gigabytes and modems. The answer is both yes and yes. Many of the crimes that we outline in this book are clearly just variations of old crimes brought up to date by the use of computers and the internet. Identity theft, for example – stealing someone's personal details to impersonate them for financial gain – is as old a criminal ploy as they come. Theft and fraud with the aid of computers and the web are in the end still simply theft and fraud, whatever the technicalities of how they are carried out.

Some crimes, however, seem to defy this reasoning. Consider the example of computer viruses. These often malicious programmes can spiral their way around the world's computer networks and emails, causing huge cost and disruption to both companies and private individuals alike; and yet they may come from the computer of one person working alone in front of a PC. It is said sometimes that virus writing is a little like graffiti writing; in other words an act of vandalism by a (usually) young man seeking attention. Yet when a kid spray-paints a wall or a fence, he knows precisely what damage he is causing and to whom. A virus writer unleashes his little programme of misery upon the world not knowing or apparently caring who or what he will damage, and on what scale. It is therefore hard to find a convincing parallel for computer virus writing in non-digital crime, and it may thus be regarded as a new form of crime.

Ultimately of course it is less important whether the new wave of cyber crime sweeping around the world are truly new crimes or old ones dressed up in modern form. What really matters is that these crimes and the people behind them are exploiting ever more ingeniously the loopholes and vulnerabilities that exist in our digital world.

Partly this stems from a reluctance by some governments to respond to the growing threat. Politicians generally have a poor grasp of matters technological (British MPs working on the E-Commerce Bill had to be sent away on a two-week crash course to learn about computers), and are usually slow to observe and react to trends; or they react to them in a heavy-handed manner that alienates law-abiding cyber users more than they disturb criminals. Meanwhile it is often claimed that our vulnerability to certain forms of cyber crime – for example, viruses – stems from the sloppy or greedy development of software by corporations that have carelessly left us all wide open to attack; a claim they naturally and strenuously deny. Perhaps inevitably that powerful and much-derided technological giant Microsoft bears the brunt of such criticism.

Yet the prime reason why the Western world is now fighting a largely unseen battle against cyber crime is simply because of the way in which technology has come to dominate our lives. Very few of us in the modern world live outside the grasp of the Digital Society. Many of us now have bank accounts either with traditional banks or with new bespoke web-based financial organisations that offer us speed and convenience in our financial transactions that would have been unthinkable even a generation ago. Even if most of us do not yet bank using the internet, many more of us have sold or more likely bought goods over the internet and a large number of us are starting to do so regularly. The total value of e-commerce in the UK in 2003 was £39.5 billion[2], while internet sales to shoppers was estimated at £15 billion for 2004[3]. By comparison, total UK high street retail sales were £19 billion for October 2004 alone[4].

Whether it is ordering our groceries online, buying books, shopping for software or using the services of online dating agencies, more and more of us are appreciating the speed and immediacy of using what is sometimes called 'etailing' (one of the many unattractive words that seem to dominate the world of technology). But we do not even have to be active users of etailing and internet banking to be caught up in the digital word. So many details are held in digital form in computer databases in various parts of society. Even such seemingly innocent information as our full names, date and or place of birth, perhaps our mother's maiden name; all these are almost certain to be logged, somewhere, by someone on a database for wholly innocent and beneficial reasons. More obviously sensitive information such as our national insurance or social security numbers, our driving license details, email account passwords, the numbers of our passports or – depending which country we live in – our national identity card details are all likely to be stored somewhere.

The point here is that in a digital world we all leave our digital traces – or digital fingerprints, if you like – in various places, even if often we are blissfully unaware of it. To paraphrase the cult TV programme *The Prisoner*, we may want to be more than just a number but, as far as a digital world is concerned, that is precisely what we are – mere data.

This development has of course brought us many advantages. The legitimate retrieval of data can be – at least when computer systems are working properly – much, much faster than old-fashioned paper-based systems. Whole aspects of bureaucracy such as going to the doctor, arranging hospital appointments, checking on benefits payments, applying for passports and other documents should be much faster and less painful than in the past.

This process would only increase if authorities introduce identity cards using biometric details. Biometric means making use of our highly individual physical forms to produce a unique set of information that can refer to one person and one person only: you. This may be our irises, fingerprints or even the shape of our heads. (The inside of our skulls occupies a unique space; by bouncing ultrasound around in our head that space can be mapped and recorded.) The US is already demanding that visitors include a machine-readable biometric in their passports, and the UK and other countries in Europe are rapidly expected to follow.

We can expect our digital footprints in society to grow ever larger and ever more visible in the years and decades to come. And as already stated, this will undoubtedly bring us many benefits. This will come at a price, however. For what is also clear – and this is one of the main themes of this book – is that our development into an information, data-driven society has also massively increased the scope for those who want to use this data for bad ends. In other words, as we evolve into a cyber society and as the internet becomes more embedded into the way we live our daily lives, we are also at the dawn of a golden era for cyber crime.

As Phil Williams, professor of International Security Studies at the University of Pittsburgh[5], wrote recently: 'The capabilities and opportunities provided by the internet have transformed many legitimate business activities, augmenting the speed, ease and range with which transactions can be conducted, while also lowering many of the costs. Criminals have also discovered that the internet can provide new opportunities and multiplier benefits for illicit business.'

It is clear from the above comment that many people on the right side of the law have woken up to this critical development and are pushing for greater and more determined efforts to combat cyber crime. In the United States, for example, after a slow start the public is becoming more aware of the issue of identity theft committed using computers and the internet. For its part, the Federal Bureau of Investigation (FBI) is acutely aware of the dangers of cyber crime and especially its economic impact. Dave Thomas, chief of Computer Intrusion Division at the FBI's Cyber Division, says:

> *The area of greatest concern for us is the attacks on the financial sector and e-commerce, because that is where it has the greatest effect on us; we're losing money, we're losing credit cards, we're losing databases of personal information that are used for identity theft. Our number one criminal priority is attacks against the financial sector.*

In the United Kingdom, meanwhile, the National High-Tech Crime Unit (NHTCU) is a newly formed group of elite police and technical investigators whose sole role it is to combat cyber crime in the UK, whether it comes from inside or outside the country. In Russia there is the exotically named Spider Group (whose uniform emblem sports the image of a spider, representing the worldwide web), the special department 'K' at the Ministry of Internal Affairs, whose task it is to tackle what is seen as a rapidly rising problem of cyber crime there. Yet while these and other Western countries such as Australia have established robust units aimed at locating and catching cyber criminals, these groups are still not well resourced in comparison with other law enforcement agencies.

Meanwhile governments and public opinion in general have been slow to appreciate the new demands and responsibilities that living in a digital world place on us. Even where governments have reacted well there have usually been civil liberties groups who have, for the best of motives, sought to limit the role of the state in cyber communications. In the 'real' world it is common practice for people to take care of their tangible possessions and their documents. Unless we live in a relatively crime-free rural area, we would not dream of leaving our car unlocked while we went off to a shop, neither would we leave our home without ensuring it was safely bolted. We are similarly careful about where we leave our cheque book, credit cards, jewellery or cash. Such precautions are almost second nature.

Moreover we expect our governments to reinforce these safety measures and educate us in new ways of 'old' crime prevention.

Yet when it comes to protecting our digital identities we are far less aware and far less safety conscious. We leave digital data around us carelessly. Passwords for email or even bank accounts may be stored in easily accessible files on our computers. The 'doors' to those same computers – the ports through which data is transmitted – are often left open for any passing hacker or virus to come in and see what is worth stealing or destroying. Basic protection systems such as antivirus software – cheaper and usually more effective than burglar alarms – are either absent or not updated.

To take just one of many thousands of examples: one elderly man in France recently bought his first computer and went online with a high-speed broadband connection so that he could email relatives and friends around the world. Later he was amazed to discover – from a cyber crime investigator – that his computer had been used for months by 'spammers' to send millions of junk emails – 'spam' – all around the world. He had simply no idea this could happen and had no internet or computer security.

On the internet or in the real world, we are often too casual in giving out other vital bits of information about us; information that if put together by resourceful criminals can be used to steal our identity and then our money.

This information might be our date of birth, our full address, our full name or a host of other small snippets of information used to build a counterfeit picture of us.

What is needed is a culture of good security with our personal data and how we store and protect it; what might be termed 'digital hygiene'. If we apply good digital hygiene and look after our information, it will certainly help deter the opportunist cyber criminal. As yet, though, there is little sign of governments overtly urging their citizens to improve our digital security.

Graeme Newman, an academic at the University at Albany, New York, and an expert on cyber crime and crime prevention in general, points out that for a period car criminals were ahead of their counterparts in crime prevention and were able to steal vehicles seemingly at will. Then the car industry and law enforcement agencies began to work closer together, immobilisers and other security devices were fitted and now it has become relatively hard to steal newer cars. The result? Newman explains: 'We are now starting to see offenders who, instead of trying to steal a car by beating its technology, go the identity theft route. They figure that if they can steal someone's identity they can buy or rent a car in that name and conceal their own identity.' Here is an example of criminals finding life tougher in older, well-protected areas of crime and opting instead to use computer and internet techniques to commit identity theft to achieve the same aims – but with greater ease and far less risk.

In the United States, recent figures suggest that ID theft costs businesses and consumers around $50 billion a year. At the moment it seems that our ability to develop a digital world has not been matched by our ability to make it safe, or rather our awareness of the need to make it safe. Currently we are behaving like a group of 19th-century city slickers, who ride into a Wild West town, tie their horses up to the nearest post and then later wonder at the fact that they have all been stolen. Cyber space – that strange world of virtual reality existing somewhere, somehow within reach of millions of computers – has often been likened to a frontier land, a kind of worldwide wild west, with all the opportunities and dangers that that implies. The more we are aware of such risks the more we are likely to be prepared for them.

To give some idea at the staggering rise in crime involving computers and the internet, one has only to glance at the figures provided by the Computer Emergency Response Team (CERT)[6], based in the United States and regarded as one of the gold-standard information sources for computer related crime. Its figures for reported attacks on computers – for example, hacking and viruses – tell their own story. In 1988 when CERT was formed by the US government's Defense Advanced Research Projects Agency (DARPA), the number of attacks – in what was admittedly not a full year of activity – was eight. In 1989 and 1990 the figures were respectively 132 and 252 reported incidents. In a decade this had risen to 21,756 in the year 2000 and by 2003 the figure had risen to a colossal 137,529 reported incidents. If one considers that one incident could have affected tens, scores or even many thousands of individual computers, and that these are just the figures for *reported* incidents, then one can begin to see the vast and multiplying scale of the problem.

So far we have really just focused on some of the more obvious ways in which computers and the internet can be used to commit crimes. These include hacking, virus writing and identity theft. These crimes are in fact among the most major problems today in terms of cyber crime, and much of this book will be devoted to looking at them in greater detail. There are, however, a bewildering number of different ways in which cyber crime – the use of computers and or the internet to perpetrate offences – can be used. Graeme Newman, together with fellow academic Ronald V Clarke of Rutgers University, New Jersey, has written *Superhighway Robbery: Preventing E-commerce Crime*[7] as part of a crime series edited by Gloria Laycock, director of the Jill Dando Institute of Crime Science in London[8]. In the course of this academic tome the authors identify a vast range of what they term computer-assisted crime. As well as hacking and viruses, this includes many other crimes that can be committed or aided with the use of a computer and the internet.

Among these are stalking and harassment, serious offences that have hit the headlines all around the world in recent years – notably in the case of celebrity stalkers – but that have not usually been linked in the public mind with the internet or computers. Yet while cyber stalking may not be well known, one of the organisations that monitors them, CyberAngels.org, estimates that in 2000 alone there were some 3,000 internet stalkers worldwide. Given the rapid growth in the number of web users since then, it is reasonable to assume this figure may be much higher now. One case involving cyber stalking that came to court was reported in Edinburgh-based newspaper the *Scotsman* on 21 December 2002. It described how a British man Christopher Kell, aged 37 and originally from Cumbria in north west England, was gaoled by a Canadian court for what the paper described as a 'cyber-terror campaign'. Kell had had a relationship with a Canadian woman whom he met virtually in an internet literature chatroom. For a while they had a 'real-world' romance in France. When the relationship ended Kell then bombarded the woman with emails, faxes and letters. Ultimately he pleaded guilty at the court in Steinbach, Manitoba and received a two-year gaol term.

A full category of computer-assisted crimes identified by Newman and Clarke is as follows:

- theft of telephone services
- video piracy
- software piracy
- copyright
- vandalism (damage caused by virus attacks)
- spying and industrial espionage
- terrorism
- fraudulent transfer of electronic funds
- hacking
- denial of service (DoS)
- cross-border crime
- extortion and/or blackmail
- cloning of mobile phone and phone cards
- credit card fraud
- accounting fraud
- stalking
- harassment
- money laundering
- investment fraud
- telemarketing fraud
- sale of stolen goods
- identity theft
- gambling
- tax evasion
- conspiracy
- aiding and abetting crime

This list of computer-aided crimes is a formidable one when written out in full, though it should be remembered that many of the offences above are old, well-established crimes simply taking advantage of new technology. It is also at the same time a useful reminder of how many areas of society depend on electronically stored data, computers and the internet, and how fast criminals have been to use technology themselves. We are often told that we now live in the Information Age; in this new age the old adage that time is money perhaps should give way to a new one: *information* is money. Once we accept the idea that most of our information either is or will be stored digitally, we should not be surprised that criminals are already hard at work discovering how to intercept, hack into or trick their way to those sources of information.

As stated earlier, crime has always been with us. Yet in the case of cyber crime there is an additional element to consider; the philosophy advanced by many early users of computers and the internet, that the computer and the worldwide web are things of beauty in themselves, machines and places to be explored, understood and shared. To them computers and the net were not – and some still say *are* not – about ownership, commerce and the storing of valuable individual or corporate data. While such early users may not quite have gone as far as the Marxist doctrine that all property is theft, they were certainly bitterly opposed to the corporate and governmental exploitation of these new technologies by companies and states. It was this philosophy, seductively attractive if rather innocent and naïve at the same time, that was ultimately to lead to what we might now regard as cyber crime.

Though it would be wrong to blame these early pioneers for today's explosion of cyber crime – criminals have little need for philosophical justifications for what they do – these views and actions did help to forge a path down which less savoury elements were to follow.

CHAPTER ONE

The Rise of the Cyber Criminal

THE AGE OF INNOCENCE

In the beginning, hackers hacked computers because they could and because they wanted to explore systems that were new and different. The same was true of phone 'phreaking', that strange phenomenon by which teenagers and college students learnt to manipulate telephone networks using a variety of bizarre techniques, including whistling. It was all simply a 'game'. Yet soon the lines between what was hacking according to the accepted original definition, and what was criminal activity, began to become blurred. This confusion was caused not just by hackers and 'cyber criminals' but also by the authorities and law-makers, who struggled to come to terms with new technology, and a series of old laws that seemed inadequate to deal with what appeared to be new 'crimes'.

Phone phreaking

The transition from old-style 'hacking' to criminality in fact started through the spread of phone phreaking, which was popular in the United States in the late 1960s and early 1970s. The idea of hacking around phone systems had always fascinated computer hackers. One of the early and most talented of telephone hackers was Massachusetts Institute of Technology (MIT) student Stewart Nelson, who knew his way around the Bell telephone system better than most people (including most of the experts at Bell). For hackers such as Nelson the exploration of telephone networks was intellectually stimulating and educational, as well as being enjoyable. They could hack into the phone system, travelling electronically around the world and talking to operators in different countries and even on occasions pointing out technical faults to phone companies. While the 'true' hackers were exploring the telephone networks – at this time in the 1960s there was no internet to explore – other students were using devices to make free telephone calls for practical, financial reasons. Effectively they were ripping off the telephone companies, a practice of which true hackers such as Nelson disapproved. Yet in the early days such actions were on a small scale, confined to a few students, and nobody took much notice.

One of the people credited with making phone phreaking a popular pastime was Joe Engressia, a blind mathematics student at the University of South Florida. Among other abilities Engressia had the gift of perfect pitch and discovered from childhood that by whistling he could imitate the 2,600-hertz command tone used by telephone company engineers to control the networks. Though he was not aware of the full implications of such technicalities at the age of eight, by the time he was at college he had been nicknamed 'the Whistler' and had become obsessed by telephone networks, in particular with hacking into the network of telephone giant Ma Bell (later to become AT&T).

Another Ma Bell hacker was John Draper, who in 1968 had been honourably discharged from the US Air Force following a tour of duty in Vietnam. Unlike Engressia, Draper did not have perfect pitch, but he did stumble across a curious fact in a cereal packet. Draper discovered that a toy whistle given away free with packets of Cap'n Crunch cereal could, with one hole covered, emulate the same 2,600-hertz tone used by phone engineers. Armed with this curiosity Draper began to explore the networks himself, earning himself the nickname Cap'n Crunch along the way.

Little blue box
Both Draper and Engressia became compulsive phone phreakers and made full use of their knowledge of how to manipulate the phones. Draper also built the now infamous 'blue boxes', devices that illegally

manipulate phone networks, allowing users to make free calls. Although Draper insisted the blue boxes were only to be used by the new elite of technology whizz-kids innocently to explore the phone network and to discover new codes, the devices were copied by others and used for other purposes. His readiness to supply wiring diagrams to accomplices, which inevitably made their way onto bulletin boards and later websites, was evidence of a naivety that seemed to allow him and others to ignore the moral problem of taking something that was not theirs.

The activities of phone phreakers as Draper and Engressia became notorious in 1971 when *Esquire* magazine[1] ran a lengthy article detailing the phenomenon of phreaking and highlighting the cases of both Draper and Engressia[2]. Such publicity made phone phreaking appear glamorous, but the authorities were not impressed and neither were the phone companies. Both men were duly targeted. Draper was arrested and tried for illegally calling Sydney, Australia, and was given a suspended gaol sentence. Engressia was initially disciplined by university authorities, but was prosecuted after law enforcement officers raided his new home in Tennessee and confiscated his telephone. Engressia also received a suspended sentence and gave up phreaking. (He later moved to Minneapolis and changed his name to Joybubbles.)

Though on a small scale, this was the beginning of the criminalisation of hacking, the point at which society – and the state – drew a line in the sand and decided what was and was not legal in the strange world of telephone hacking. The conviction of phone hackers such as Draper (and there were similar trials of phreakers in England in the early 1970s) did not of course stop the practice. Indeed, the notion that such vast systems as telephone networks could be manipulated for financial gain attracted the attention of people who until this point had appeared largely uninterested in new technology: criminals.

Draper himself was not able to stop phreaking; hacking was in his blood and he continued to break the law. As he explained in the *Esquire* article, what he was doing was learning about a system. 'The phone company is a System. Do you understand? If I do what I do it is only to explore a System. That's my bag. The phone company is nothing but a computer,' he argued.

This reasoning would probably have met with the approval of the old MIT hackers, who were also interested in understanding so-called Systems. But it was of no interest to the criminals. What they cared about was whether this strange manipulation of a telephone network could make them money, give them power or provide valuable information. The exploits of people such as Draper clearly showed it could. Thus when Draper was targeted and convicted for a second time – in 1976 – for his phreaking compulsion, his subsequent experience of prison was eventful and instructive.

Despite his military background, apparently Draper had an unworldly air and seemed too wrapped up in technology to be able to cope with four months in the Lompoc Federal Prison in California. He desperately needed a survival technique and soon found one; he held impromptu phone-phreaking classes to fellow prisoners in the prison yard. This apparently saved him from several beatings, though he did reportedly turn down one approach by organised crime to work for it. Draper was later quoted as saying: 'I went out of my way to teach every criminal I came in contact with on how to do this.'

This information sharing marked a significant turning point. For the first time the world of technology and hacking had crossed paths with everyday criminality, and the smarter criminals liked what they saw. For example, drawn by the traditional criminal lure of getting something for nothing, the Vegas Syndicate of the US mafia asked one phone phreak to build a thousand devices for $300,000; it used the boxes to place bets undetected and free of charge.

Professor Neil Barrett of the Royal Military College of Science explains the significance of this cross-fertilisation between hacking and criminals. 'You had criminals, organised crime, gangsters in fact, who were able to communicate with fellow gangsters without paying money. But not only could they set up free phone-call services, they could also sell this service to other people.'

Professor Barrett adds: 'I've seen figures quoted for how much Draper cost the telephone network prior to his arrest but I have never seen anything for how much the cost was of the people that he trained. In terms of criminal use of computers this was the first hack.'

Such developments highlighted a trend that would hasten the ultimate use by criminals of hacking techniques. As more and more hackers were to face prison sentences for their activities, so the chances of cross-fertilisation inside gaol with hardened criminals increased. Criminals were becoming 'technologised'.

The greatest network of them all

The phone phreaking phenomenon turned out to be a dress rehearsal for the 1980s, the decade when hacking hit the headlines and when the authorities in the Western world began a determined attempt to criminalise hacking. The days of hacking innocence were over, a process further increased by the technological development of telephone networks. In the US these had become computerised as early as 1960. By the 1970s their operation was becoming increasingly reliant on the Unix operating system that was developed by AT&T Bell Laboratories at the end of the 1960s. To manipulate the phone system, therefore, hackers had to understand the language that the telephone network and computers talked in: Unix. This meant that hackers who became proficient in hacking telephone systems could also apply this skill base to computers and their own local networks. Ultimately this would allow them to hack using the greatest network of them all: the internet.

One of the first reported cases of a hacker being prosecuted involved a character who went by the colourful nickname of Captain Zap. Zap's real name was Ian A Murphy, a young American phone hacker who in 1981, with three others, was arrested and later convicted of breaking into the computer system of AT&T. According to reports, Murphy and the others changed the internal clocks of the computers; as a result some customers received evening discounts despite using their phone during the more expensive daytime period, while others who used the phone in the evenings were faced with unexpectedly large bills. As a result Murphy, AKA Captain Zap, received probation for two and a half years and was ordered to do one thousand hours of community service. The activities of Captain Zap are sometimes credited as one of the sources for the 1992 hacking movie *Sneakers*, starring Robert Redford, Sidney Poitier and the late River Phoenix.

Child's play

One eye-catching operation was carried out by a group of hackers known as 414, named after the area code of their home town Milwaukee. The 414 gang was a group of youngsters aged 16 to 22 who, during 1983, hacked its way into some 60 different computers around the United States. By far the most striking intrusion was into computers at the Los Alamos National Laboratory in New Mexico, a centre for nuclear weapons research.

Though no important data of information was accessed, the very idea that a bunch of (mostly) high-school kids could bust into such a centre sent shock waves through the security establishment. Another high-profile victim was the Memorial Sloan-Kettering Cancer Center in New York. The 414 gang gained access to a computer programme that contained details of the correct doses of radiation to be given to individual payments. Some data – fortunately none of it critical – was lost as a result of the hack, even though the financial cost was put at $1,500.

The young hackers had not, it seems, needed to be that ingenious or technically proficient in their hacking. It later transpired that they had simply been able to dial into their victim's computers using the old Telenet system (a telephone system that allowed people to dial directly into computers and bulletin boards) and exploit the fact that most of the systems had not changed their default passwords (that is, they had kept the initial password used by the manufacturer and system builder). Since these passwords are designed to be obvious, easy to remember and then to be changed to something much harder to crack, it made the work of these young hackers mere child's play.

Undoubtedly the system administrators bore some responsibility for leaving the doors to their computers if not open, then effectively unlocked. Not for the first time in the story of cyber crime, however, the young hackers justified their intrusions using immature logic. One unnamed supporter of the group was quoted: 'If this information is so confidential or so private, why is it accessible via Telenet? Why don't the system managers change the default passwords?' This is akin to a burglar claiming that the break-in they had just committed was solely the householder's fault for not fastening the windows securely enough. It is surely hard for anyone to justify breaking into a patient's cancer treatment files; though the young gang later claimed they did not know exactly where or what they had broken into.

The six-member 414 gang was later arrested by officers from the FBI; one was given immunity from prosecution in return for testifying against the group, while the others all received probation. Notoriety, even fame, briefly resulted for the group; the picture of Neal Patrick, one of the hackers, appeared on the cover of *Newsweek* in September 1983. Patrick insisted to newspaper reporters at the time – and the evidence supports his claim – that the group never intended to destroy any data. 'It was more curiosity than anything else,' he said. 'It's like a mix between the curiosity and the challenge. It's like knowing a foreign language and being able to read all those signs you couldn't read before.'

One of the few activities the gang indulged in once it had entered a computer system – other than looking around and playing a few games – was to open a few accounts named 'Joshua'. This was in honour of the password used by the hero of the recently released 1983 movie *War Games*, a film that helped to heighten both hacker interest in exploring systems and official fears about attackers being able to get inside supposedly impregnable computer networks.

The film's young hero, played by Matthew Broderick, is a computer-game addict who finds his way into the US military computer network and accidentally starts the countdown to a huge nuclear strike on the then Soviet Union. It is a rather far-fetched scenario, but the actions of the 414 gang now seemed to suggest that it contained at least a kernel of truth.

War games

The US federal authorities were accordingly becoming increasingly alarmed at this new crime of 'hacking'. More and more government data was being stored digitally, and so the country's national infrastructure – for example, utilities – was becoming more computer dependent. The internet was growing rapidly in scale and importance. Moreover the military, which had its own version of the internet called Milinet, was concerned at the potential vulnerability of its closely guarded secrets to outside hack attack. *War Games* and the actions of the 414 group only made those fears grow.

The result of all these concerns was the US' Computer Fraud and Abuse Act of 1984, which sought to protect information on federal or government computers and to guard against financial frauds. Although this ground-breaking legislation's focus was narrow to start with, by 1996 an extended definition of a target as 'any protected computer' has effectively meant that any attack on any computer connected to the internet could be prosecuted under the Act.

In truth the activities of hackers such as Captains Crunch and Zap, and the 414 gang could alone hardly justify the passing of major new legislation. The US authorities – with the rest of the Western world looking on, waiting for a lead – were clearly insuring against a day when top-security networks and the very fabric of computers and the fledgling internet would come under attack from sustained attack from determined criminals or enemies of the state.

Unfortunately for the authorities, however, the legislation did not immediately trap the kind of criminals they were expecting – and fearing. Howard Zinn, another teenage hacker, was a 17-year-old high-school dropout from Chicago. Zinn, who used the handle 'Shadow Hawk', broke into a variety of US military and AT&T computers during 1986 and 1987, during which time he stole around 55 software programmes. These included software relating to computer design and artificial intelligence, plus software used by the Bell Operating Companies for billing and accounting on long-distance telephone calls.

Though Zinn reportedly gained access to no militarily sensitive files, the case unnerved the authorities, who decided to throw the legal book at him, trying Zinn under the updated 1986 version of the Computer Fraud and Abuse Act. Zinn's online activities – he was caught after boasting of his exploits on a bulletin board – earnt him a nine-month stint in a juvenile prison, two and a half years' probation and a $10,000 fine.

Though Zinn was, in hindsight, a rather harmless teenager, his case did highlight the growing phenomenon – still an issue today – within the world of hacking and computers: the way in which hacking tactics, techniques, passwords and ideas for targets are regularly swapped around the hacking community.

During Zinn's trial, Assistant US Attorney William Cook stated the defendant obtained the information that gained him access to AT&T/Illinois Bell computers from fellow members of computer bulletin board systems (BBSs). At the same time, Zinn gave out passwords, telephone numbers and technical details of 'trapdoors' (hidden ways of entering) that he had built into computer systems, further boasting on the BBS that he would 'shut down AT&T's public switched network' (its main telephone network). What Zinn did not know, however, was that the same BBS was used by AT&T staff, who eventually set their own electronic trap for the mysterious 'Shadow Hawk'.

During the trial Assistant Attorney Cook dismissed members of such BBSs as 'street gangs' but the way in which someone like Zinn could learn from them and then pass on his own knowledge demonstrated the grim potential of computers, networks and ultimately the worldwide web to spread crime. A technological breakthrough by one hacker in one part of the world could be passed on almost instantaneously to another on the other side of the world. For any real criminals – that is, criminals seriously intending harm or financial gain – looking on, the implications were clear. Prisons may be known as finishing schools for crime, but the world of computers, bulletin boards and the internet offered something even better; a 'finishing school' for cyber crime.

The second person convicted under the 1986 Act was also not a major league criminal. In fact he turned out to be a super-bright computer student with impeccable family credentials who wanted to test out a theory; only for his experiment to bring the internet very nearly to its knees. His name was Robert Morris and his case is discussed in detail in Chapter 5, on virus writers. In brief, this former Harvard undergraduate and current Cornell University postgraduate released a programme into the Harvard University computer network in 1988 to check out a flaw he had discovered in the Unix operating system code. To his horror the programme began to replicate itself, spreading throughout many networks and taking scores of computers offline, causing millions of dollars of damage in the process. His programme became known simply as the Internet Worm. Morris was prosecuted under the 1986 Act even though his lawyers argued that he lacked the necessary intent to cause damage, an intent they said was implied in the legislation. The undergraduate was given three years probation and a $10,000 fine.

Once again the law had succeeded – however understandably – in criminalising a person who no real proven desire either to destroy data or to steal from anyone.

Across the Atlantic in the United Kingdom, scores of wannabe hackers were catching on to the new craze for home computers. This was partly inspired by events in the US, while also perhaps motivated by the exciting depiction of computers in the *War Games* movie. Mostly, however, they were young people – nearly all male – who were eager to explore a new world that suddenly opened up with the wide availability of computers. Like the original hackers from MIT and Stanford in the 1960s, these were young people who simply wanted to explore systems.

Among these young hackers in the UK were Neil Barrett and Peter Sommer. Barrett, a real computer whizz-kid, has since become a respected professor and one of the UK's leading experts on computer-related crime. Sommer wrote the immensely influential *The Hacker's Handbook*[3] under the pseudonym Hugo Cornwall and, like Barrett, has become an academic and leading expert on computer forensics.

In the UK, however, a notorious and long-running hacking case and subsequent legislation was to change the status of hacking for ever. The case involved, improbably, the Duke of Edinburgh Prince Philip, an accountant, a magazine journalist and an electronic mailbox account.

Hackers fight back

In 1984 two computer enthusiasts, Stephen Gold, an accountant from Sheffield, and Robert Schifreen, a computer magazine editor from London, hacked into what was called Prestel. Prestel was a dial-up electronic mail system and combined features of the telephone, computer and television, and was based on the technology known as Videotex. (Prestel, run by British Telecom in the UK, never really caught the public imagination; in France, however, the Minitel system flourished and only in recent years has it become superseded by the internet.)

Gold and Schifreen were fascinated by Prestel and both hacked into the system by dialling up random numbers and then using obvious default passwords – in this case a string of zeros – left in the system to make their way around it.

The pair were later accused by the authorities of making unautho-rised changes to data. More crucially, however, in terms of the notoriety and importance the case was to assume, Schifreen managed to gain access to a mailbox belonging to no less a dignitary than Queen Elizabeth's husband Prince Philip. British Telecom and Prestel were deeply embarrassed, the police initially taken aback and the tabloid press understandably enjoyed every second of it.

The 'culprits' Gold and Schifreen were eventually traced and arrested. The question was, what could they be charged with? There was no legislation that seemed to fit the pair's case, and for a while lawyers debated as to the best course of action. Gold and Schifreen were ultimately charged with forgery under the Forgery and Counterfeiting Act 1981, a piece of legislation not designed with the computer age in mind. Nonetheless, in 1986 the two hackers were convicted at Southwark Crown Court in London. Inevitably Gold and Schifreen appealed; how on earth, they reasoned, could they have been guilty of forgery? The Court of Appeal and then the highest court in the UK, the House of Lords, agreed with them and in 1988 – four years after their hack – they were formally acquitted. One of the five law lords – they were unanimous in their decision – Lord Brandon argued: 'Their object in carrying on these activities was not so much to gain any profit for themselves as to demonstrate their skill as hackers. It never occurred to them that they might be com-mitting any offence under the Forgery and Counterfeiting Act 1981.'

Even more tellingly Lord Chief Justice Lane had said in the earlier Court of Appeal ruling: 'Their conduct amounted in essence to dis-honestly gaining access to the relevant Prestel data bank by a trick. That is not a criminal offence. If it is thought desirable to make it so that is a matter for the legislature rather than the courts.'

The distinguished judges may not have approved of Gold and Schifreen's activities but one thing was clear; the kind of hacking they had carried out was not against the law. They had neither damaged nor stolen anything, at least in any meaningful sense.[4]

The game is up

If this seemed a victory for the hacking community, however, it was short lived. The British authorities decided that hacking, even its more seemingly innocent forms, had to be outlawed and within two years the Computer Misuse Act 1990 was on the statutes. This wide-ranging legislation was designed to outlaw any obviously criminal acts such as the commissioning or covering up of a crime, but it also outlawed any unauthorised access to any computer. At one stroke hacking in the UK was now illegal.

For most UK hackers the game was up, and many did realise that the new law ended their days of hacking. Sommer, who abandoned it to stay on the right side of the law, explains the mood change.

I use the analogy of trespass and I say that it's a little like walking across someone's field when you're not formally invited to do so. On the whole you think that people don't mind – and on the whole people didn't mind. I was doing that sort of thing between '82 and '83 – my country rambles as I called them – and by the end of the decade you were getting people who were plainly not operating to that sort of ethic.

Sommer says it was a conscious decision to change his approach to hacking:

You have to take the view that – as I did – that Parliament had now passed a law about it. I think my experiences were a fairly common one, but not universal. I think there were people who were interested in showing off and maybe inter-ested directly in crime.

The darker side

By using legislation to make criminals of hackers, the authorities were imposing a tough choice on many in the hacking community. Hackers either had to quit what they were doing – much of it genuinely harmless, if a little irritating – or face the full force of criminal law. Many, such as Zinn and Morris after their convictions, went on to live blameless lives and use their talents for constructive purposes (Morris became a professor at MIT). Others, though, resented being forced to make what they saw as a false choice. The hacker ethos was freedom of access for all; they saw nothing wrong with going into someone else's computer or telephone network as long as one did not cause any damage or steal anything.

The result was that some hackers turned to the darker side and moved further away from what the law now dictated. Inevitably this would lead them on a path towards the true criminals.

Schifreen, too, was aware of the change of attitude between the earlier hackers and those who were to come later. 'I was merely keen to learn more about how systems worked, and to see how many I could get into. I had no intention to damage anything or anyone, and I never did.' He adds: 'People now do it for money, or to cause damage or to see how many machines around the world they can infect.'

Meanwhile, criminals were more eager than ever to pick up tips on technology from the young hackers who were being made an example of by the authorities. Nicholas Whiteley, the UK's first hacker to be gaoled and who served time in London's Brixton Prison in 1990, said he was regularly approached by inmates asking him whether he could hack into bank computer systems. Another hacker confirms this curiosity among criminals, even if he is scornful of their expertise. 'They were interested in the hacking but in fact they didn't know anything about it at all and kept asking stupid things; can you hack into this bank or can you get details out of Manchester United's computers. They thought you just tapped on a few keys and then started trying passwords. They didn't realise it was nothing like that.'

But while their knowledge of technology was poor, the fact is that criminals had become curious about technology and had seen the future. The age of cyber criminals had arrived.

THE AGE OF CYBER CRIMINALS

In the United States the stakes were already getting higher. For a while the notorious hacker Kevin Mitnick (see Chapter 4) became high on the FBI's Most Wanted list and achieved incredible publicity for hacking, even though his motive was never to make money. Mitnick, who now writes and consults on security issues, cites an obvious reason for the growth of crime on the internet: the fact that more and more business is done online means the pickings for criminals are greater. This, he says, was a fairly inevitable development: 'When the internet went commercial and there was money involved – business transactions from B2B (business to business) and B2C (business to consumer) – it was going to attract criminal elements.'

Cyber vandals

The 1990s also saw the arrival of a hitherto unknown phenomenon: the cyber vandals. Otherwise known as virus writers these young (again, mostly) men sent out their destructive programmes neither knowing nor caring what damage their creations could to do businesses and individual computer users, and in the process earning the disdain of most hackers, who deplored their destructive intent and relative lack of programming ability. The decade began with the Tequila virus, and ended with the Melissa virus, with other damaging 'malware' such as Michelangelo and Back Orifice causing havoc in between.

Meanwhile other phone phreakers and hackers were beginning to appreciate how their talents could be put to gain tangible benefits. Hacker Kevin Poulsen helped to rig a Los Angeles radio station competition and won a Porsche car as a result; he later served three years in gaol for his troubles.

On a much larger scale a Russian hacker Vladimir Levin was arrested in March 1995 for what was the world's first known hack attack on a bank's network. Working from a PC in St Petersburg, Levin and members of his hacking group gained access to Citibank's US network and then used the account names and passwords of customers to siphon more than $3 million into personal accounts they had set up around the world. Levin was later extradited to the US and gaoled, while Citibank recovered most of the stolen money.

Significantly, it appears that the talented Levin may have been put up to the hack by members of organised crime. According to a security source Levin came back from a bar one night in his home city to find two members of the Russian mafia in his room. 'They offered him a small amount of money or an "attitude-correction course" as incentives to help them with their proposition,' says the source.

Not long after Levin's hack, in 1996 a drug-smuggling gang operating from Southend unsuccessfully tried to hack into the computers of a mobile phone company to obtain records on two cell phone numbers. The organised gang had been put under surveillance by the Metropolitan police. Suspicious that it was being watched, the gang had been using a scanner to monitor the surrounding area and had picked up the signal from the mobile phones used by the surveillance team. Identifying the network from the numbers, it then tried to find out whom the phones belonged to; a clear awareness of the possibilities technology had.

This was the start of the most frightening development of all within cyber crime. No longer was the main adversary simply frustrated teenagers writing damaging viruses or the lonely obsessive trying to hack into a US Air Force base or the Ministry of Defence. Organised crime was beginning to muscle in on the patch.

Hi-tech crime

In fact, it had taken a surprisingly long time for organised crime to realise the potential that lay within hi-tech crime and to move into the area. Even now there are few signs that 'old' organised crime such as the Italian mafia has yet embraced it. In part, believes Chief Superintendent Len Hynds, head of the UK's National Hi-Tech Crime Unit (NHTCU), which was founded in 2001, this is because long-established crime syndicates are already making substantial money from their traditional areas of drugs, people trafficking and arms smuggling.

'The process of diversifying into hi-tech crime is not something that they have grasped as quickly as they might; and that was good for us, of course,' he says. 'It meant we could get a foot in the door first; in fact law enforcement in the UK has got one step ahead of the game. Much of what's happened in the last three years we have anticipated.'

Gradually, however, the syndicates realised that hi-tech crime could gain access to vast amounts of untapped financial reward. As the world of business and banking became digital so the criminals realised they had to become digital, too. The question was, how would they acquire the technical skills they needed? The answer was simple: by recruiting highly qualified IT professionals.

Detective chief superintendent Hynds recalls one of the NHTCU's first cases that involved a well-known English crime gang – whom he would not identify – who sought out the services of such an expert, and succeeded in stealing substantial amounts of money. Hynds describes how the gang operated: 'This particular gang was an organised crime group operating throughout the UK but with some links to associates on the near continent. It was involved in other areas of criminality but it had identified an opportunity and had targeted people who it believed – and rightly so – would have valuable inside information and access to IT systems.' He goes on to explain that the gang, 'researched the individual concerned, identifying where that individual socialised, and then made proactive efforts to engage that individual in conversation in a social setting. Over a period of months it gained the trust of that individual to the extent that the gang felt able to offer him lucrative opportunities to work on the inside for that crime syndicate.'

Hynds says the man the group targeted was working for an IT company and that he was of value to them for two main reasons: 'One, because he had access to all the premises that the company would utilise and therefore access to the IT systems; but two, because he was a key person responsible for the management of assets that the company owned.' The IT professional was eventually recruited by the gang, who used him 'very successfully' to make it money until the NHTCU's investigation put an end to its scam.

New recruits

According to Detective Chief Superintendent Hynds the recruitment of IT experts is now much more frequent and sophisticated than it was just a few years ago. Chat rooms and newsgroups used by IT professionals are often monitored by members of international organised crime syndicates, with likely recruits then approached online. 'They offer high financial incentives but they have also – we are aware of this – coerced people through intimidation to move out of legitimate work and into work for them,' says Hynds.

Another recruiting ground for organised crime is specific websites used by IT industry staff, who are encouraged to put up their CVs. Again, gang members will sift through the CVs and approach those they feel most fit their required set of skills.

'It's actually very difficult to determine just how many of those people who put their CVs up are aware of whether they are getting involved with organised crime,' says Hynds. 'I think that some of them are attracted by the potential to earn large sums of money and have a degree of awareness and knowledge of what they are getting into; but clearly there is also scope there for people to unwittingly become involved in organised crime groups.'

He says we should not be surprised that criminals use the web in this way. 'If organised crime is looking for a particular skill set and the internet is a wonderful open resource, we should anticipate that it's going to make use of that resource.'

Once the experts are recruited – often for ten times the pay they could expect in their day job – they can expect a varied life in the employ of crime. The senior police officer explains: 'I do know that the programmers concerned have been set a whole range of different tasks including the management of websites, the development of phishing scams [setting up bogus websites to trick people out of their money] and the control of "bot net armies" [used to launch DDoS attacks on commercial websites], so a whole range of different skills are being utilised.'

Bot armies or bot herds are commonly-used expressions to describe collections of software programs which, because they perform tasks semi-automatically, are called robots. Though such 'bots' often have a benign purpose, such as in search engines, when gathered together and used to attack websites and servers they can cause immense damage.

Meanwhile Tony Neate, industry liaison officer of the NHTCU, describes the way that organised crime regards the issue of hi-tech crime and the extreme lengths to which it may go to expand its knowledge. 'They see a new opportunity come up in crime and they set up a new section,' says Neate. 'There certainly is a Research & Development department in these organisations. They're even prepared to put people through universities. They place them in university in order to educate them to a certain level to get them into a business.'

This unexpected criminal enthusiasm for higher education is confirmed by one hacker who had links with a London-based crime syndicate in the 1990s. 'One member put his daughter through university so she could get a job in a bank and then they set up the crime. Apparently she "made a mistake" as she trans-ferred around £500,000 into a dodgy account and the bank sacked her; but the deed was done already,' the hacker reveals.

Hynds is reluctant to discuss details about where these internet-literate gangs are based, though reports suggest that many of them are from the former Soviet Union, the old Warsaw Pact countries and in particular Russia itself. Dr Mark Galeotti is director of the Organised Russian and Eurasian Crime Research Unit at Keele University, managing editor of the journal *Global Crime* and an expert on Russian crime gangs. He explains why they are more tech-nologically inclined than some others. 'Russian organised crime is the first post-modern form of organised crime to explode in the modern era,' he says. 'A lot of the people who have moved into it are youngsters, disenfranchised. They are very bright, very highly edu-cated middle-class elite who now have no prospects in the commer-cial sector and who are more pre-disposed to technology than traditional organised crime.'

Dr Galeotti says that the Russian gangs – including the biggest, called Solntsevo – tend to hire their IT experts as and when they need them.

'If you take an organisation like Solntsevo, which has transna-tional interests, you will not find it taking hackers into the organisa-tion. Instead, if it needs hackers it will bring on in those it has used before. Hackers are just part of a whole number of services that is available to be bought in.'

Vladimir A Golubev, director of Computer Crime Research Center (CCRC) in Ukraine, confirms the connection between crime and technology in the former Soviet Union. 'Generally organised criminal groups use high-skilled IT experts in their criminal intentions, for committing both traditional crimes and cyber crimes,' he says.

'The internet can be used in information exchanging and plan-ning crimes. For example, in one case in Ukraine the police data-base was hacked with the aim of deleting records on stolen cars, allowing criminals to sell stolen cars without any problems.'

Detective Chief Superintendent Hynds says that the organised syndicates they have encountered operate in a cell-like structure. The technical staff will be in one group, managing the technology the syndicate is using, the security staff will be in another and will help recruit IT staff and protect the gang's interests, while the finance section will deal with money laundering and recruiting any necessary staff to deal with that. 'They manage the process by keeping each of the cells unaware of the rest of the business. It's only the management group that has a broad understanding of the overall crime syndicate,' he says.

Dr Galeotti points to the role of former KGB agents in Russian gangs and says that some security officials have remained in administrative posts even though they have been recruited by organised crime. 'A good example of this is the SAPSI, which is the Federal Government Communications Agency,' he says. SAPSI has now been absorbed by another agency but it has the lead role of information gathering by electronic means.

'A lot of the SAPSI people were moonlighting for organised crime and corrupt business or they were allowing SAPSI resources to be used often for espionage; this might mean that they were phone-tapping on behalf of a company or that crooked SAPSI agents were selling on wire taps to criminals,' he says.

There is also a legacy from the days when the KGB exploited the abilities of technologically gifted groups in eastern European countries. In Bulgaria, for example, there is a significant number of hackers and virus writers, trained by the Durzhavna Sigurnost (DS)(the Bulgarian secret police) but overseen by the KGB. Dr Galeotti says:

> *Now there are new generations of hackers coming from those places, who have been taught by the old hackers. With groups such as Solntsevo, who are transnational and have outposts in Bulgaria, they will have access to that talent.*

Another group that has been working in technology is the Tambov gang, which is headquartered in St Petersburg and whose zone of influence extends from Northern Europe to Scandinavia. It has been drawn to technology crime because of the high number of maths and computer science students in the St Petersburg area.

Cyber turf wars

Law enforcement agencies believe that more and more organised criminal gangs are beginning to move into cyber crime as they see how much money is being made by other groups in such activities as phishing and by extortion using the bot herds to threaten DDoS attacks (the shutting down of a site) unless money is paid.

Len Hynds says: 'We've seen how the groups themselves will look to copy successful exploits and enterprises. So that one group for example might make a particular success from extortion involving the internet and we see other groups adopting similar tactics and following those leads.'

As a result the police is now beginning to witness a phenomenon familiar to anyone with a knowledge of organised crime, namely turf wars – only this time in cyber space. Syndicates are so worried that rivals might steal their pitch in various areas of cyber crime that they are using their 'security' personnel to smash hardware such as computers belonging to other gangs – and even to harm specialist IT staff.

'I remember saying three years ago that there were no turf wars in cyberspace – that's actually not true now,' says Len Hynds. 'We've got some very high-grade intelligence suggesting these turf wars spill over from the internet and into the real world.'

This he says might mean using one set of bot armies to attack a rival's bot armies (these are software robots that can be directed at targets in cyber space) or more likely simply a physical attack on the other organisation's programmers.

Dr Galeotti believes there is also a new trend emerging specifically among Russian cyber crime: 'virtual' organised crime gangs. These are groups set up by and wholly consisting of IT experts, unlike the other cases where existing gangs have simply diversified into hi-tech crime.

'With these technology groups we are now at a cusp point,' he maintains. 'Until now, the computer people still had their own jobs during the day. Now they are at the point where there is enough activity for them to drop those jobs. Virtual mafia gangs are now forming particularly in the St Petersburg area.' Ironically, however, there are areas of 'business' for these virtual gangs where they need to turn to the experts in existing crime gangs – for example, in the long-standing problem of how to launder stolen money.

What is undeniable now is that the modern equivalent to gangsters of old – such as the Kray brothers in London – have established a foothold in cyber space and are there to stay; with worrying implications about the likely growth in cyber crime. 'I have to say that I was not even sure if we were going to find the modern day Ronnie and Reggie [Kray] in cyberspace when we were first set up in April 2001,' says Len Hynds. 'But I can tell you now that the modern day equivalent is definitely there; they are operating at international level, and they have an awareness of what the internet offers to the criminal mind.'

The FBI too has been charting the growing involvement of organised crime in the internet and computers. Dave Thomas, chief of the Computer Intrusion Division in the FBI's Cyber Division, says that the new 'mobs' seem to be faster to exploit this area than the better-known groups. 'I don't know that the traditional mafia in Russia is any more ahead technologically than the Italian-based mafia groups that we see here,' he says. 'But I think that they are learning very quickly that they can use the services of these people to make money so they are blending together really quick.'

He adds: 'We have identified organisations in the former Soviet Bloc that seem to have that sort of expertise and we are constantly trying to determine the makeup of those groups and who is involved. Some of them are more loosely knit than others. Some of them will migrate across groups.'

The Computer Intrusion Division is conducting around 2,000 'intrusion investigations', as they are called, at any given time. 'They go across the entire gamut of intrusions but the overwhelming percentage of those would be the Eastern European groups that are targeting the financial sector in the US, UK and Canada, and anywhere that they can obtain money. There are many, many systems out there that are misconfigured and easily accessible by anyone with a decent skill set,' Thomas warns.

He does not believe there is one controlling mastermind or 'Cyber Don' behind the groups, pointing out that the crime is being committed by loose-knit groups, though he concedes that the idea of a cyber mastermind is one that 'may evolve in time'. He also points out that while criminals believe they can use the internet to jump from jurisdiction to jurisdiction, ultimately this will not help them evade justice. The FBI was created to deal with exactly this kind of threat, says Thomas, and it is co-operating well with other agencies around the world. In that respect, the prevalence of internet crime may even have done it a favour; 'Cyber crime has probably brought us together as a global law enforcement community better and quicker than anything else I can think of,' he says.

Though cyber terrorism is not a major theme of this book, it is worth noting that there is evidence that terrorist groups such as Al Qaeda – hampered by new restrictions on it and its finances – are turning to organised crime groups because of the latter's expertise in sophisticated hi-tech money laundering techniques. Dr Galeotti, Russian cyber crime expert, maintains that, 'On the whole they are looking to buy in expertise rather than depend on people they have indoctrinated because it is easier and quicker and there are less links.'

However, buying in help from Russian gangs – who are not naturally well disposed towards Al Qaeda – comes at a heavy price. 'Al Qaeda is paying three times what Russian organised crime is charging the Cosa Nostra, which means paying interest at around 75 per cent,' says Dr Galeotti.

It is well known that the US has been trying to stem this flow of money, which comes in part from bank accounts. After the attack on the twin towers on 9 September 2001, US security agents unofficially approached at least one private computer security firm to see if it would be willing to launch DDoS attacks against specific banks at specific times of the day; times when the internet traffic revealed that terrorist groups were transferring funds.

One person who was approached – and declined the offer – says: 'The targets were Arab banks, large banks that were moving funds and were thought to have been involved in financial transactions that facili-tated the attack – and that there was other money going through it. I know the hack was carried out but I don't know any success rate.'

A senior former intelligence source, meanwhile, reveals that Al Qaeda has recruited top-grade com-puter experts to hack on its behalf against Western targets. '[The US were] investigating four or five cases of Al Qaeda cells recruiting computer science professors from Eastern Bloc countries. They were moving them

to Africa and then they were hacking from there.'
Targets were thought likely to include the computer
systems of airports, power grids and water supplies,
and the attacks would be DDoS attacks using whole
cyber armies of bot software.

CHAPTER TWO
The Fight Against Cyber Crime

Near a small village deep in the English county of Hampshire runs an unremarkable dusty track. Winding up the side of a hill past a couple of council houses, it has no signposts and seems to lead nowhere in particular. Yet once you climb up this quiet little path and reach the top you are suddenly greeted by an incongruous sight. There, behind a sagging wire fence and battered old sign displaying the name of a long-since departed company, is a car park packed with expensive, gleaming vehicles.

There are no guards, no buildings, no one and nothing; just two shabby concrete towers, the obligatory communications tower, and a couple of strange grass-covered shapes, over which two buzzards lazily circle. Otherwise nothing stirs.

Beneath the concrete towers lies a nuclear bunker. And inside this cold war relic is an information-age listening centre, a symbol of the 21st century. Hidden beneath a carpet of wild flowers is what is called the Security Operations Centre (SOC). Its entrance is via another path, one that winds a little down the hill, before abruptly turning and vanishing into the hill itself. Before any visitor thinks they have chanced across some quaint Hobbit-style underground home, such thoughts are quickly dispelled by the sight of the apparatus fixed above the foot-thick steel doors. It is only now that you realise you have been watched from the moment you arrived, by a bank of cameras scanning the top of the hill.

To gain entry to this stronghold, the security tag handed to every prospective visitor is not enough. A security man has to punch in a code to open the steel door, and the visitor must stand in what feels like an airlock while the guard waits for the door's time-lock to operate. That done, he repeats the exercise at another, even heavier door. You are now inside the hill – or more accurately inside a former reservoir inside the hill – about to embark on a voyage into the depths of the internet. For this is the property of Symantec, better known to many people as the providers of Norton antivirus software, and this curious location, the Security Operations Centre, this world of artificially light and massively thick steel doors, is at the front line in the worldwide fight against cyber crime.

The Hampshire SOC is housed in one of the last bunkers to be built before the end of World War II. Not far away is the still-pretty town of Winchester, yet down in this bunker it is hard to shake off the impression of being in a cold war submarine, with its specially designed steel cups that allow the building to be pressurised to keep out the outside atmosphere, and the door thresholds raised to stop flooding. The bunker is one of five SOCs that the firm operates around the world; the others (even larger in scale) are in the United States (two), Germany and in Australia. It is their job to monitor the internet 24 hours a day, 7 days a week and every day of the year, looking for something – anything – that might be a threat to the smooth running of the internet.

The SOC teams work in global relays, each passing responsibility on to the other as they follow the daylight around the planet, each centre running shifts from 9.00 am to 3.00 pm. Specifically the job of this highly trained team is to watch out for new viruses and worms as they slip onto the publicly-accessible parts of the internet – or being in the 'wild' as it is often described. They will then track them, ignoring the weaker ones, but keeping a careful eye on those that might look as if they are a threat. Once they have detected a programme that looks dangerous they immediately alert one of Symantec's three Security Response teams – based in Dublin, Santa Monica and Tokyo – whose staff also work 'following the sun' shifts.

Run by a former army intelligence officer, Graeme Pinkney, the Hampshire SOC sails the deep waters of the web, sampling 480 million logs a day for any signs of unusual activity. Cold war parallels or not, there is certainly a struggle going on here, a battle to keep the digital world safe from attack from the 'enemy'. This enemy may be, as we have seen, hackers, virus writers or organised criminals out to extort money using the latest technology. But just as the enemy is becoming increasingly organised, so is the security of the internet and the world of computers. And as we shall see, the organised crime-busters are not just the traditional law-enforcement agencies.

MALWARE

One of the biggest players in the fight against worms, viruses, Trojan programmes – a Trojan programme being a malicious programme, usually disguised as something useful or desirable – and other forms of what is generically called 'malware', is the antivirus industry. In the mid 1980s this industry did not even exist and few could have foreseen its rapid emergence. Now the antivirus business is worth billions of pounds a year worldwide; by 2007 some estimate it will be worth $3.98 billion[1]. It employs thousands of people in scores of different countries and has spawned a number of highly visible brand names; as well as Norton there is McAfee, Sophos, AVG, Kaspersky, F-Secure and a host of others. The core products have spread from antivirus software to include personal firewalls to protect against hackers, anti-spyware to protect against commercial and malicious 'spies' being put on your machine, and even anti-spamware.

Symantec, with its string of futuristic control centres and banks of computers analysing the world's internet traffic, is right at the heart of this battle. Despite its rather dramatic setting in a wartime bunker, Pinkney says there is a good reason to base its UK SOC in rural Hampshire rather than in the capital.

'We could run this operation from anywhere. The key thing about the bunker is that it allows us to maintain real-time threat response;

any disruption takes that ability away,' he explains. 'If we were in the middle of a city like London or Dublin, a bomb threat could cause us disruption or the electricity supply may be brought down or there could be flooding. We don't have that problem; we are in the middle of nowhere with few cars and little to attract disruption, and we have 40 days of backup electricity supply. The bunker is perceived as physically very secure.'

Pinkney describes his team's work, how it analyses traffic on the internet and is able to detect changes in cyber activity against the everyday background 'noise' of digital communications. When one considers that this is done from looking at 480 million logs a day, one realises just how tough this task is.

One difficulty for Symantec's array of analysts is to determine whether any new activity seen on the net is the start of an 'attack' by a worm or virus, or whether it is someone preparing for a future attack. The analysts are aware that if a criminal wants to release a virus, the writer will sooner or later have to give it a trial run in the 'wild' (rather like testing a new weapon in a live firing display for the first time).

'If they are looking for a vulnerability they have to ping [test it on a real computer "victim"] to find that vulnerability,' Pinkney says. 'What we have to do is look at that and say is this activity really the activity – and is it really targeting the intended victim?'

It is an elaborate game of cat and mouse. Pinkney says that once they find a pattern they can start to understand what is happening and do something about it; the hard bit is building that pattern. He cites an example: his team was able to predict a big worm attack from amidst the blur of internet traffic in 2003 – a blur that turned out to reveal the Blaster worm that hit the internet in August of that year.

'With Blaster we saw the pattern two weeks before and we put out a global alert. We were able to tell our customers when it was going to hit and what it was going to do,' says Pinkney. 'Those warnings can help people to change their defences.' But he is under no illusions about how complex and tough their work is. 'If you want an analogy for the job, it is that you have to stop a bullet that's already been fired,' he says with a smile.

Raising the alarm

The antivirus industry has often been criticised for being too willing to scare business and the public with dire warnings of what particular worms and viruses might do, but the former intelligence officer rejects these complaints. He insists that they are very cautious before raising the alarm.

'If we do see something we don't immediately put out a warning because we don't want to cry wolf.' Instead the experts go through a rigorous question and answer session to test the strength of what they have seen and to test it against other intelligence they might have received. Or they might relate it to any new technology recently released that might have altered traffic activity for different and entirely innocent reasons.

Worryingly, Pinkney is beginning to see signs in his 480-million piece 'jigsaw puzzle' of greater subtlety in the activity of worms and viruses. If 2003 was the year of aggressive attacks, then 2004, for example, was the year of a more cautious and possibly more sinister approach. 'There has been a lot of reconnaissance activity going on. They could be harvesting bots or they could be looking for other vulnerabilities.' He adds grimly, 'If the reconnaissance stops then it doesn't mean that the army's gone.'

Instant updates

Pinkney works closely with another key figure, Kevin Hogan, in Symantec's European operations. Hogan runs the Symantec Security Response (SSR) team in Dublin, the centre to which the Hampshire bunker will pass on its findings. If Pinkney's team are the advance scouts, scouring the horizon for signs of enemy activity, then it is the task of Hogan and his team to decided how to deploy their technological troops and how to defeat the enemy by coming up with the right software solutions.

'The purpose is to respond to internet threats, to protect our wider customer base and to protect the public, too,' he says. 'We are the eyes, ears and mouth.' Much of this response work means alerting customers to potential and upcoming risks – as with Blaster – and producing near-instant updates for their clients' software so that they will be able to detect the new threats.

This is no easy task. 'You have to remember that we are now seeing 15–20 of these things a day, with the bulk being Trojans and back doors,' says Hogan. The teams are also sifting through an astonishing 200,000 submissions – reports of virus activity – a month from corporate customers, though many of these can be dealt with automatically. On average, he says, they are releasing 2.2 updates every week. These are usually new 'signatures', software enabling the clients' machines to recognise the new malware.

'If you think about what we do for a lot of the time, it's looking for a small needle in a haystack and we have to pick that out from a lot of noise. So we have to spend a lot of time just listening. It's not very glamorous.' Even when solutions and procedures have been put in place to meet a particular problem, the team's work does not end there. The situation is constantly changing, says Hogan, and they may have to change their procedures. 'You also have to realise that many of these threats don't go away.'

When Hogan's team is confronted with a new piece of malware, its approach is to take it apart to see how it was made; a process sometimes called reverse engineering. 'To do that we have isolated networks where we run the code to find out what it does,' he says. Hogan says his engineers are responsible for the analysis, the testing and the 'deliverables' (in other words the updates they send out to deal with the new threat).

'Because of that we have to ensure that the information we provide is accurate. Our engineers do both white box and black box analysis. We run the threat on a black box [a sacrificial computer] while on a white box [a computer used for investigations] we do analysis on what it might do,' he says.

A constant headache for antivirus teams in all companies is the risk of malware aimed at exploiting new advances in technology. An example of this was the long-predicted first worm to hit mobile phones, the so-called Cabir worm. It was devised by a member of the 'elite' European virus-writing group known as 29a, and details of its existence were revealed in June 2004. Though there were no immediate signs of the worm spreading into the real world (the 'wild') and it may remain simply a 'proof of concept' for a while, 29a proved that what had always been a possibility became a reality.

Hogan says that his team is ready for such challenges. 'We examine the problems that new technologies might bring, so with Cabir we weren't taken by surprise. We had brainstormed the potential, so that we would know how to react if something did happen.'

The same he says was true for viruses such as Rugrat, discovered in May 2004, which affected computers using 64-bit chips in their processors rather than the current standard of 32-bit chips. 'We don't wait for something to happen, we prepare for it; with the 64-bit viruses we had looked into what might happen two years before Rugrat came out,' says Hogan. 'And when I say we investigate that does not mean we look for vulnerabilities. What we do is to look for the potential tools that may be available, and think of the things that a virus writer might do, so that we know how to respond.'

Hogan and his team say there is typically a two-year gap between the time that new technology appears and someone produces a new virus or worm to attack it. This is because the writers need to get their hands on the correct documentation for that technology, so they can analyse how it works and unearth any flaws. Companies such as Symantec take advantage of this two-year breathing space to prepare necessary defences against the new threat.

The Symantec Security Operations Centres use five different categories to determine how menacing a new piece of malware might be. Category 1 describes viruses that are in what is known as the 'zoo'; that is, they are confined to laboratories and are not a threat. Category 2 is for a virus that is in the wild (out and about, and potentially dangerous) and already propagating. The next level – category 3 – is used for malware where the propagation rate has reached potentially dangerous levels. (There is also a 2.5 category, which is a warning that they might be about to reach category 3.)

Category 4 describes all the worms and viruses causing major threats; typically these will include the ones we hear about in the media. The final level is the scary one (though fortunately one that has yet to be seen); category 5 is for internet meltdown, the Armageddon of the digital world. Many experts believe that it is possible to create a worm that might achieve effective melt-down of the internet and emails; though whether there is anyone with the necessary high-level ability to do this and who would want to achieve this is open to question.

Inevitably much of the media coverage of worms and viruses concentrates on the people behind them, the virus writers. But Hogan warns against focusing on individuals and against treating the malware as if they were real biological entities. 'I think the thing about dealing with a virus is that for us it's just a programme that does something bad. It's not a big beast; at the end of the day we are dealing with a code. It's just a malicious programme and that's the challenge.'

Hogan's most memorable moments so far with one of these 'malicious programmes' came with the arrival of the notorious Slammer, a worm that smashed rapidly around the world in January 2003. He recalls: 'I was rung at 5.30 am in the morning. We don't really want to drag people in from other sites because we want them to be fresh. If we make a mistake on a signature we can cause as much damage as a worm and produce something that could disable the functionality in a programme.'

On this occasion, however, the Security Response team in Japan wanted to alert the Dublin team's boss to the fact that a new worm had gone round so fast they had not had time to come up with a signature that would allow customers' machines to detect it. 'Slammer had happened so quickly that they had to switch from analysing and trying to get a solution, to remediation, or helping customers get it off their systems,' he says.

At such times Hogan says one is unaware of the stress involved, because there is so much information coming in from their SOCs and elsewhere. 'It's only when you look back that you know what you're dealing with,' he says.

Conspiracy theory

Hogan and his experts believe the malware phenomenon simply have to be accepted as part of the digital scene. He says: 'I don't see malicious code going away. It will evolve – malware follows technology.' In line with many others in the industry he does not believe the classic viruses – for example, those spread by opening email attachments – will be the main threat. Instead this will come from constantly changing combinations of worms, Trojan programmes and back doors, what are known as blended attacks. 'I think viruses are now few and far between and when we see them they are unusual,' he says.

Like others he also attaches some of the blame for the current malware problem to companies that produce software that is not focused enough on security. At the same time, firms such as Microsoft should not take all the blame. Instead we should all learn to get used to updating – 'patching' – our operating systems as part of our digital hygiene, Hogan says. 'I think there is responsibility on both sides; patching is a fact of life. At home on my computer I'm patching every week.'

Yet if the need for robust anti-malware security seems stronger than ever, the antivirus (AV) industry is not without its critics. Ever since the lucrative emergence of AV software in the 1980s there have been dark mutterings that the industry may, on occasions, have been behind some viruses itself. After all, say the critics, where would the industry be if there were not constant scares and the frequent appearance of new viruses and worms on the horizon to perpetuate those scares?

It is a good conspiracy theory, and conspiracy theories are very popular in the digital world. Despite the constant whispers, however, there has never been a shred of evidence to suggest that any AV firm has ever released a virus. Matthew Ham, consultant to the influential Virus Bulletin[2], is extremely doubtful of such claims. 'There are always rumours but there are none that I consider to be in any way founded.'

French virus expert Marc Blanchard, the head of the European Virus Research Centre run by Kaspersky Labs, says it is absurd to suggest that either companies or their employees would write such stuff. 'For a start, people who work for antivirus companies are on very tough contracts and would not just lose their job; they could go to prison if they were caught.'

The nearest a company might get is if, during the course of its work, it comes across a new idea that might be written up as a proof of concept, he says. But this would be kept in the lab or 'zoo' and never allowed near the wild.

Ham says there have been rumours that some firms have, in the past, recruited former virus writers to their staff. He doubts, however, whether most virus writers would have the correct set of technical skills to be of much use to an antivirus company. In any case AV firms doubt whether such a person could ever have the right kind of 'social conscience' to work for, rather than against, the industry. 'Now whether that is correct, that a virus writer will never reform, it is in any case not going to be good publicity for an ex-virus writer or a current virus writer to be seen working for them,' says Ham.

This view is echoed by Carole Theriault, security consultant at antivirus company Sophos. She says, 'I have heard these stories where people claim that the antivirus industry would have a vested interest in writing computer viruses but that is simply not the case. We have never had anyone with a dodgy background working for us, because it's not worth the risk.'

Hyping the threat

Perhaps the most realistic charge against the AV industry is that it has been guilty sometimes of hyping the threat of potential viruses and worms, and afterwards exaggerating the amount of damage they have caused to firms. Among the most costly so far have been the Code Red worm, which caused an estimated $2.6 billion in lost productivity; the LoveLetter virus, whose cost may have been $8.8billion; and the Klez virus, at $9 billion[3]. The problems with such estimates is that they are just that, estimates, averaged out over the world and based on numerous assumptions about how companies might be affected. Critics point out that some estimates of 'loss' include the time and expertise spent by the computer security staff of large organisations in dealing with virus and worm attacks; this ignores the fact that this is what such staff are paid to do.

Matthew Ham believes that antivirus companies have become more cynical and that their marketing departments have become better at understanding what makes a good media scare story – and will thus give them free publicity. He cites the example of the Harry Potter virus that was prevalent in the first half of 2004. It was spread by email and contained Harry Potter in the subject line, an attempt to cash in on the enormous popularity of the books and films and induce people to open the attached file.

Ham says that this worm was part of the Netsky 'family' of viruses and could therefore already be detected by existing scanners and software; and there was no reason to think that this Harry Potter virus would be particularly important or dangerous.

'However, [AV] companies look at this and say, Harry Potter, this is something that we can sell, because Harry Potter is very popular at the moment. So we can send information to a news agency that there is a new Harry Potter virus discovered and it's a massive danger, and that it is appealing to children, and watch out, the sky is going to fall in . . .' Ham adds: 'The companies are too subtle to say "and you need to buy our software" but it has been noticeable that with large virus outbreaks the stock price of large antivirus companies does rise.'

There is a clear warning for the antivirus industry here, one that the more insightful individuals working in it have already grasped. Over-hyping the threat from worms and viruses could have unfortunate and unforeseen consequences for the internet. One consequence might be to make people far too blasé about the risks that really are there. If the average user hears all the constant publicity about dangers to their PC and yet personally experiences few problems, they may well conclude that the whole fanfare is a crude marketing exercise and relax their 'digital hygiene' – and possibly leave themselves and others open to attack. The opposite reaction would be that users become so scared by the endless threats that they literally switch off altogether – with disastrous consequences for e-commerce.

DEFENCE STRUCTURES

The work carried out at such sites as Symantec in Hampshire is just a part of the massive security effort aimed at keeping computers and the internet from being attacked by criminals and terrorists. As the industries of Western countries have come to depend more on e-commerce, and as utilities such as water, telecommunications and power have become more reliant on information networks, so the protection of these networks has become of paramount importance.

Industry partners

The steps each country takes to police its information highway vary considerably (though they all involve complex organisational structures; this really is the land where bureaucracy and acronyms rule supreme). They all share two similarities, however. One is that all governments realise that, in the digital world, no nation is an island and therefore their defence structures have been built from the start with international co-operation in mind. There is no point in being able to stop a DDoS attack being launched in your country if one can be started just as easily from another nation and aimed at you. So the swift and reliable transfer of information between jurisdictions is essential.

Secondly, and most striking of all, is the heavy reliance that governments place on private industry to protect the information networks – including the network of networks itself, the internet. The reason for this is quite simple. The vast majority of private networks and the internet are run by private industry; and they alone have the knowledge and expertise to know how to protect them. Left to themselves, most governments would simply be unable to sustain the information networks to anything like the level they exist at now.

The United Kingdom's own Cabinet Office – the heart of the spider's web in Whitehall – openly acknowledges this core fact. On its website the department states: 'The UK is an "information society". Information systems are now an essential part of the way we live . . . Information systems are so deeply embedded in our everyday lives that we tend to simply take them for granted.'

It then adds, 'Government cannot make the UK's information systems secure by itself. Most information networks are neither owned nor operated by government so we must each play a part in protecting all our information systems – from home computers and the IT networks behind large companies to local and central government systems.'

The role of government in the UK then is essentially one of co-ordination, to make sure that all the various interested groups and private companies are sharing information and can build a bureaucratic framework within which mutual co-operation can flourish.

Mutual co-operation

There is a good example of how the public and private sector work together to protect networks in the United States. Since the mid-1990s a programme called InfraGard[4], sponsored by the Federal Bureau of Investigations (FBI), has been playing a key role in information security. Infragard is essentially a US-wide group of small, medium and large businesses who act as the eyes and ears of the internet-protection bureaucracy.

It sprang out of the work of one regional FBI officer and now has 14,000 private sector members across the US. The chair of the InfraGard Board of Directors, Phyllis Schneck, emphasises the importance of industry in keeping 'critical infrastructures' such as the internet running.

Dr Schneck, whose day job is as Vice President of Strategic Development for CipherTrust, says: 'About 85–90 per cent of that which is defined as critical infrastructure is owned and operated by the private sector. When you look at all of the different critical infrastructure and given that the private sector owns and operates so much of it – and given that we are the eyes and ears – we're seeing a lot more than in some cases what the government is seeing.'

She adds: 'So they want a vehicle by which to report, investigate and correlate, nationwide and globally, things that you and I, common people, see every day; the analysts then are trained to correlate this to something that might be useful.'

Dr Schneck points out that not only are the national information networks critical infrastructures (CI) in their own right, but that other CIs such as water and power are increasingly depending on their open networks to function. In other words an attack on information networks is potentially an attack on a country's entire critical infrastructure; which shows why the threat to information highways is taken so seriously.

She explains how the idea for InfraGard began. 'It started out of Cleveland Ohio when an FBI agent had something that he was investigating and he went to people in the private sector. He quickly discovered that getting them to help with his investigation was extremely successful. And the FBI realised that if it did this on a national level, it would have far more analysis and far more ideas to gather and distribute information.'

After the events of 11 September 2001, InfraGard has been moved to the overall umbrella of the US' new Department of Homeland Security (DHS), though it remains an FBI programme and its success still depends on local businesses keeping look out for suspicious cyber activity. 'We call it neighbourhood watch for the internet, cyberspace and all our critical infrastructures,' says Dr Schneck.

The FBI says it continues to value the role of InfraGard. Dave Thomas of the bureau's Cyber Division says: 'We maintain our liaison with Infragard because it really does know what's going on on the internet and we need that capability out there. You can't work crime on the internet without your industry partners – it's not something the FBI can work on alone,' he says.

'The industry partners and Infragard own the internet where the infrastructure sits, so we have to maintain those partnerships,' Thomas continues.

Industry partners

Dr Schneck suggests there are similarities between the work of InfraGard and what is known as the National Infrastructure Security Co-ordination Centre (NISCC)[5] in the UK. In fact the NISCC is far more governmental and bureaucratic than its US counterpart, sitting as it does at the heart of Whitehall. The nearest true equivalent in the UK to how InfraGard works is probably the National Hi-Tech Crime Unit (NHTCU)[6], which liaises closely with British businesses, and whose work is discussed in detail in the next chapter.

NISCC describes itself as an 'interdepartmental organisation' set up by the Home Office in 1999 to 'minimise the risk of electronic attack against the UK's Critical National Infrastructure (CNI).' Its role is to work with both private and public sectors, offer advice on how to protect information systems, liaise with international bodies and issue alerts and warnings of new threats. Another UK body charged with protecting the nation's information infrastructure is the Central Sponsor for Information Assurance (CSIA)[7], which, unlike the NISCC, is based in the Cabinet Office. Confusingly, it also describes its role as 'promoting the understanding that it is essential for government and business alike to maintain reliable, secure and resilient national information systems.' Other organisations involved in UK network security include the Computer Electronic Security Group (CESG)[8], which is part of the country's eavesdropping Government Communication Headquarters (GCHQ), based at Cheltenham in the west of England.

If nothing else, the prevalence of such overlapping organisations proves that when it comes to promoting bureaucracy, it is hard to beat the world of the internet infrastructure. And in spite of the avowal of government units such as CSIA and NISCC that part of their remit to inform the public of technological threats, it would be interesting to know just how many members of the public have ever heard of them. One suspects that it would be a small fraction of 1 per cent.

HYBRID CYBER CRIMINAL HUNTERS

The crossover between the public and private sector in computer and internet security is a consistent theme. Experts in the private sector and academic institutions are able to understand, far more than government and law enforcement counterparts, the intricacies of systems that they themselves built. The nature of crime itself may not have changed that much, but the way in which it can be carried out on computers and on the internet has transformed beyond all recognition. Therefore if you cannot understand and manipulate the technology, you cannot hope to trap and convict the criminal – or defend yourself from attacks. The result has been the development of hybrid cyber criminal hunters.

Indeed, uniquely in the history of modern crime, it was in the private sector that the assault on cyber criminals first began, and in some people's eyes where the skill and expertise is still at its greatest. Before computer-related crime became a major issue for Western police forces, private companies and particularly financial institutions feared the deployment of new technology against them by determined criminals. There was a feeling among businesses in the early 1980s that the police neither knew nor much cared about computer crime, and that in any case going to the police meant dirty linen might have to be washed in public.

No one to turn to

This was the time when computers were the ultimate in big business accessories and, as James Bond films never tired of showing, to have a computer room meant you had a company worth possessing; you had tycoon power.

The computer was thus the symbol of a modern go-ahead business and any attacks on the system were quickly seized on by armchair sceptics as evidence of the futility of placing trust in the use of these mere machines. Indeed, the term 'computer error' became beloved by a largely Luddite public (aided by sections of the media), who saw computers as agents of redundancy and objects of fear associated with vague notions of 'Big Brother' control. Therefore, by admitting that these systems could be entered and interfered with by an outsider not only put the company's reputation at risk, it even called into question the judgement of the people who had invested in the new technology in the first place.

This reinforced the feeling that calling in the police was not always the best solution. In any case even if the police had any familiarity with the technology – which it almost certainly did not – the direction of police investigations could not be controlled and could become very public and very conspicuous. In the eyes of many in business it was, therefore, far better to bring in private investigators skilled in computers who you could pass off as 'consultants' and whose efforts you controlled – and whose findings you could act upon discreetly.

'At the time there was no one else to turn to,' insists Paul Carratu, managing director of the London-based private detective agency Carratu International, a company that saw very early on the opportunities for crime that the computer offered and quickly created its own computer investigations unit. He continues:

I think at the time the private sector was beating the police in technological know-how by ten years. The police has still not caught up with fraud. The first cases were in fraud and at that time the police did not have a clue how to understand a computer.

We'd be asked in because we knew how to pull files on a computer and a lot of the people in the company didn't. It wasn't like today when everyone has got accounting packages. In those days they were all bespoke systems made by a whole range of different companies, all of them doing roughly the same thing but doing it differently. If they had called in the local police they would have been wasting their time so they called us in.

Another private security expert – who asked us not to name him – adds that even today, with the arrival of modern specialist police units, some companies still feel their security problems are not always adequately dealt with. 'The problem is that a business will go to report an incident to its local police and be met by a man from the local CID who has 20 years' service; whose eyes will glaze over as soon as they tell him what has happened,' says the expert.

'He will take a few notes, say he will get back to them and refer the case to the NHTCU just so he can say he has. The police will not be interested if it's not "serious and organised" and so nothing will happen. Then they will call us in.'

Bounty hunters

As a result, private industry in the form of security consultants has rushed in to fill the gap in the market. In the early days of UK computer security there were people such as Ken Wong of BIS Applied Systems; Martin Samociuk of Network Security Management; Peter Sommer, a consultant, investigator and former hacker (and author of *The Hacker's Handbook*, see Chapter 1); Paul Carratu himself; and, even further behind the scenes, Kroll, the US private investigations company set up by the former CIA agent Jules B Kroll.

One can liken such characters to the work of the agents of the world-famous Pinkerton detective agency; the men who 'never slept' and who policed the West before the law came. Like the Pinkerton men, the security consultants in those pre-computer law days of the 1970s and 1980s hunted down and ended the careers of computer criminals though, unlike the Pinkerton agency of old, discretion was always their main watchword.

Alternatively the consultants and security firms are sometimes described as 'bounty hunters', a term made even more credible by the tendency of large organisations such as Microsoft to offer huge rewards – up to $250,000 – for information to track down cyber criminals.

Bounty hunting can certainly be a lucrative business. The top consultants can charge around £2,000 a day for their services. Such large fees might, for example, pay for them to secure a firm's computers discreetly over a weekend, set traps on them to catch culprits or take a copy of a computer disc and examine it to find out who has been moving files. These freelance cyber private investigators are able to carry out the most detailed forensic examinations of computers and, especially, the hard drive, the part where all the past actions of that computer are stored. It is unsurprising that these consultants are able to carry out examinations to the same standards as (or usually higher than) the police. After all, very often these are the same experts who are also teaching the police how to examine hard drives and sift for cyber evidence. Often their equipment will be more powerful, too.

One computer security company based a little more than a stone's throw from the Houses of Parliament in

Westminster boasts a safe for holding computerised evidence that would be the envy of a local bank, and employs former officers from the intelligence agencies and the police. This combination mirrors specialist police units in every way except that its staff have been practising the trade for much longer, have better tools and work directly for major financial institutions (among the most exacting masters of all). These computer professionals and scientists can even rebuild data from discs that have been erased, a function they occasionally carry out for the police.

Industrial espionage

There is of course another side to the private computer security industry, one hidden even further from public gaze. Most of the time these experts focus on protecting information on behalf of clients and on helping to catch cyber criminals.

However the authors have been told that in some cases it is the experts themselves – at least, a small minority of them – who are paid to go out and search down information. Much of this is innocent and perfectly legal, such as when they carry out so-called 'penetration tests' on a client's computer security system to see how effective it is against a genuine attack.

Yet in some instance the experts might be hired by one company to 'retrieve' information about a competitor. Industrial espionage is a crime simply made for the use of sophisticated computer techniques – such as hacking.

'I was asked to carry out a penetration test on one of the companies during the Distillers takeover,' says one computer security professional. (In 1986 there was a fierce battle in the UK between the companies Argyll and Guinness to take over drinks firm Distillers, a fight eventually won by Guinness in a £2.6 billion deal.) 'They asked me to get into the company computers to see what information I could get. So I turned up at reception as a BT repair man and asked to be taken to the computer room.

'Coincidentally they did have a phone problem and someone thought that I had been rung for. I asked for a phone terminal and they took me to an empty room in the computer suite. I plugged in my computer and came back every day for a week. The only people who weren't happy were the company who employed me, who said that I had "cheated"!'

Black knights, white knights

According to Paul Carratu such events are not uncommon. There is of course a huge incentive in being able to search through a competitor's data. Firms store not just traditional items such as payroll data in digital form, but more importantly the sensitive work a company is doing now and is planning for the future. The theft of such data from a computer can determine an organisation's very survival.

'We worked on one case where a major PLC in the drugs area had all of its research and development work stolen. It was worth £20 billion to the company but more importantly it lost its competitive edge in the marketplace for two years,' says Carratu, adding that it is well known in the industry that there are people who can obtain information on your behalf. 'We know that information is taken to order and that there are people out there, former intelligence people, who can get it for you. It's like everything – there are black knights and there are white knights.

'You don't see these people very often – they only need to do about three jobs a year and that's all they will do.'

Simon Janes, a former sergeant with the Scotland Yard's Computer Crime Unit and who now works with the computer forensics specialist Ibas, believes that much of the spying goes on from within a firm; the classic inside job.

'Espionage is big money and a lot of companies don't know it's going on 95 per cent of the time, and that it's internal,' says Janes.

One of the biggest threats are 'information brokers', people who steal information and sell to the highest bidder. He says that there has always been a suspicion among the police that this was going on but it had never been able to get a handle on it. 'Rather than going to the police, [businesses] will bring in companies like mine to find out why, who and how something was done.'

One of the distinctive features of computer security all over the world is how former law enforcement officers now work alongside colleagues from the 'dark' side – former hackers themselves.

It is not of course unusual for police officers to move into private security work after a number of years of public service; the pay is usually better, there are fewer bureaucratic restraints and the work can be more varied. In the UK, Janes is a veteran of the Metropolitan police's pioneering Computer Crime Unit, as is his former colleague Mark Morris, who is now Head of Forensics at IT consultants Logica CMG.

The best example of a police officer turning private is the astute officer who set up the Metropolitan police's Computer Crime Unit (CCU) unit in May 1984. John Austen was Britain's first 'cyber cop'; indeed one of the first in the world. He is a now a consultant at Royal Holloway, University of London, course director for the Royal Holloway Diploma in Information Security and a director of QCC InfoSec Training Ltd.

Austen, who had worked with computers before joining the police, was an obvious candidate for the pioneering post. 'They wanted something in the fraud squad who would be able to counter fraud and who knew something about computers,' recalls Austen. It was still a daunting task.

'They gave me three guys who didn't know anything at all about computers and to be perfectly honest I myself had to undertake quite a bit of research – very rapidly.'

Austen knew enough about computers and programming, however, to know that he needed help – and where to find it. 'I started contacting people that I knew in banking and then made friends with people in government departments, universities and business. It was so I could get to know people who were quite good on the different operating systems – so that we could produce evidence.'

He adds: 'The next task was to get some staff who understood or were capable of understanding the technology, and to do that I actually had to establish training courses. I ran the first course in 1985 and that has carried on ever since.'

Austen says that though his unit lacked resources, he was lucky that his superior officers did not interfere with his work and let him develop the specialist group as he saw fit. 'The bosses at the Met and at the Fraud Squad actually gave me quite a free rein, it was amazing. Nowadays it wouldn't happen; I don't think it had happened before either.'

Morris explains that though the unit was London based, it became in effect a default UK-wide police force. 'At that time the CCU was really the only dedicated computer unit in the country. We weren't just Metropolitan – we did actually have a remit to investigate international-type crime, which of course computer crime by its very nature is.'

Hackers turned officers

Yet if the path from law enforcement officer to private consultant is a well-trodden one, the route from hacker to security consultant is no less common. Perhaps the most infamous hacker of all, Kevin Mitnick, once one of the FBI's most wanted men, now advises and writes on security issues. Steve Gold, the Briton prosecuted over the hacking of the Prestel system in 1984, now writes on security issues. Meanwhile Nicholas Whiteley, who hacked into Queen Mary's College, London, computer system in the 1980s, also works as a security consultant.

Another example is Peter Sommer, now a successful academic and security consultant. He wrote *The Hacker's Handbook* under the name of Hugo Cornwall and was for many years a hacker (though it should be stressed that his hacking was performed at a time before it became illegal and before the term 'hacker' took on its darker meaning of recent years).

Another former hacker from those days of innocence is Neil Barrett. Barrett is the hacker who came in from the cold and went on to become the youngest-ever university computer studies lecturer; the original whizz-kid. Barrett has been one of the moving forces behind high-tech policing in the UK and sat on the panel at the media launch of the NHTCU in the Science Museum. Barrett has advised GCHQ, the then Defence Research Agency (now QinetiQ), worked in Northern Ireland with Special Branch and MI5, and sits at the core of many of the activities aimed at countering today's hackers. But as well as his establishment links – he is also professor of Computer Criminology at the Royal Military College of Science, Cranfield University – Barrett also works in the private sector and is non-executive technical director of a firm called Information Risk Management Plc, which specialises in testing the security of e-commerce sites.

Across the Atlantic, a key figure who again underlines the exceptionally close links between public and private sector in computer security is Paul Strassmann. Strassmann served on the side of the

Allies in a guerilla combat unit of the Czechoslovak Army from 1944 to the end of the war in 1945, and in a sense has been fighting for much of his career. However most of the time his 'enemy' has been cyber criminals, and especially hackers. Strassmann's career has spanned time with huge corporations such as Xerox, combined with a period spent in public service first as director of Defense Information at the US Department of Defense and more recently as chief information executive for National Aeronautics and Space Administration, better know as NASA.

As well as a successful administrator, however, Strassmann is an important theorist, a sort of Hegel of the information age. One of Strassmann's main arguments is that the protection of the digital world should be done rationally, logically and with each part of the world working together and helping each other out. At the moment he feels this is not happening, but cites as a potential model the way that countries such as the United States fight national health problems. Strassmann explains:

> *You must understand that the reason why disease control works in the US is because every nurse that is certified in the emergency room of every hospital or clinic is under law obligated to report certain things. There is a whole infrastructure of people who do autopsies.*
>
> *It's a very, very rich spectrum of institutions and people and charters and so forth that individually are serving certain things – but in aggregate they work admirably well. With this part of the infrastructure the whole idea is how you get the private industry and the various police departments and so forth to work together. How do you create the law and the infrastructure they have in health certification?*
>
> *We are absolutely at the most primitive stage today of dealing with this whole issue of how you get an electronically based society function. At the moment we are in an almost Victorian industrial stage in relation to the internet.*

Governments get wise

Yet despite Strassmann's somewhat gloomy view of how we are coping with the digital age, there are signs that governments and law enforcement agencies are waking up to the threat of cyber crime.

We have already seen one approach in the United States, with the collaboration of the FBI and industry. In Germany specialist units of the BKA police are charged with tackling hi-tech crime, while in Russia there is the already mentioned Spider Group, a special department 'K' at the Ministry of Internal Affairs. And there is a Hi-Tech and Intellectual Property Crime Unit at the Ministry of Internal Affairs in Ukraine.

The authorities in Australia have set up their own Australian High-Tech Crime Centre to co-ordinate the fight against hi-tech crime and attacks on the country's information infrastructure. In Britain too there is the new specialist unit dealing exclusively with cyber crime, also mentioned previously. Set up in April 2001, the National Hi-Tech Crime Unit (NHTCU) marks the emergence of a new hybrid form of police force; part investigative, part computer forensic, part liaison between industry and law enforcement. Unlike previous police forces it is not outside the 'machine' – the world of the computer and the internet – looking in, but now operates within the machine itself. How it and similar bodies fare in the coming years could determine whether the battle against cyber crime is won or lost.

CHAPTER THREE
The Rise of the Cyber Cop

In the background one can hear the constant din of the air-conditioning system as it struggles to cool two powerful eight-feet-high servers standing in the corner. Meanwhile all around the anonymous room sit sleek black computer terminals and processors, churning through endless megabytes of data, each under the expert eyes of their user. On the desks are numerous sets of earphones through which the users listen to their favourite music as they methodically plough their way through the information in front of them.

One, Marc Kirby, barely seems to notice the incessant noise of the cooling system; he is focused on the computer in front of him, its VDU glowing with letters, numbers, files and curious grey areas in between. 'This,' he tells you, pointing at the bewildering array of computer data on the flat screen, 'is a crime scene'.

CYBER-HIGHWAYMEN

At first glance this might appear to be an unlikely statement, but then this is an unusual room in an unusual unit in an otherwise unremarkable building. Even Marc Kirby's full and rather wordy job title – Digital Evidence Recovery Manager – does not really give a clue as to the vital work that he does. He is, in fact, Detective Inspector Marc Kirby, a member of the United Kingdom's National Hi-Tech Crime Unit (NHTCU), the world's first purpose-built national law enforcement agency dedicated to the prevention of cyber crime and the trapping of cyber criminals. Here, in this tall building located somewhere in London's Docklands – the authors have agreed not to identify the exact location – the UK's fight against the growing menace of cyber crime takes place.

New kids on the block

The unit was set up in April 2001 after a series of high-level reports and studies revealed a disturbing weakness in the country's ability to combat cyber crime. It has a daunting remit. Its official and stated aim is, couched in the usual language of Civil Service-speak, to 'combat national and transnational serious and organised hi-tech crime within, or which impacts upon, the United Kingdom'.

In reality however the unit has an even bigger, if unspoken, challenge; nothing less than keeping the country's entire internet structure safe from attack and to make sure that Britain's growing e-commerce industry is able to flourish. If the internet revolution has brought about a whole new way of doing business and communicating with each other, then it has also spawned its very own form of law enforcement.

There are interesting historical parallels between the development of this new kind of cyber cop and the growth of traditional policing in the 19th century. The 'real world' police were born partly out of a need to prevent lawlessness on the streets but also, and crucially, to ensure that the belongings of the propertied classes were protected and that the conditions needed for the growth and expansion of trade in society were met. Its power and structure grew with the triumph of the Industrial Revolution. So it is with the new hi-tech police force. If there is no one to police the cyber highways then, as we have seen, they will quickly become taken over by the growing number of cyber criminals; the 'cyber-highwaymen' as they have been dubbed. The inevitable result; a potentially catastrophic loss of public confidence in internet and e-commerce and an almost complete reversal of the massive growth of internet-based trade in recent years.

The challenge facing the unit, the self-styled 'new kids on the block', is explicitly recognised by its own members. The job of detective constable Tony Neate, a personable career police officer from Wales, is to act as the NHTCU's liaison with government and, crucially, industry. This includes many of the country's leading businesses, huge multinationals that are growing to rely on the internet to do ever more of their business. He is, therefore, well placed to know just what is at stake.

He says: 'What we've all got to be concerned about is keeping the trust of online e-commerce alive because as soon as customers start thinking I'm not going to buy anything online, then they think I'm not going to bank online, I'm not going to buy my air-line tickets and I'm not going to buy my holidays online.'

DC Neate adds: 'The work that I'm doing is to keep industry informed about what's happening in other sectors so we keep consumer confidence. Because it's all about what we were set up to do: to make Britain a safe place to live and work and the best place for e-business.'

The unit's senior analyst Helen Saunders also paints a grim picture of what could happen to public trust in the internet without effective policing and security. 'Yes it could crumble, this is the concern,' she says. 'All this stuff [people hear] about just going to a website and their computer being infected . . . it might reach a point where people say I am not going online, as simple as that. They might say, I am unplugging my machine and I can live without the internet and I will go to a local bank like I used to ten years ago.'

Unfortunately, of course, it is not as simple as that; there may not be any bank branches to go to. As one well-placed computer security analyst told the authors: 'A lot of companies now are built on online commerce. Barclays bank is a prime example; it has 3.5 million online customers all run by just seven people. If customers were to go back to the high street, there just wouldn't be enough branches to cater for them.'

If online banking failed, the costs of banks having to re-establish real branches would run into billions and billions of pounds. All of which explains the decision by the then Home Secretary Jack Straw in 2000 to agree to set up the National Hi-tech Crime Unit and charge it with maintaining Britain's e-commerce infrastructure; ensuring that public trust is maintained in the internet[1].

This second requirement explains another of the unit's current key pre-occupations: child pornography and abuse. Much public ire has been aimed, in recent years, at the way in which paedophiles have used the speed and anonymity of the internet to form private networks and exchange information, photographs and videos. A great deal of the unit's current workload is spent investigating large-scale paedophile rings online and in helping other UK forces in their own local investigations. While the paedophiles themselves may pose no direct threat to the internet, public disgust at their use of it might well do so.

Yet e-criminals and paedophiles are not the only cyber criminals in the sights of the NHTCU. Its brief can cover any form of hi-tech crime as long as it is 'serious' and 'organised' and their targets may include hackers, virus writers, phishers and gangs carrying out DDoS attacks on websites. Their fight may be against 'old' crimes in a new form such as the exchange of paedophilia material via the internet, as well as brand-new types of crime such as hacking and virus writing. An officer's skills therefore need to cover both old and new; traditional policing combined with advanced technological ability. In other words, he is a cyber cop.

Global beat

In the days of Dixon of Dock Green the criminal mind was no less cunning than it is now, but a villain's ability to use technology was severely restricted. On a typical beat, a police officer might come across an opportunist thief trying to break into a car, a cat burglar shinning up a drain pipe or, just possibly, a local professional committing some kind of white-collar fraud on his firm.

Nowadays the modern cyber cop may still have a beat; but it is one based on bytes, bits, servers and international networks. While the traditional police officer's patrol will take him or her within a few miles of the station, a cyber cop's patrol could cover the entire global network; they might visit, literally, anywhere in cyber space. And if cyber criminals now have vast technological skills and resources at their fingertips, then the cyber police officer must adopt the same techniques and acquire the same mental approaches as their prey.

Helen Saunders explains their mindset. 'You have to put yourself in their shoes. It comes down to thinking laterally. It is the business of a career criminal or organised criminals to commit crime, and it is our business to stop them. If they spend 8 hours a day or 24 hours a day working out how to get a vital piece of information, then I have to spend an equal amount of time working out how they would do it. There are close parallels in the way we work, research and use intelligence.'

The unit is split into four main groups: Investigations, Intelligence, Tactical and Technical Support, and Digital Evidence. It is the first of these groups that most closely mirrors other traditional policing units. Its role is both to initiate its own investigations into cyber crime and criminals, and also to help other police forces and other law enforcement agencies – for example, Customs and Excise – around the UK. The criteria governing the unit's involvement are that the crimes must be both serious and organised and involve some use of High-Technology, such as making sophisticated use of the internet or computers.

The unit's Intelligence group has an even more wide-ranging role than Investigations. Its staff sift and examine evidence of cyber crimes not just from the United Kingdom but from all over the rest of the world; its beat truly is global. Information may be passed on to the unit from, for example, fellow officers in Germany, France or the United States, from other law enforcement agencies in the UK or from non-government private industry sources. This information will then be assessed and if necessary acted upon; the unit might launch an investigation itself or pass the information on to the police force most affected by where the crime has or is expected to take place, be it in the UK or elsewhere in the world.

The Tactical and Technical (T&T) Support group combines two key roles. One role is to act as a central clearing-house for information and technical advice for local UK police forces. Although each police force in Britain has its own specialists in computer-related crime, few have the concentrated bank of knowledge and expertise developed by the NHTCU in London. These forces can therefore call upon the T&T unit as an additional resource to help them understand different techniques and trends in cyber crime law enforcement. The unit's other job is to liaise between the police, industry and government; a unique role in law enforcement that we shall examine in more detail later in the chapter.

The fourth unit (and most technical and in many ways arcane of them all) is Detective Inspector Marc Kirby's Digital Evidence Recovery group. Kirby's team operate in a room behind closed doors, doors that are closed even to the rest of the NHTCU squad, except with prior permission. On the days that the authors were allowed access to this secretive investigative lair, much of the sensitive material that might usually be worked on by the unit's four-member team had been locked away. The reason for this secrecy is soon clear; Kirby explains that while this closely knit unit is part of the NHTCU, it is also a separate entity, a unit-within-a-unit. Their job is to provide a detailed forensic examination of any computers that are seized by NHTCU or other investigators and to demonstrate what evidence is – and is not – contained on them. In other words their job is to provide an accurate, unbiased view of exactly what a suspect's computer contains.

DI Kirby explains: 'The only people allowed access on the entry card are myself and the team. Access to this room is restricted so we can maintain the integrity of everything that we work on . . . for evidential reasons and because we are impartial in what we do.'

The T&T unit is supported up by some formidable computer power, storage capacity and ingenious software. The storage capacity, for example, is almost mind-boggling for a home-computer user. The office has those two servers, one running a primary domain server, the other a backup. Combined with six computer terminals, this means the forensic unit's storage capacity is around sixteen terabytes. That is 16,000 gigabytes of capacity, no small amount when the top-of-the-range home computer may just stretch to a 250 gigabyte hard drive.

Yet even this substantial capacity is not enough. When the system is full – and at the moment it is 'almost full' – then much of the vast amount of data is stored onto discs and transferred to a secret location for the day that it might be needed as evidence. Elsewhere his computers are running various ingenious bits of software, some of it available in the high-street, some of it less familiar – each of them the computer forensic expert's tools of the trade.

The real key to the forensic examination of cyber crime is a computer's hard drive. Exactly what is or is not on the hard drive will determine the fate of an investigation and whether prosecution of a suspected hacker, virus writer, paedophile, phisher, fraudster or extortionist can go ahead. DI Kirby explains: 'People bring hard drives to me and say, "Can you look for X, Y or Z?" That's what I do. If X, Y, or Z is there I tell them; if it's not there I tell them.'

The hard drive of a computer is like an all-seeing, all-knowing witness, silently recording all that the computer (and by extension the computer user) is doing, and keeping its secrets intact until the moment when someone chooses to interrogate it. Then, like any compliant witness, it divulges the clues and evidence the investigator is seeking. Kirby regards the hard drive his 'crime scene'. 'And it has to be investigated in exactly the same way as any other crime scene,' he says. 'So you apply "ABC"; Accept nothing, Believe nothing, Challenge everything.'

There is even more to it, however, than the application of tried and tested police investigation techniques. It is in this room where the policing that might have been familiar to Dixon of Dock Green meets the computer forensics of the 21st century to create the cyber forensic investigator. Each of Kirby's men – all serving police or military officers – is put through a masters degree course in forensic computing at the Royal Military College of Science at Shrivenham, the self-styled Defence Academy of the United Kingdom[2]. On this elite course the investigators will hone their skills in systems programming, e-crime, forensic networks and understand how different computer operating systems work, how networks operate, how computers connect to the internet and where potential evidence is likely to be stored – or hidden – on a server or network. Above all they must be expert in what is called disc geometry; essentially, knowing how a hard drive works.

DI Kirby believes his team is just about the best in the country and intends to keep it that way. Kirby says he looks for 'natural investigators' among his team; they do not necessarily have to come from police or military backgrounds (though these two professions tend to perform investigative work so it is natural that they should form the core of his unit). What his team must all have in common is a certain passion for computers, software and increasingly the internet; it is a trait shared right across the NHTCU, beyond just the 'techies' who carry out the forensic work.

Kirby himself is no exception to this. Powerfully built and engagingly direct in manner, it comes as little surprise to find out that his favourite sport is rugby, and in many ways he appears to be a very conventional career detective. But then you discover his other side. His entry into the police in 1982 was roughly the time when personal computers were becoming popular in Britain, when machines such as the Commodore and the Sinclair Spectrum were being launched upon a curious public. Kirby, who had studied statistics as part of his university degree, and was comfortable in the world of figures and data, knew he had to get involved in this PC revolution.

For much of his police career his work was as a hands-on operational policeman (investigating murders, for example). One day he heard that the Home Secretary was announcing the formation of something called the National Hi-tech Crime Squad. Kirby suddenly realised that his dream job had been created. He applied and was accepted.

Aladdin's Cave

All of this training, computer power and software is aimed at one thing; unlocking the secrets of hard drives belonging to suspected cyber criminals. For the skilled forensic investigator the hard drive can be a real Aladdin's Cave of hidden or apparently 'lost' information.

Kirby points to the screen in front of him again, a screen that shows a sample hard drive designed to show where information is stored on a computer. What appears to the untrained eye as no more than a list of different drives becomes, using the software used by Kirby's team and other forensic experts, a series of colour bands, broken by small grey zones, and it is these dull, nondescript areas that shout one word: evidence. For these are known as 'unallocated space' on the computer's hard drive and it is here that vital evidence may be found. 'When you delete files they are not always deleted, and this is where they end up,' says Kirby, pointing to the grey zones. 'Similarly, if you want to hide files, this is where you would put them, so they are full of data.'

The detective then goes onto explain, using the analogy of a filing system in a library, how difficult it is to delete a file completely from a computer's hard drive. 'If you go to a library and look for a book, for example by Bert Smith, but do so when the first letter is taken away, the indexing system becomes useless and you can't find the book,' says Kirby. The book is still in the library, of course, it just cannot now be located by the normal indexing system. 'And that's what is happening here . . . when you delete an item from your computer, it only deletes the first letter and marks the file, saying "available for use for over-writing",' says Kirby. 'So unless the file has been overwritten – and that does not happen until a hard drive is really quite full – the chances are probably 70:30, maybe even better, that the file still exists and can be recovered. All you do is just put the first letter back!'

File slack holes

These mysterious grey areas are not the only places where secret data can be discovered. Delving ever deeper into the mysteries of computer hard drives, Kirby discusses the existence of what is called 'file slack' and 'slack space'.

'When a file is written to a computer it is allocated a certain amount of space but it does not always use up all that space,' he explains. 'What it does not use up is called "slack". The operating system Windows does not like slack so it will put anything in there – gobbledegook, from anywhere – to fill up the space so the operating system works.' In other words, crucial phrases, names or numbers could be tipped, like so much builders' rubble, to fill up these 'file slack' holes, and lie there awaiting to be unearthed by the skills of a forensic examiner.

According to Kirby, even if one overwrote a file one hundred times, the chances are that some of the data would be left somewhere on the machine. Each time one writes a document, one starts not just the original file but a temporary file, too, and there is also data being stored in the computer's memory (RAM), all of which are potential repositories of important data. The chance of someone being able to overwrite all these areas exactly, while ensuring that no data has 'leaked out' into areas is small, says Kirby. 'There are four areas where all of your data has gone and you have got to overwrite all of those data areas a hundred times for it to completely, completely disappear; and the chances of that happening are not great because Windows leaks everywhere.'

To demonstrate how recovery of leaked data works, an investigator asks the diagnostic computer to search the 'suspect's' hard drive for the word 'Orlando' (which the suspect had deleted), asking it at the same time to search among the file slack. Within seconds the screen displays a deleted file, its contents marked in black. Here, among the coherent sentences, there is no sign of the word Orlando. Scroll a little however and there are lines of random words, letters and symbols marked in red; this is the file slack. It is here, among this 'rubble' of jumbled words that the word Orlando appears.

'It could be for example a credit card number,' says Kirby, pointing how it could be a valuable piece of evidence. 'It might be nowhere on any of the files . . . but it is on that machine in slack space. When I give evidence, I say that I was asked to look for credit card number 123456, for example, and that here, clearly, is that number, and I found it physically on that hard drive.

The chance of that number appearing in that sequence by chance is a million to one.' To counter this evidence, a defence expert would have to find an explanation of why that may not be a credit card number. 'But they can't,' says Kirby.

Yet criminals are always exploiting new developments in technology to conceal their tracks in this cyber cat and mouse game with the investigators. One such technique is known as 'steganography', defined as the science – or art – of concealing information in apparently harmless-looking files or areas. Steganography can be likened to the use of a false bottom in a suitcase to make it look as though there is nothing else below it, when in fact there is a concealed compartment. Using this technique – and there are programmes that can do it automatically – a person can bury secret data (such as credit card numbers) within innocuous documents and files on the hard drive. The problem with this ruse is that the concealed compartment still has to occupy a certain amount of space, and a skilled observer is likely to notice the discrepancy between the outside bulk of the suitcase and its inside volume.

'If I look at a word file and see the average size is 1kb, and all of a sudden I look at this word document and it's 50 kilobytes I think, that's a big number, lets have a look at it!' says Kirby. 'And if it's got just five sentences in it I know there is something else in there. Once again it comes back to your analysis of the crime scene. Looking for all of those things that are not quite right.'

A stealth technique more commonly employed by criminals – as well as by many other legitimate computer users – is to use encryption to protect data. To read the encrypted code you need to know – or to find – the key to the code. Though the team have come across encryption, they have usually been able to break the code. On the few occasions where they do struggle, they send the hard drive to the National Technical Assistance Centre (NTAC)[3], a specialist unit that works from the headquarters of MI5 building in central London.

An example of this outside help occurred in the case of David Ward, a British paedophile who was later gaoled for taking and distributing obscene images and for sexually assaulting a baby. Ward had gone to great lengths to hide his activities and had used what are called 'encrypted magic folders' to hide much of his material. While Kirby's software was able to detect the presence of the encrypted magic folders, the unit was unable to break it because Ward has used a 'cracked' (pirated) copy that was tricky to unlock. 'We tried every which way but could not [get into them] so we fired it off to NTAC. They got back quickly with the password, and we used it and found more of what we had already found: hundreds of paedophile pictures.'

Freezing a hard drive
To carry out an investigation, the forensics team needs an exact copy of the hard drive to be investigated. Actually, the word 'copy' does not accurately describe the meticulous nature of the process: to ensure that investigators – and ultimately any courtroom – has a complete and true representation of the suspect's hard drive, its contents have to be 'frozen' and preserved. In the same way that a 'real world' murder crime scene cannot be contaminated and altered while an investigation is continuing, the hard drive crime scene must be kept secure too. If even a minor change to the image is made after the moment of 'freezing', then it cannot be used as evidence in law.

Freezing is done by taking what is known as an 'image' of the hard drive; more than just a copy of the data on the hard drive, it is an exact replica of the drive itself. To prove the image's integrity, a complex algorithmic verification number, called an MD5, is made at the time the image is made. A kind of electronic fingerprint of the image, when the image is reloaded onto a machine back at the unit's laboratory, the MD5 fingerprint is checked again against the original. 'If they are not identical the programme will just not work,' says Kirby.

As well as taking the image of the hard drive, the team will usually physically open up the computer to ensure the suspect has not tried to conceal hard drives. 'Some people are very clever and are able to disguise hard drives by pulling out the plug so, when you turn on the machine, they are not noticed by the operating system. So we might have four hard drives in there but only one is plugged in,' says Kirby.

Building a picture

This detailed examination of a person's hard drive means the forensic team often build up a clear picture of that person's life. Understanding how the suspect works and his personality is important for Kirby.

At the start of each investigation he typically takes a clone of the hard drive, puts this into another hard drive and then boots up a machine so he can see the way in which the person arranged their computer. 'I look at it as they would look at it,' he says. This includes how they arrange their desktop, their favourites or bookmarks on the internet, the way they store and arrange their data and files. 'It's like going into someone's bedroom or into their car; you get a pretty good idea of what they are like,' he says.

Kirby recalls one case in which, after a short examination of a hard drive, he had an insight into the complex life of one male suspect. 'After about half an hour I had his mobile phone number, his mistress' mobile phone number, the fact he sent her flowers on a certain day, the time and place, his four or five Yahoo email account passwords, copies of quite a few of his deleted emails he sent using Yahoo – because there were traces left – his credit card number and that of his mistress' . . . all with a minimal amount of work.' He adds, 'So immediately you knew, for example, that he was having an affair, the woman was living in America, and what her address and mobile number were in America. From a quick look, you can start to get an idea of what someone is like.'

Simply how someone stores their data can be a clue as to whether they might be involved in a suspected activity. For example, says

Kirby, if there is disorganisation and 'clutter' all over the place, this might cast doubt on whether that computer user really is, say, at the centre of a highly organised distribution of paedophilia online.

Perhaps the most important part of a forensic examination, though, will be to see the time and date at which files were created, deleted, or when emails were sent or received. One of the first tasks of any investigator is to put the image of the suspect's hard drive in the order of time and date; this soon builds up a picture of their activities and, crucially, can link their online and computer behaviour to events in the 'real' world.

'The time and date are for me the most important,' argues Kirby. 'For example we have had investigations where a corporate email has been sent.' In such cases the person suspected will often claim he did not send the email, even though it came from his machine. He will argue that everyone in the office knew his computer login name and his password. However, says Kirby, if a time and date examination shows that, close to the time the email was sent from the machine, personal documents relating to the suspect were changed, 'You think the chances are that it was him who has sent the particular email.'

Analysing cyber space
Along the corridor, Helen Saunders, too, is in her element surrounded by computers. Saunders is a true child of the computer age; her father encouraged her interest in them while she was still a young girl and they remain a passion. 'My dad could see that computers would be the big thing – he told me to go out and understand them.'

Now her life revolves around using the machines. Using the internet and email for research and communication is as natural to her as it might be for others to open a book. 'I cannot imagine my life without a computer,' she admits. 'If I need to find out something I will look on the internet, that's the first place I look.'

This affinity for computers and the internet is crucial for the job. Saunders is the NHTCU's senior analyst, head of a small but important team of analysts, the unsung heroes of the world of law enforcement. Analysts are routinely used by criminal investigation units throughout police departments, yet they rarely feature on police and crime dramas. Saunders is philosophical about the analyst's low public profile. 'Someone sitting at a computer analysing data is not as interesting as someone going and kicking in a few doors, is it? We are supposed to be the engine room of the unit but no one wants to see a greasy lump of metal do they?' she adds with a smile.

At the heart of Saunders' job is the use – or in the jargon, 'manipulation' – of vast amounts of information and data, out of which the analyst's task is to make some sense and find a pattern.

There are two different types of analyst, strategic and tactical, in crime detection generally and at the NHTCU. The role of NHTCU strategic analysts is to examine reports and information from, for example, recent cases, other law enforcement agencies, government departments and media reports, and out of this establish future trends in cyber crime, draw lessons from what has happened in the past and establish standards for future approaches or 'best practice'. Their work helps establish where the unit should be concentrating its focus for maximum effect.

'It gives you an idea of the main threats and helps you decide priorities,' says Saunders. 'For example, denial of service (DoS) attacks [attacks on websites to extort money from the owners] are a big thing at the moment.'

If Marc Kirby and his team work on the microscopic level of cyber crime, minutely analysing the workings of a computer hard drive, then the strategic analyst is working on the opposite extreme, at the macro level.

By contrast, tactical analysts are case based, typically working with an investigating officer to establish patterns, spot links, and highlight the holes in an investigation's knowledge, so the investigator has a clearer idea of what needs to be done to crack the case. In a sense they are joining up the dots of the raw material uncovered by an investigation. Many of us may already be vaguely familiar with some of this; those crude whiteboard drawings so beloved of senior TV detectives as they explain a case to their team are, in more sophisticated computer form, the stock in trade of the tactical analyst.

Cyber links

Saunders, herself a former tactical analyst at Scotland Yard, explains how they work in practice. 'An officer is assigned a case that involves, for example, getting server logs [reports of email and internet traffic held on web servers] from all over the country or world. If they look at them and don't understand what they are seeing, they will ask an analyst to get involved. I would then examine the logs, and explain what picture I see emerging.

'I could see from the data that "X" knows "Y", that they frequent a particular place, that kind of thing. I would start building up a picture.

'I might then say that we have data from this area but, if we had data from another source – for example another witness – then we would be able to fill in the part of the picture that we don't understand at the moment.' She adds by way of summary: 'We give an overview so investigating officers do not get drowned in information. We are like a filtering mechanism.'

Usually an analyst will reduce a hugely complex web of information to one or two sides of A4 paper so the picture of the investigation can be kept as clear and uncluttered as possible. One of the main differences between the traditional analyst and the cyber analyst, however, is that the patterns, links and networks they are seeing may not just be between people, but between, computers, websites, email accounts and servers. Slowly the analyst builds up a picture of how these different parts of cyber space link together to form a pattern showing criminal association.

Ultimately, insists Saunders, the goal and outcome is the same as with other analysts. She says: 'I think there is almost a fear among some people that technology gets in the way and they think they can't handle it and that it must be a very different world. But it's not. You have just got the real world with this layer of technology over the top of it.'

Investigators are still dealing with criminals and the workings of the criminal mind. 'At end of day, you are still looking at criminal relationships, networks, how they work, the inter-relations, who they communicate with. You are just maybe replacing a phone call with an email. You are still looking at the fundamentals of communications and associations. It just so happens it takes on another guise.'

In some senses the work of Saunders and her team is reminiscent of a sheriff in the old Wild West, doggedly tracking down his foe by moving methodically from one footprint left in the wilderness to the next. The difference in the case of the NHTCU is that the trail they are following is in cyber space and the tracks left behind are digital rather than human footprints. They are also permanent and lasting footprints. Saunders herself prefers a slightly different analogy. 'It's almost like following bread crumbs.'

One investigation Helen Saunders and her team worked on concerned someone who was suspected of launching denial of service (DoS) attacks. She was able to track him down through some old clues – or crumbs –

he had left years earlier on the web. 'We had the guy's website and a nickname. By researching old versions of his website on the internet, we found that in the past he had given out personal information, his first name and his date of birth; but in the version of the site up there now that had all disappeared.' The hacker had obviously deleted any references to is real name and background details to safeguard his identity.

In this case the hacker probably assumed his trail had gone cold; but not, as it turned out, too cold for the cyber analysts to follow.

Though the cyber analysts all have standard tools for sifting and analysing the date they find, they also need to think laterally to anticipate how a criminal might react and try to cover their tracks.

'The key thing is not just know how technology works, but where data is stored on the internet,' Saunders says. She points out that while the technology they use may be logical and, in a sense infallible, the people using them are still, of course, just people. 'In the end, criminals slip up; that's the way we catch them. It's human nature to make a mistake.'

One particular mistake it is hard for cyber criminals to avoid is to create patterns of behaviour on their computer and on the internet. 'For example, everyone tends to use the same user name or password for ten different things; people are creatures of habit, we cannot randomise very easily.'

Even if users are smart enough to change a user name they might still use the same or similar passwords, and this too can help show analysts those crucial links and patterns they are looking for. Indeed there is something of a paradox here; we are constantly told that the internet is anonymous and that criminals and others take advantage to hide behind this anonymity. And yet when they are using the internet these criminals cannot help forming patterns, using similar names, contacting similar people. In other words, they start to create their own cyber identities.

As Saunders says: 'In the end it is still just technology sitting on top of the world.' This explains why she still finds it useful to try to anticipate the suspect's moves. 'You have to put yourself in their shoes.' She gets access to every bit of intelligence and evidence in an investigation, and is therefore well placed to understand how a suspect thinks, and even what makes them do what they do.

'The best example is in the case of child abuse. When they talk to each other you do get their personalities and an understanding of where they are coming from, what their "morals" are. It's people talking to people.'

Cleaning data

A lot of the work carried out by Helen Saunders and her team is the time-consuming business of 'cleaning' the data she is given, which means putting it into forms from which true patterns and trends can be extracted. It can be a laborious process but is, according to Saunders, a necessary one.

'By cleaning the data you understand what's in the data set. By understanding what's in the data set you understand which is the best way to manipulate it. Then once you have manipulated it and you get a set of results, the analysis starts [to make sense of these results].' This brings its own pleasures to the unsung heroes of the NHTCU: 'There is a certain satisfaction in being given this absolute mess of data; and to have created something out of it,' says Saunders.

INDUSTRY LIAISON

Like many of his colleagues Tony Neate has long had an interest in computers and in computer crime. In his native Wales the detective constable has headed up a cyber crime unit, and he has also been involved with the Association of Chief Police Officers (ACPO)

Computer Crime Working Group, giving him a good strategic overview of the issue and how it could and does impact on society.

It was a natural progression, therefore, for him to move to the NHTCU and take on one of the more unusual roles in British policing. His title is Industry Liaison Officer, which means he spends his time talking to UK businesses about the threats posed by cyber crime and ensuring that vital information on specific cyber crimes, such as phishing, viruses, hacking and denial of service, is passed both to and from industry. Neate's job therefore underlines one of the key aims of the unit: to keep the e-commerce arm of UK PLC running smoothly and ensure that public confidence in online transactions is maintained. His beat is the Cyber City.

It is a job for which DC Neate is well equipped. His name suitably describes his appearance and manner, and he combines the reassuring air of a detective with the assured poise of one used to speaking at conferences and mingling with the great and good of industry. When he took up the position, Neate also understood that it was a job that is probably unique in UK policing.

'I thought it was going to be a great new way forward; brand new for the police force to actually have a police officer detective with some experience who was specifically employed to liaise with industry.'

The buzz words – trust and confidentiality – in Neate's vocabulary reflect the delicate nature of his task. It is commonplace in Western societies around the world that many big businesses – especially financial institutions – have routinely failed to disclose that they have been victims of cyber crime. Their reason is simple; the financial damage caused by the cyber attack is usually dwarfed by the potential damage if word of their loss leaked out and damaged customer confidence. The banking industry in particular is built largely on trust; when we hand over our money we trust that they will be able to return the money whenever we ask for it.

There were other reasons too for the non-reporting of cyber crimes. Many in business traditionally felt there was no one to report it to or that the crimes were too complex for local police forces. Others were not even sure that the 'offences' against them were really crimes. This lack of reporting has meant that police forces all over the planet have been unable to assess the true scale of computer-assisted frauds, or the methods used or personnel involved. Ultimately this means that the whole of industry has suffered by not being warned of impending new attacks.

Trust and confidentiality

The response of the NHTCU has been not to try to name and shame the reluctant businesses but instead to enter into a unique confidential agreement with them, an agreement nurtured by Tony Neate. The agreement is enshrined in the unit's Confidentiality Charter, whose aim is to reassure industry that it can 'safely' report hi-tech crimes. In its summary the Charter states: '. . . It is essential that commercial organisations in the UK and elsewhere who are targeted by hi-tech criminals are given the assurance that they can report such attacks without fear of adversely affecting their business.'

Allowing for the bureaucratic nature of the language, there could hardly be a stronger sign of just how closely the unit works with industry on this crucial issue. The flow of information is not just one way. In return for revealing their own secrets, companies can expect to be briefed on threats they might face; threats gleaned from the police's own intelligence work and private discussions with other firms. The police are, in effect, acting as an honest information broker between different and competing companies and the security industry.

Tony Neate says that already in the unit's short existence industry has become far more open. '[Businesses] are happy to give us information as a third party and for us to disseminate it; and the trust and confidentiality over the last three years has certainly gone through the roof.'

The detective constable realises that what they have achieved is a first. 'It's something that doesn't happen in other areas of crime. They [the firms] now realise that they do need us. In a lot of these sectors they don't talk to their counterparts because of competitive edge. They've learnt to talk to each other – certainly in the financial sector – about fraud a lot more but, as for the high-tech crime side of it, the security side of it, they haven't really thought of [doing] it.'

Neate says the police are well suited to building up trust with industry because it is part of their culture to keep certain items of information concealed. 'The police is good at keeping secrets in relation to, for example, informers.' He also recognises however that if it loses that trust, even once, by breaching a firm's confidence, then it is 'dead in the water'.

Keeping up-to-date

Interestingly the sort of agreement that business in the UK has with the NHTCU cannot operate in countries where the right to know information can on occasions outweigh even the demands of commercial secrecy.

'The Confidentiality Charter we've got [in the UK] wouldn't work in the United States because it's got Freedom of Information – you tell the government something and the government has got to tell the people,' explains Neate. 'Society [in the UK] understands why there is a necessity to have confidentiality.'

The system that the NHTCU has established means that Neate is in constant dialogue with British firms, as well as the Department of Trade and Industry (DTI) and other parts of the British government.

He explains: 'We run briefings in the financial sector and in other areas, where we bring them together every six months. We tell them what the current trends are, what the current threats are, what we're seeing coming.'

Speaking about the threat of phishing (the spoofing of emails and websites by criminals to lure the unwary into handing over financial information), which began in the autumn of 2003 and has been growing ever since, Neate says: 'At the moment phishing is a massive problem and increasing; but that threat is going to move from the financial sector where we're seeing it to other sectors. So we can pass that information on to other sectors.'

For many companies, especially the smaller ones who might depend on the web for much of their business but do not have the resources and expertise to employ full-time cyber security staff, the problem of knowing what to defend against next and how to do it can be an acute one. Such is the speed with which criminals role out new technology and techniques, it can even be tough for the larger firms to keep in touch.

Neate recalls: 'I was at this meeting where there were some top-quality guys and they were astounded at the things that are coming out. It's tough keeping up to date with them. Now if you've got a company that's not the biggest company in the world and its core business is producing widgets, how is it going to keep up to date? How does it know what the latest scam is? How does it pick its way through the reports?' He adds, 'It is a nightmare both for the consumer and for those smaller enterprises that just happen to use a computer for their communications but whose core business is producing widgets.'

The police acknowledges that one problem facing small businesses is viruses, which can cause both disruption and potentially damaging costs for smaller companies as well as undermining public trust in the sites they run. Neate says that thanks to the NHTCU the issue is being dealt with more seriously nationwide in the UK, but he believes that one country acting alone can do little to stop the menace:

We've got lots of people looking at the virus attacks but it's so global and massive that all we can be is part of a blended effort with other agencies around the world to look at the issues when they come out and to work with other law enforcement agencies.

The issue of viruses is so large that it's impossible for us to take on as a whole; but we take it seriously. We look at the web

*scans, we've got connections with every antivirus organisa-
tion in the country, they let us know anything that's coming
through and we might pass that onto other law enforcement
agencies in other countries or they contact us and we run the
lead here.*

Asymmetric vandalism

For example, the unit might glean information from abroad that a
virus writer is active in a particular UK city, and they would set up
an intelligence cell to monitor and gather evidence for a prosecution.

Neate believes that rewards offered by companies – for example,
by Microsoft – for information leading to the arrest and conviction
of perpetrators have helped to deter would-be virus writers. Yet he
accepts that the ability of a virus writer to cause so much damage on
his own – what some have dubbed the phenomenon of 'asymmetric
vandalism' – makes it hard for the police to smash the practice
completely.

'There's nothing else like the virus community really, because it's
where an individual can affect the world and cost billions. How do
you break into that if you're a law enforcement agency? It's not the
same guy and the same group doing it every time. You look at the
variances in some of these viruses and there can be hundreds in a
matter of weeks.'

One answer he says is to put more effort into demonstrating the
damage that individual writers can cause. This would ensure that if
and when the vandals are caught, judges would be able to hand out
tougher sentences. For example, more effort could be put into taking
statements from companies affected by the viruses, he says, in the
way that victim statements are routinely taken in other crimes.

However, Neate says there is also a responsibility on smaller UK
firms to make sure they take the basic security precautions – firewalls and virus protection for example – and not to assume they are
too small to be hit.

'There is some protection in the numbers,' he admits. 'It's like being on a housing estate; there are only a certain number of burglars and you might survive.' But he adds, 'I've always given the example of walking down a street and seeing that every house has got a burglar alarm except one. Well, I know the one that I'd go for.'

He points out that sophisticated hacking techniques routinely scan the networks for systems that are insecure and vulnerable to attack, using software robots, or 'bots', to retrieve all kinds of information about the victim's computer and software.

'The bot comes back and has found these things – these are the IP numbers and they are on broadband and they are running Windows XP – because it tells you everything about the system.'

Though cyber attackers are using evermore sophisticated attacks, such as bots, Neate says it is important not to glamorise them. He also confirms one of the themes of this book; that hackers and virus writers are using their dark skills more and more for financial gain rather than just for recreation or out of disenchantment.

'Don't put them on any pedestal; they're criminals and they are just like any criminals in the real world. There are eleven-year-olds up to eighty-year-olds,' including people such as computer systems administrators who might work for a major firm and who when they get home start writing viruses and hacking.

'We're certainly seeing more of the latter. The well-known "pimply youth" is now older and has got a family and starts to need money. And that's something that I have seen recently.'

Forensic intelligence analysis

Detective constable Steve Adams became hooked on computers out of frustration at the police force's slow administrative system. Having demanded a password to the office computer so he could type up his own reports, his interest in computers quickly snowballed.

'I was given the responsibility for data protection and I also used to build computers and break them and fix them. I naturally liked computers, I like the software side of it; basically problem solving.'

That was in the mid 1980s when home computers were just becoming popular. As Adams' interest in the machines grew so did his family's; they now own a number of computer shops.

In many ways Adams typifies the new hybrid officer that is emerging from the combination of traditional policing and the use of modern technology. A down-to-earth character from Merseyside, Adams is an investigator, a detective to the core. But his aptitude for technology means that the officer is also able to delve into an area that remain mysterious and incomprehensible for many of his colleagues around the country; the inside of a computer.

His current role at the NHTCU is team leader on the Paedophile Investigation Section, which means that much – though not all – of his time is spent dealing with the grim subject of child abuse and in tracking and catching abusers. In many ways this is quite a traditional form of police work; forces all over the Western world have for years been hunting down those who photograph and sexually abuse young children. Now however many paedophiles have switched to using computers and the internet to disseminate and swap their images, and police detection techniques have had to adapt accordingly.

This is where Adams' technical skills come into play. One of his key roles is to find intelligence to discover hitherto unknown paedophiles who are using the internet. At the centre of this hunt for vital clues is the hard drive. The hard drive is not just the key to finding evidence that will convict a suspect, the corner stone of Marc Kirby's work. It can also store vital intelligence clues. And one thing Adams knows about, with the help of forensic people, is how to examine hard drives.

The detective constable actively seeks out the hard drives of paedophiles who have been convicted by local police forces. These regional forces may have gleaned enough data to gain a conviction, but Adams is aware that they will not have had the time or resources to have made an exhaustive search for extra nuggets of intelligence.

This however is part of Adams' job; and he will re-examine the hard drives from old cases for their treasure troves of secrets. He says: 'With every hard drive that comes in we analyse it for intelligence, because what you'll find is that the internet is people's main source for communication.

'They will speak to people – not so much in emails now – but chat forums; IRC [Internet Relay Chat] and ICQ [another proprietary chat system – its initials don't really stand for anything, they are simply a play on "cq", the ham radio signal for seeking conversation]. There are always logs and always traces of people talking to like-minded people.'

Such investigations always seem to yield results, he says. 'Out of every hard drive I've examined I've always traced someone else who needed to be arrested; I've never failed yet.'

This 'forensic intelligence analysis', as the unit calls it, can even involve hard drives used by criminals convicted in other countries. In one recent case the examination of a hard drive from overseas that had not been used by the suspected paedophile for more than a year was able to bring about convictions of paedophiles in the UK.

Adams recalls: 'A guy was arrested in the United States – he's since died in prison – and we asked the US Secret Service and US Customs for a copy of his hard drive. From an analysis of it and a model of the chats that he'd done we were able to identify a large number of people.

'In particular two were people in the UK who were part of a very small paedophile group; one was a school headmaster from Liverpool who has since received five years, nine months [in gaol] and the other was a computer contractor who did all sorts of different contracts for the government, and he's doing five years, six months.'

> Even this was not the end; the information that came from the prosecution of those two men also led to the arrest and eventual prosecution of four others. Adam says: 'They were only identified because we had the foresight to say, "Give us a copy of the hard drive."'

Sometimes, if the offences are serious enough, the unit will initiate its own prosecution of suspects. In other less serious but still important cases Adams and his team might pass vital information onto regional forces for them to take action. The process is constantly generating new leads, he says.

'At the moment I have people assessing cases all around the country for me. They'll come back and tell me there are ten cases around the country I may well want to have a look at. As long as my bosses are happy with it I will go and get copies of those drives. I won't be doing it as a priority because I've also got other duties to do. But I can look at a hard drive in a matter of days and tell you whether or not it's going to be worth doing any work on it.'

As well as finding and assessing their own intelligence, Adams and his team will also be receiving potentially important information from foreign law enforcement agencies about cyber crimes carried out abroad by British-based suspects.

For example the paedophile David Ward was trapped in part thanks to the work of an undercover policeman working online in Germany. The unnamed officer, from the federal police the BKA, was offered a trade in paedophile pictures by the British man, and passed on this vital information to the NHTCU. He did so by using established international procedures designed to ensure that cross-boundary crimes are dealt with swiftly, an important feature of the way the unit works.

Adams explains that, 'Every nationality that we're involved with in Europe does some sort of monitoring. If someone trades with them, they have a responsibility to disseminate it to us.' Though such officers get to know each other and can share information informally, formal contacts have to be made through the correct channels, he says. 'For instance I'm doing some work at the moment for a South American nation and that's come through Europol; what we do for them will go back through Europol. So we have a set procedure that we stick to.'

Human error

A common theme among all the NHTCU staff is that while computers may work logically, there is always a weakness that can be exploited in any criminal enterprise: human nature. Adams' experience is no different. He recalls how his team was tracking one group of paedophiles, who were hopping from website to new website as the unit shut down each one. At one point Adams says his team were 'just eleven days behind' the paedophile gang.

'The way we were working we'd have been right behind them,' he says. 'We knew who they were; it took months and months and months to identify them because they used nicknames. But people make mistakes, not everybody in a particular group sticks to the rules.'

However, as the investigator points out, while it is possible to track criminals across cyber space, first they have to find out who to track. 'Any network administrator can tell you that you can monitor everything that comes in and out of a server,' he says. 'The problem is actually doing it.'

Adams continues: 'If it's hosted in this country then we have legislation in place but if that server is hosted in another country where we don't have relations or there's no legislation in place ... Or we notify that we're going to do [some monitoring], so the people paying the money for the site are then told – so they move and jump servers.'

The FBI's number one priority

In the US the FBI has also been busy accumulating experience in combating cyber criminals. Its cross-frontier jurisdiction and history of combating organised crime in theory makes it uniquely well equipped to deal with the global nature of cyber crime.

Dave Thomas, chief of Computer Intrusion Division Cyber Division at the FBI, explains how it operates[4]. 'The bureau has adapted to cyber crime the same way we've adapted to other violations over the years.

'We've migrated our traditional investigators that have been very good at working with drugs, organised crime, white-collar crime and any other areas, into working with cyber crime and we've given them the technical expertise they've needed to be able to do that.'

These officers can then be moved around other parts of the FBI. Thomas says that, as with the NHTCU, the key quality is still to be a good investigator. 'If you bring me a good investigator I can teach them the technology they need to investigate these crimes, but if you bring me a technology person it's going to take me longer to make a good investigator out of them.'

He adds, 'Certainly there is the development of the cyber cop, there are specialists now, and we certainly have that capability here where people just deal with cyber. We're constantly trying to build up that expertise within the FBI.'

Thomas is head of the Computer Intrusion Division, which is part of the Cyber Division of the FBI. 'We deal with all computer intrusions, whether it's counter-terrorism, counter-intelligence or criminal. I also have the responsibility for gathering and disseminating intelligence, what's going on in the internet. But we also have sections that deal with our traditional cyber crime, whether it be white-collar crime, crime that has migrated to the internet, child pornography; we have technical units here that deal with nothing but technical issues if we need something done.'

He explains that half the workload of the cyber division involves 'traditional' crime that just happens to take place with computers or on the internet, while the other half is internet-specific, the 'intrusion' crimes, such as hacking. In total the bureau has up to 3,500 people dedicated to dealing with cyber crime at any given time. 'Cyber crime is [the] number one criminal priority of the FBI so we do have a lot of resources involved with working cyber crime matters.'

Indeed Thomas admits that they have been well looked after in terms of funding for the equipment and training needed to fight cyber crime. 'Congress and the director have been very good to us. We have been able to keep up technically with what we need to keep up with and we've been able to keep up financially with what we need to keep up with,' says Thomas.

'Our biggest problem has always been our human resources, getting the agents trained and getting them proficient to be able to work the type of cases they need to work. We've got a very aggressive training programme that's both domestic and international to assist us with that.'

The problem of tracking cyber suspects and then being able to obtain the necessary evidence to prosecute them is one of the greatest difficulties facing the FBI, the NHTCU and other law enforcement agencies around the world. Cyber criminals are no less cunning and resourceful than their 'real world' counterparts and are able to take full advantage of the different laws and jurisdictions in which web servers can be based. And in this digital game of cat and mouse, it is possible for the resourceful cyber criminal to stay one step ahead of his or her pursuers.

Among the most resourceful of all of these are the hackers. Once upon a time a hacker was a benign person, someone who loved systems, who loved to explore but had no desire to cause damage or make money. Those more innocent days have largely gone. New waves of hackers are less scrupulous, less dedicated to the true hacker ethic; and a constant thorn in the side of today's cyber cops.

CHAPTER FOUR
The Hackers

It has dominated his adult life and even now, twenty years later, he can still recall how he first got involved in hacking. 'I was a hacker,' he explains with a smile, 'not just because of computers; [I liked] hacking stuff like taking clocks apart, electrical things, just to see how they worked.' In his childhood this included trying to rewire some electrical device he had been given as a present. 'It wasn't about defeating anything in a sense to compete with the creator of it – but just to get that extra mileage out of something,' he insists.

Our hacker is now aged 40 and though he was a late starter – he did not own a computer until he was 20 – hacking has been his life for 2 decades. The authors know his true identity but have agreed to refer to the hacker by his handle in cyber space: Fungus the Bogeyman. Fungus is black, articulate and self-educated and lives in southern Europe, where he enjoys a comfortable existence, flitting from job to job and working as a web designer and consultant. The one constant factor in his life has been hacking.

Fungus describes the impact that the arrival of personal computers in the early 1980s had on an intensely curious teenager. 'There was this big massive electronic box of tricks and not only could it do the electronics and the lights; it could do stuff with images and text and so on. And the goal then was to try and learn that system, which is what I did. There was an MS-Dos operating system and I learnt nearly every single individual command, every single flag [hardware setting] it had.' He adds, 'I was a computer nerd, basically.'

Just find a hack

Surviving on just four hours sleep a night, Fungus combined a hectic social life with the calling of his chosen path. Painstaking step by painstaking step (and after having managed to scrape together enough money to buy a Commodore 16 computer at the age of 20), he taught himself everything about computers, hardware, software and programming.

At night Fungus would pore over magazines and manuals, at first simply following the instructions but then gradually starting to understand the principles that underpinned what he was doing and why. Slowly he was being pulled into the system and beginning to appreciate what was really happening at a far deeper level on this rickety old TV screen. Without fully realising it at the time, he was becoming a hacker.

Before long Fungus had discovered modems, the device that allows computers to 'talk' to each other via telephone lines, and began to make contact with like-minded individuals through bulletin boards. Gradually Fungus began to realise that there were whole banks of computers out there, run by companies, government and academic institutions, all waiting to be explored. He soon realised that the process of discovery – self-discovery – and education went hand in hand. 'You're sitting there thinking, I need to get in, and you keep on trying and you realise, Oh wow, you just find a hack.'

He says that he knew what software a system was based on, and how it worked, and he would sit at his screen wondering if he could send controls remotely and break into the programme. 'More often than not you couldn't – but sometimes you could. And then you would maybe get a copy of the programme yourself and although you couldn't get a copy of the source code you'd find lots of ASCII code [American Standard Code for Information Interchange, the code that represents English letters as numbers] hidden in them. And you'd find password strings and methods in there.'

Fungus explains the process of getting inside a system and inside the mind of that system's human creator. 'Slowly you'd study it and study it and this is one of the skills I and a lot of the other hackers have. Rather than understanding the system fully, as a hacker you understand the methodology of the person who created it or how it actually works; what its function is, what it's doing. That way, you can find a way in. You can find what the intention was.'

Once inside an organisation's system, Fungus explains how, assuming you had done your homework on the programme so you knew how to react to it, you could roam around creating user accounts for yourself, giving yourself greater privileges or access, and learn for example how to stay inside for a full hour rather than half an hour.

Unlike many of his fellow hackers Fungus had little formal education, came from a poor immigrant family and was, at 20, older than many other hackers. Thus he had to find a job to earn a living as well as fund his passion for computers. It was now that his hacking collided with the world of crime, and he saw a way to combine the two.

'I had to find work. Luckily for me I met a criminal who owned a computer shop. He got me working for him removing evidence of data from hard discs and so on, and I got to play with all the computers I wanted to. He paid me extremely well.'

This new way of 'earning' a living meant that Fungus had the time to fulfil an ambition and get a university education. His lack of formal education was no obstacle, for the young hacker did not need to enrol at a university; he just hacked his way into one. Fungus explains:

When I was 23, I lived 800 yards away from a university and I went in there. For me it was a whole new world, for me this was a place that was for white folks, money. I know it sounds crap but this is what I always saw university as.

I was always a good social engineer [good at deceiving and persuading people], which is one of the great skills. Part of the stance was that I would always take my books in under my arms. I'd go in and I'd develop skills that I'd read about in one of the best books that got me hacking – The Hacker's Handbook *by Hugo Cornwall* – *and I practised shoulder surfing [looking over people's shoulders to get passwords], which he'd recommended.*

And once I got that I got accounts and learnt about Janet, the Joint Academic Network. [This was a part of the early internet in the UK.]

When I say 'learnt' it, I did not know it inside out, but they were never suspicious. I'd go to the printer room and pick up 400 sheets, and print out on that green-lined paper on the sprockets. It was a dot matrix printer. I'd have to wait two or three days for my print-offs to be done! That's where I did all my homework.

Some years later, at the age of 28, Fungus did go to university by a more conventional route just at the time when the internet was becoming well known. Before that however the hacker had been honing his skills with groups of like-minded individuals around the world. He describes the camaraderie he felt with fellow hackers:

'I started writing small applications that would do things for me, like password-guessing programmes and so on, and slowly they started appearing on the network.

'I felt that I was part of an elite set as well because I would turn up to "copy parties" [this was a party in the real world where you took your software along to and shared it around; a sort of Tupperware party for computer hackers] or get onto discussion groups. I found that most of the people didn't know what they were talking about, and I found that out quite quickly.'

Hippy-head hackers
Nonetheless Fungus soon found there were people whose ability he could admire and with whom he became cyber friends. 'You start

talking about your personal lives and you realise that you've got this friend who you've never seen before in your life.'

Fungus adds: 'You know that maybe they're from the United States or from Algeria and you know you don't know nothing else about them really; you know they're into computing. And typically they play the guitar! They were into music and they were into peace and they were anti-capitalist and there was that bond and you felt a unity and a strength; and even though you were working alone at night I felt there were other people doing the same.'

For a period Fungus did flirt with the idea of becoming a serious 'cyber criminal' and on occasions clearly broke the law at the request of criminal gangs who wanted to use his talents. 'I got pretty good at faking MOTs by hacking into computers and then using a printer to produce the fake certificate; and I even broke into someone's business and stole their database for an ex-employee who wanted to set up in business in competition with them.'

He later took a job that placed him in high-flying financial circles and he began to think that one day he could use his well-honed skills to make real money. 'I kept learning and learning, thinking, "Well, one day I might be able to transfer money," and that got me interested. But in the end I got bored because I didn't like the grind I was in.'

He left his high paid job and enrolled on a university course; but that too became a grind. It frustrated him that the computer science course he was taking did not include the internet as a subject, and the emergence of the worldwide web at the start of the 1990s was what really fascinated hackers such as Fungus. Instead, as he had in the past, he taught himself all the basics of how the internet worked – file transfer protocol (ftp), telnet, HTML, web servers – and left the university where he was unable to learn about such things.

Though not active in party politics, Fungus did, like many of his fellow hackers, possess a default sense of anti-capitalism, an anti-big business stance, coupled with a dose of the usual paranoia and conspiracy theories that often go with such views. 'I had a big hippy head on and my argument was that the system's going to try and destroy us; and we had got to learn the tools that they are going to use against us.'

He also saw the hacking opportunities that the emergence of the internet could bring; he now likens it to the early pioneers travelling to the United States. 'I thought, Great, I can now break into all of these computers via the internet and the early adopters – these people haven't got a clue!

'They've got loads of money, they're going to buy into this. It's like me going to the United States on my own right like right at the beginning and seeing it all lying there in front of me and thinking, "fucking hell this is a big place," and I can go anywhere I want. I think that's what hit me about it.'

Fungus also sums up what he sees as the essential difference between the hackers of his generation and the earlier 'pure' hackers of the 1960s and 1970s.

'The true hackers, they were thinking, This is broken, let's fix it. And then there was me – and I think our new breed – who were thinking, "Right, this is broken, which means that they're using this protocol at Debenhams stores out on the street – we could get into Debenhams!"'

Fungus believes his most inventive and enjoyable times as a hacker were when he had to work hard to identify the telephone numbers that companies might use for their modems so he could dial into their system, or work out the Internet Protocol (IP) addresses they might have.

'Those were the days that I'm proud of because there weren't many tools around; you had to make your stuff to break in. That was the hacker in me and I did some really neat stuff then. We used to put back doors on and we used to write Trojans [programmes] in our time. Nowadays you just get them off the shelf and that's the way that the new hackers are.'

Perhaps predictably he is quite scathing about most – not all – of the new generation of hackers, many of whom are dismissed within the older world of hackerdom as 'script kiddies'. It is a common refrain among many hackers of a certain vintage, and may partly be explained by the natural rivalry between one generation and the next. Fungus is aware of this.

'Am I just envious of the new hackers, is there a rivalry there? Are they the new kids on the block? Part of me says that must exist. But part of me says, well, they're not like the old school.' Once again he is drawn to an analogy with the creators of modern America.

'It's like new pioneers. OK, I know they were Indian-killing mother fuckers who went to America. But they went to a new land and they did something, they built this country. A new set of people have gone over now and moved into the houses that are already in place and it's not the same – they're not really making anything new with it. They've walked into it, they're using all the resources and they're being more malicious than ever; they're nuking the Indians, basically.'

Fungus concludes: 'I understand there are some people there who have read their history and they've got respect for the old hackers and they are trying to find something new. But you've got a lot of script kiddies out there and they're not hackers at all; they don't deserve to be called hackers.'

Good guys versus bad guys

Fungus' story may not be the typical story of a hacker; indeed there is probably no such beast as a 'typical' hacker. But his story contains some important truths about the nature of hackers and what they represent. As Fungus relates, the actions of a hacker have often been on the very borders of legality, sometimes falling over into outright criminality.

When describing the world of hacking, the distinction is often made between 'white hat' hackers (the 'good guys') and 'black hat' hackers (the 'bad guys'), using terminology that appears to spring from a discussion about witchcraft. But, as in witchcraft, where the distinction between white and black magic is often hard to make, so too in hacking the line is hard to draw. As Fungus' case perhaps shows, a hacker can be white or black hatted, depending on their circumstances, their mood and of course other people's points of view.

Another expression often used to distinguish the 'good' hacker from the 'bad' hacker is 'cracker'. According to this definition, a hacker is someone who explores or repairs systems while a 'cracker' is someone who breaks them. While this is a more practical and less mystical distinction, it can nonetheless meet similar objections; a 'good' hacker may sometimes 'crack' a system if they feel it is 'justified'.

The 'operating system' of cyber crime

Whatever the problems in distinguishing between good and bad hackers, there can be little doubting the prime importance of hacking when it comes to discussing cyber crime. Hacking could be described as the 'operating system' of cyber crime. The skills used in hacking – the understanding of software (and sometimes hardware), the familiarity with systems, the ability to programme to very high levels, the flexibility of mind, the patience, the perseverance – are all key qualities for anyone wishing to commit crimes in cyber space. This does not mean that anyone who possesses these skills is a criminal or potential criminal; just that hacking provides the necessary skill set for the cyber criminal. The particular crime may involve the use of viruses, worms, Trojan programmes or software robot (bot) armies, but behind all these is – usually – the ability of a hacker.

The most famous hacker in history, Kevin Mitnick, the man who was on the FBI's Most Wanted list and who faced a life gaol sentence, regards hacking as a talent that many disparate people might acquire.

Interviewed for this book Mitnick says, 'I would see hacking as a skill, it's a skill set. There are people from all different walks of life that can use that skill, whether it is for a criminal act, to exercise their curiosity or their interest in gaining more knowledge in an area. There are some people that are purely malicious, who write worms that have destructive payloads.'

He concludes: 'I think it is really hard to stereotype a hacker. I do not think you can just equate crime to hacking.'

In Mitnick's case he is speaking from bitter experience. He was a talented hacker who used his skills to penetrate some high-profile victims in the 1980s. But thanks to some sustained publicity, the importance of his hacks were blown up out of proportion and he became demonised as a dangerous criminal on the run. For many he became the ultimate criminal hacker, even though his actions pale in comparison alongside those of today's organised cyber criminals or even those virus writers who cause such immense damage with their nihilistic programmes.

Exploiting systems

Mitnick grew up in an ordinary working-class family in the San Fernando Valley area of California. He was a shy and overweight teenager who early on developed a talent for getting around and exploiting systems. He played with ham radios, learnt how to get free rides on buses by punching bus tickets and was also a phone phreaker (someone who hacks into the phone network to make free calls, as detailed in Chapter 1). Even as a youngster, however, he was in trouble with the law for stealing computer manuals from the Pacific Bell corporation, and he was put on probation.

Mitnick was hacking computer systems from the early 1980s, during which time he perfected his greatest ability as a hacker; 'social engineering'. He used his personality to persuade – or con, if you prefer – computer users and technicians into divulging valuable pieces of information such as passwords and clues as to how systems worked. The use of social engineering by hackers puts into context some of the myths that have grown up about how hackers work. They are usually very technically proficient and understand how systems work; but they also rely on cunning, subterfuge and bluff to get information they need to break into systems. The image of a teenager sitting in a lonely bedsit and hacking into military computers through sheer technical ability alone is not always an accurate one. There is nearly always an element of social engineering in all the best hacks.

Using the information he got from various ploys, Mitnick was able to hack into numerous companies, though he was not always smart enough to evade detection. In 1987 he was arrested for breaking into a firm called the Santa Cruz Organisation, even if his lawyers were able to get his charges reduced and he was given three year's probation. Not long after, however, Mitnick was caught for breaking into Digital Equipment Corporation (DEC) and this time he could not escape a custodial sentence. However, his lawyers were able to argue that Mitnick suffered from an 'addiction' to computers and he was allowed to serve his one-year sentence in a centre for treating people with similar disorders.

Mitnick was released in 1989 and began work for a computer security firm, yet within a few years was in trouble once more, accused of violating probation by hacking into voice mail boxes. This time Mitnick did not hang around to see what the consequences might be; fearing that he would not receive a fair trial, the hacker went on the run in 1992.

Mitnick – who was also known by his online handle Condor – had already attracted a fair amount of notoriety at this time as a gifted but dangerous hacker. Now the hunt for him across the United States propelled him into something approaching Public Enemy Number One. Partly this was because of the involvement of a *New York Times* journalist John Markoff, who wrote about the hunt for Mitnick and his alleged exploits, and partly because a computer expert named Tsutomo Shimomura, who claimed to have been hacked by Mitnick, turned from victim to hunter and set about tracking him down.

While on the run Mitnick assumed false identities, was spotted in various locations around the country and was accused of several high-level hacks, against various companies and institutions including NEC, Motorola, Nokia, Fujitsu, Novell, Sun Microsystems and the University of Southern California. The more lurid media reports claimed the damage caused by Mitnick during these hacks was as much as $80 million.

Whatever the truth of these claims, it was an absorbing story and the legend of Mitnick grew and grew. It was even claimed that the hacker had, during 1982, broken into the North American Defense Command (NORAD), a claim Mitnick has always dismissed as nonsense. (It was even improbably claimed that Mitnick was the real inspiration for the lead character in the 1983 movie *War Games*. He is one of at least two hackers accorded this 'accolade'.)

Even when, with Shimomura's help, the FBI finally got its man in 1995, the drama did not end. Partly through the complexity of the case, Mitnick's trial did not take place for a further four years, during which time he was kept in custody for fear that he might abscond again.

Eventually a deal was struck; Mitnick pleaded guilty to a variety of hacking charges, in return for which he was allowed to set the four years he had already served against a new five-year sentence. This meant he would be freed within a year. There was still one more sting in the tail, however. By this time Mitnick had become credited with almost supernatural abilities as a hacker and he was required to stay away from computers, word processors, the internet, email – anything to do with the world of computing – until 2003.

All through his pre-trial incarceration his lawyers insisted – as he himself continues to insist to this day – that Mitnick was not a thief, a vandal and certainly not a terrorist. His attorney Donald Randolph said before his 1999 trial: 'He's a recreational hacker. He didn't do it for economic gain, or damage anything, and there's no allegation that he attempted to damage anything.'

It is hard to escape the conclusion that Mitnick, for all that he undoubtedly caused a major nuisance and embarrassment, was being made an example of, in order to dissuade future hackers who might be more likely to cause harm.

Though she is understandably biased, his grandmother Reba Vartanian perhaps had a point when she described the government's treatment of Mitnick as 'foolishly paranoid'. She pointed out: 'He loves technology, he wouldn't hurt it.'

Now rebuilding his life as an author and writer and adviser on security issues, the convicted hacker reflects on the differences between hacking in his time and hacking now.

'I think what has changed between when I was doing it and today's world is that you get a lot more hacking; it has become easier in a sense. In the past hacking was more challenging because there were not the tools and tricks that you could find on the internet. Pretty much you ended up doing it on your own or writing your own code.

'There are many tools and lots of information on the web [now] to help people hone their skills in this area,' Mitnick says. 'On the other hand it has also become more difficult because governments, companies and academia are much more aware of security issues. They try to bring up their security to a reasonable level and try to exercise some standard of due care.'

Computers and politics
Mitnick's view of hacking was fairly straightforward; he wanted to understand and explore systems. For him it was an addictive pastime,

a 'recreation', as his lawyer said, albeit a fairly serious one in his case, and ethically he traced his hacking 'heritage' back to the old MIT hackers of the 1960s.

In other parts of the world, notably in Continental Europe, hacking has been more overtly political. A prime example of this was the formation of the Computer Chaos Club (CCC) in West Germany in the early 1980s. Its founder Wau Holland, who died in 2001, saw a direct link between computers and politics. Holland, who was on the left of the political spectrum, thought access to computers could liberate the people from the 'oppressors', who were big business and state monopolies such as the German telecommunications industry at that time. For Holland and the early CCC members hacking had to have a political and moral purpose.

This resulted in spectacular hacks by the Club, details of which it then shared with the media and the German police, the intention being both to highlight security flaws and also to embarrass its political 'enemies'. For example its first 'hactacular' was against the BTX online service network of the German postal and telecommunications giant Deutsche Bundespost.

Holland and co-founder Steffen Wernery had earlier warned the organisation of a weakness the pair had detected in the corporation's system. When it failed to react, the two men hacked into the system using a password belonging to a savings bank, and switched some £30,000 in credit to the CCC's account. The story caused an outcry in West Germany and helped to put hacking and the philosophy of the CCC on the map.

There were of course socially aware computer movements in the US, too, and there were also technological activists. Lee Felsenstein, who was involved with a Californian group called Community Memory Project[1], was a good example of this. But such hackers and movements never achieved the prominence that the decidedly hippy-ish CCC enjoyed in West Germany.

Yet the purist theory of CCC policy was not always reflected in the behaviour of all of its hacker members. Some resorted to criminal hacking and even espionage, forming a direct link to many of the criminal and organised crime hacking in Europe today. The most notorious example was the activities of certain CCC members who publicly admitted to stealing secrets and software from Western military, industrial and nuclear establishments and selling them to the KGB via East German agents[2].

One of the hackers involved in this remarkable story was a young German called Karl Koch. Koch was a CCC hacker and also a drug addict; it was thought he had sold secrets to the KGB in part to fuel his cocaine habit. (The use of drugs was another feature of European hacking that tended to distinguish it from US counterparts.) If the selling of the secrets was not bad enough, Koch later decided to sell the story to the media in Germany to get yet more money for drugs. Koch was found burned to death in a forest near Luneberg in May 1989, just months before the fall of the Berlin Wall[3]. He was aged 22.

Koch's death has always officially been described as suicide; he was certainly unbalanced and dependent on drugs at the time of his death. But there are those who still believe that Koch may have been punished for embarrassing and showing disrespect to the KGB by going public on his exploits. The truth will probably never be known.

What the episode does illustrate is a link between the spying agencies of the Eastern bloc and hacking, which was to have important consequences in later years. After the break up of the Soviet Union and the fall of the Warsaw Pact, many of the former security agents found their way into organised crime throughout Russia and Eastern Europe. They brought with them a knowledge of hackers and how to use them; this encouraged the involvement of organised crime in cyber crime.

The episode also underlines the point that beneath the ethical theories and politically correct hacking of the Computer Chaos Club, some of the hackers were prepared to use their skills for less exalted purposes.

East meets West

Hans Hubner was a hacking and CCC colleague of Koch. He headed the CCC's West Berlin branch, though he was eventually booted out of the club for his role in the espionage scandal. Today Hubner denies that he was personally involved in the stealing and selling of any Western military secrets to the KGB, but he does admit to having been aware of it, and to having met spy masters in East Berlin.

The West Berliner says that a hacking colleague called Peter Karl made the initial approach to the KGB. 'We had this guy Peter go to the East and offer them our services, telling them, "I have this hacker group that is unique in the world; nobody else can do it and they have access to information that nobody else has."'

Hubner says the Russians were not particularly impressed by this approach, but instead made it clear that they had their own needs. At the time the COCOM Treaty – signed by mostly NATO countries – restricted the export of military and nuclear details to the Soviet Union and her allies, and these restrictions covered software. So the Russians gave the hacking group a shopping list of software they wanted.

'The treaty prevented Western software from going to the East by legal means and they [the Russians] specifically asked us to get particular sources codes and particular software versions for particular systems; that's what they were actually interested in,' recalls Hubner.

From the start however the organised and very focused KGB operatives were wary of this group of hairy hacker hippies. 'They would not allow any information to flow from them to us because it was completely clear that [to them] that we were a group of drug addicts doing things that were interesting in a way – but that we were not by any means trustworthy.

'What they did is they asked us to get them ware, like specific products, and they were able to pay for that,' he recalls. Hubner describes how Peter Karl remained the person with the contact in East Berlin, and how he would regularly call the hackers to see if they had 'anything to deliver' before he went to visit the agent. He even persuaded Hubner to go into East Berlin with him. 'Peter was convinced that we were doing really big things and he wanted to convince the Russians too. As he couldn't do [the hacking] himself, he wanted me to come along to show me as the living embodiment of a hacker.'

Hubner recalls how impressed he was at how Peter Karl's contacts gave him unusually swift access to the communist-controlled part of the city.

'For me as a West Berliner it was totally, totally spectacular.'

At one point he and Karl – who was ostentatiously smoking a joint – went to one office called Casanova, which appeared to house a Russian import–export company. 'This guy came and interviewed us – he called himself Serge – and we sat in a little conference room and had a talk. He gave us some money and Peter gave him some tapes and some floppies, so it was pretty businesslike. The guy told us that he was from Moscow – it was not hidden.'

Hubner is open about the extent of his involvement in the spying operation. 'I was involved in the transfer of the information from the West to the East. I could not deny that I knew something was going on that was criminal, illegal.'

When the spying activities of these CCC members came to light in 1989 – thanks to Koch's need for drugs money – the club's leader, Wau Holland, was apparently furious and rounded on Hubner for his behaviour. 'Hackers must trust each other,' said an aggrieved Holland, Hubner remembers. 'They must work together, all information should be free. You broke that, you gained information and you sold it.' At the time Hubner, who was thrown out of CCC as a result, denied he had broken 'hacker ethics'. 'We were fascinated and wanted to be the first and best technical geniuses among hackers.'

Where to draw the line

This approach to the philosophy of hacking is one advanced by many practitioners; they insist they are interested in technical ability, exploring and mastering systems, not in criminality or causing damage. Yet it is at best a naïve argument. If one can use such rationale to justify working for a political system that wreaked massive damage on the world, and threatened freedom and democracy in the West, it can just as easily be used to 'justify' working for criminal gangs or conceivably even terrorists. Hackers do not always seem to realise that they do not live in a moral vacuum; that their actions have consequences.

Today Hubner accepts that hacking and criminal behaviour can coincide and openly concedes that hacks may be acts of crime too. 'To me hacking means using the technology as it can be used and not looking into the manual to find out how it is supposed to be used.

'In a way the gains that criminal gangs get from using computers – not using them in the way they are supposed to be used – is not right. But the activity is the same as what I would call hacking. So I am not quite sure whether I would be able to draw the line and say that criminal activity is the thing that makes something not hacking. Indeed this is not true in my case; what we did was criminal. Criminal activity and hacking is something that can go together.'

Hubner's views echo those of Kevin Mitnick, in suggesting that hacking is a skill set and can be used for good, bad or morally neutral purposes. Yet Hubner himself is doubtful whether the skills used by hackers such as Mitnick really constitute hacking at all.

'There is a broad definition that to do a hack is to do something cool. Kevin Mitnick calls people and tricks them to give them their user IDs, and he calls that social engineering or social hacking. And I'm not sure that it is.

'I think hacking is to do with computers originally; and to use the phone is not something that I can admire for any creativity,' insists Hubner.

Techno-anarchists

Elsewhere in continental Europe hacking has also relied on a strong social and political ethos, notably in Holland. There, a hacker by the name of Rop Gonggrijp established a magazine called *Hack-Tic* in the late 1980s. Though it has since been closed, *Hack-Tic* had an enormous influence on continental hackers in particular. The magazine described its target audience as 'techno-anarchists' and had a very clear political agenda about the need for open and free access to information.

Yet once again the lines between politically correct views and behaviour on the one hand and criminality on the other were blurred. For example, *Hack-Tic* ran items on how to make free phone calls on the telephone networks, how to break PIN codes, and also gave its readers the latest information on software for entering databases belonging to organisations such as universities and private companies. At the same time the magazine stated: 'The information contained in *Hack-Tic* is for education purposes only. Making use of this information might be illegal/criminal/un-constitutional/nasty.'

Interviewed in 1995, the year the magazine was closed, Gonggrijp admitted: 'It was still the Wild West at that time. There were no laws on computer criminality. It was only we, the hackers, who realised the immense potential of such a computer network.'

However Gonggrijp always insisted that it was the philosophy behind the hacking that came first. In the same 1995 interview for the Dutch newspaper *Trouw*[4] he confessed: 'I've never been a truly great hacker myself. What matters to me are the ideas behind hacking: free access to information for everybody. In our society, information is no longer stocked in libraries and archives, but is burrowed in databases and spread over the network. It is a knowledge machine that 90 per cent of the population can never access.'

Free access

Out of this philosophy sprang the idea for the Dutch Internet Service Provider (ISP) called XS4all, which not only gave ordinary people internet access but also made Gonggrijp a wealthy man and turned him into, in his own words, a 'respectable citizen'. A senior police officer from Holland's cyber crime unit even turned up as a guest at *Hack-Tic*'s farewell party.

Yet despite the apparent transformation, Gonggrijp is still able to find a justification for hacking. 'Never take what is written in the user manual for granted is one of our sayings. Hack it. And only then you'll know how secure it is. The whole world around us is fast changing into systems. It is important that we learn to think about it for ourselves, and not to trust blindly that small self-appointed elite that allegedly knows it all,' he told *Trouw*.

This is another argument often found in the hacking community; that the world of technology needs hackers to help keep large corporations 'honest'. For example hackers take great delight in exposing security flaws in Microsoft's operating systems. It also explains the presence of many former hackers in computer security firms, where they can use their expertise to test client's vulnerability to attack – quite legally. But it would be naïve – and just wrong – to suppose that this is what all or even most hacking nowadays is about.

The recruitment of hackers by organised crime, the constant hacking of private firms and universities, the hacking of individual computers by criminals to turn them into 'zombie' machines (taking them over to use for their own purposes, see Chapter 7) – all these are testament to the huge crossover between hacking and criminality.

In January 2004 a case came to light in Israel in which the branch of the Israeli Postal Service was hacked using a wireless network device. According to reports of the case, there had been a mysterious break in at the Haifa branch of the service, during which nothing was taken or damaged. A few weeks later security experts noticed that money – around $13,000 worth – was being transferred unexpectedly from old existing accounts at the branch into a string of recently opened accounts.

It appears the hack operation had started with the break-in, during which a wireless network device was planted among the organisation's computers. Then a number of individuals involved in the conspiracy had opened up – quite lawfully – new accounts at the same Haifa branch. Using a laptop a hacker had then connected to the previously installed wireless device, got inside the computer system and started transferring money into the new accounts. On this occasion the hack was spotted and a number of arrests were later made. But an Israeli police spokesman was quoted as saying: 'This computer crime takes us to year 3000.'

Back in 1999, meanwhile, hackers carried out one of the most audacious hacks yet; they moved a satellite while it was in orbit. The loosely organised group, called the Masters of Downloading, and who included at least one British hacker, moved a satellite belonging to a North American telecommunications company. No one was ever prosecuted for this extraordinary technological feat[5].

Economic espionage

Each day, it seems, brings stories of new and ingenious ways of hacking for criminal purposes. There is also a considerable crossover between hacking and industrial espionage. We saw in Chapter 3 that the 'acquiring' of information about rival firms is big if discreet business in the Western world.

A well-placed security source, with experience of both government and private security, reveals how secret security staff sometimes use their talents to make money when they leave government service.

'There are ex-intelligence guys who go out with this spying expertise and take it to a commercial level; you can hire them through law firms to acquire "competitive intelligence",' he says. 'I see quite a lot of that. I don't call it hacking; I call that competitive intelligence gathering. It's a very, very grey area but it's a commercial thing that is in a way almost sanctioned.'

One extraordinary case that the authors have been told about involved a government's own secret agents apparently stealing highly valuable commercial information from the private company of another country.

The country involved is France and its target was a company called Philips Consumer Communications (PCC), a joint venture then partially controlled by the Dutch-owned electronics giant Philips and by a US firm Lucent.

PCC's main business was the design and manufacturer of telephone handsets. Its leading competitive advantage at the time of the industrial espionage was Philips' ground-breaking voice recognition software. According to an extremely well-placed source, who has asked not be named, but whose background and identity the authors know, French secret service agents – working with freelance operators – infiltrated PCC's Paris headquarters during an extended period at the end of the 1990s.

Our source reveals: 'We found that the local French intelligence agents were literally coming to the office for intellectual property and taking it. They also had a list of 30 employees that we had working at headquarters. We knew they were French intelligence because we got one name from a photo-ID.' They ran it through photo scanning and sent off the photograph to a contact who specialised in identifying agents, who confirmed that person's identity.

The source says that the company's security then looked at some of the firm's own staff more closely. What they found was extraordinary. 'We identified about ten staff who were reporting off-site directly to the DGSE [Direction Générale de la Sécurité Extérieure, France's external security agency equivalent to the US' CIA or the UK's MI6]. These were French nationals, working for a Dutch-American operation, who were literally walking into the local mairie [town hall] and sitting down with an agent every two months!'

The source says that the spying operation was not just taking details about new technology but also internal business plans, personnel information and even whole personnel files. Some of the material taken by staff may have been used by private individuals to help set up small product design companies. But he believes that the French agents had other priorities. 'Our understanding, our belief and our hypothesis was that they were feeding this information directly into our competitors.'

However Dutch and US owners of the joint venture took no action. The source says: 'When both Lucent and Philips were formally made aware that local intelligence firms were walking into their doors and their offices in Paris and pretty much acting as employees, they came back and said "That's the price of doing business in Paris." We had started to draw up papers to protest to the French government but the company did not want to know both for political and commercial – tax – reasons.'

It is impossible to verify the claims with French authorities who, in common with many other Western countries, traditionally refuse to comment on the activities of their secret services. Meanwhile PCC has since been transferred to China, where it remains a Philips subsidiary.

A spokeswoman at Philips denied that 'espionage' had taken place in those offices. She added: 'There was a case that had nothing to do with economic espionage, but was more an indiscreet treatment of information we shared with a customer. As we did not find it necessary to legally prosecute or publicly speak about this indiscreet behaviour, we also do not feel inclined to go further into this matter.'

However the source's impeccable credentials and insight into the affair least raise at the very least some intriguing questions about the use of government espionage agents against individual companies.

In late 2004 the North Korean government started training more than 500 hackers, whose purpose apparently will be to wage 'cyber war' on the United States, the country most reliant on new technology, and to glean intelligence.

South Korea's Defence Ministry claims that the military hackers have been educated in a five-year university course, and that the graduates would be targeting Japan and South Korea as well as the US. 'North Korea's intelligence warfare capability is estimated to have reached the level of advanced countries,' claims the ministry.

Whatever the truth of these particular reports it is clear that hacking still remains at the centre of cyber criminal and potentially terrorist activity. Professor Neil Barrett explains why. 'You now can go and get all of the tools that you need; if you like you can go and get the electronic equivalent of a lock-pick. But it's fair to say that hacking – ie knowing the vulnerabilities – sits at the bottom of all computer crime. For example modern computer viruses – which are really worms – are just automated hacking tools that are designed to exploit the vulnerabilities that you know are there.'

Über hackers

There also lurks a fear among some in law enforcement agencies around the world that there is a top layer of people – the über hackers – who are so technically proficient and so good at hiding their tracks that they are never traced – and never caught.

Bob Jones, chairman of Interpol's European Working Party on IT Crime, voices these concerns. 'My feeling – and quite a few us share this feeling – is that there is a group of hackers out there who we never see,' he says. 'These are the Premier league hackers, the über hackers, if you like. I think the ones we see – the ones that get caught – are the ones who are perhaps in the next division down. They might be good, but are not that good. They might be using some of the tools and techniques used by the real top hackers but are not good enough to remain unnoticed. I think that there must be hackers out there who are better than the ones we see.'

Though they vary in motive and ability, however, there is near-universal agreement among hackers about their reaction to a newer breed of cyber criminal: virus writers. While hackers admire the technical ability of the best virus writers, they despise the actions of the 'script kiddies' who transform viruses and worms from theoretical possibilities to real-world problems for ordinary computer users. Even hackers can get hit by computer worms and viruses.

Fungus the Bogeyman sums up the mixed feeling many hackers feel about the subject. 'Virus writing is very interesting; but it's been put to a bad use,' he says. 'Now virus writers have just got silly – they're just writing and putting out rubbish.' It is to such people we now turn: the internet's very own cyber vandals.

CHAPTER FIVE
The Virus Writers

WREAKING HAVOC

Lunchtime on 26 January 2004 will long live in the memory of many antivirus experts. It was at this time across parts of Western Europe that the sophisticated 'early warning' systems in use by leading antivirus (AV) software firms detected a new virus. At first many experts on the cyber frontier, whose daily job it is to evaluate the risk of new discoveries arriving over the horizon, were inclined to play down the appearance of this new virus. After all, new viruses appear regularly – every day – and many if not most of them are so badly written they pose little threat to anyone's computer except perhaps the writer's. Even the fact that this virus was in an attachment on an email coming out of Russia – one of the hot zones for viruses – did not concern the cyber patrolmen too much. There were other viruses to be concerned about at the present, and just one more Russian virus was not going to make anyone break into a cold sweat just yet.

That confidence seemed justified when in the first few hours the new virus seemed to be picking up only modest speed as it lumbered its way around cyberspace. Then the AV experts suddenly began to sit up and take notice. Almost unnoticed the new virus was beginning to build an ominous momentum. The number of infected emails rose through 50,000 and quickly onto 100,000 and beyond as the working day dawned in the United States and millions more users came online. By nightfall in Europe the new creation had gone into overdrive and AV companies were frantically trying to get out new 'signatures' to their customers all around the globe. Signatures are the parts of the AV software that identify a particular virus and warn the user that an email or its attachment is infected. They can then act to remove the threat; usually by simply deleting it. If your AV software does not have the right signature for a new virus, then you will not know if you receive the rogue programme – at least not until it is too late.

This was what happened with this mega virus, which was to become known as MyDoom, Novarg or Mimail.R.

Unsurprisingly the more powerful name MyDoom stuck, a name that was given to the virus by AV experts after they spotted a repetition of 'my domain' in the code. Craig Schmugar, virus research manager at Network Associates Inc., who has suggested names for about 200 viruses and worms, says he tries to pick a name that refers to something unique or memorable about a virus' coding or behaviour. In this case, he first shortened the reference to 'mydom' and then stuck in an extra 'o'. 'I steered away from the non-catchy names, because I knew it was going to be big,' says Schmugar. 'When I saw the word "doom" as part of it I thought that might be appropriate ...'

Within a couple of weeks of its disarmingly slow introduction, MyDoom had become the fastest-growing email worm since this peculiar type of technological plague had first been noticed back in the 1980s. At its peak MyDoom was infecting as many as 1 in 12 of all emails being sent in the world.

Though this virus caused worldwide disruption, as well as keeping the AV firms busy, the real apparent purpose of the virus was to launch an attack on a US software company called SCO, based in Lindon, Utah. Using the combined force of more than one million or so computers it had infected, MyDoom launched its expected assault on www.sco.com on 1 February and the company was soon forced to close down its site. The virus was programmed to stop spreading on 12 February when it effectively became 'sterile' (unable to propagate itself) and SCO was able to re-open its site.

But even this was not the end of the story. A less virulent variation of the virus, called MyDoomB (the original MyDoom now renamed MyDoomA), was designed to launch similar attacks on Microsoft and SCO again, though with little serious effect. Even so, some AV experts believe that the attacks and disruption may have been a smoke-screen to disguise the programme's true aim. One of the main effects of MyDoom on the computers it infected was to open a 'back door'. This, as its name suggests, means that a way is left open for later pro-grammes to sneak into the machine and potentially steal passwords and other valuable data from it.

For some observers at least the technical sophistication of MyDoom, added to its multi-pronged attack, clearly exhibited a new and even more dangerous trend among the many viruses and worms that are constantly being released. No longer were they 'just' being produced by teenagers who wanted to dazzle and show off, by would-be cyber gurus who wanted to highlight software flaws before anyone else spotted them or even by lunatic vandals out to cause maximum damage with little regard for how this could affect people's lives.

For what the presence of MyDoom and other similar viruses now suggests is that money-motivated criminals have either become – or teamed up with – virus writers to provide yet another new sinister threat to online security. The 'launch strategy' alone of MyDoom indicated some criminal cunning worthy of a bank robber or small-time fraudster. It was programmed so that the virus and its infected emails would not initially be sent to antivirus companies, govern-ments and military institutions, the very bodies that would be the first and the fastest to raise the alarm. The criminal brain was now being engaged with the logic of the programmer. Virus writers are no longer content with just harming our computers; now it seems they want our money too.

Viruses spell money

Matthew Ham, consultant to the authoritative Virus Bulletin, believes that criminals are now taking advantage of the greater opportunities for cyber crime and have adopted viruses as part of their armoury.

He explains: 'In the past if you took someone's password, you might get their passwords to a bulletin board or their email account. Now you might get the password to their online bank account or to their work accounts where a lot more information is stored. You might therefore get information that is directly and easily financially valuable.'

Another important feature of the MyDoom episode was the size of the 'price tags' put on the heads of the writer or writers – who at the time of writing remain uncaught. Bounties to be paid on the capture and conviction of suspects had been issued before, after the Sobig.F virus – a fast-spreading virus released in August 2003 and thought to have been created by spammers – and Blaster virus (see Chapter 2), but this time the stakes were raised spectacularly higher.

As Carole Theriault, security consultant at antivirus company Sophos, explains: 'SCO started to offer a bounty on MyDoomA because it attacked its website so it was offering £250,000. And then Microsoft announced that it was going to offer a bounty pool of £5 million.' She adds: 'We saw the bounty as a sign that people were getting very desperate. The thing that you have to realise is that viruses are very difficult to track.'

Meanwhile there was soon yet another twist to the MyDoom story, further underlying the complexity of this strange world of viruses and worms. Soon after MyDoomA had been active, another worm appeared, which was labelled DoomJuice. This worm sought out those computers that had already been infected with MyDoomA. Carole Theriault explains the significance of this: 'If it found [a computer infected with MyDoomA], it opened up a back door and then downloaded the source code for MyDoomA so that it could be cleaned out. We think that the reason for that was because the writer was cleaning up their tracks.'

Coming from hell

Of all the various digitals threats that we face from our computers and from the internet, viruses are probably the most infuriating and, proportionally, the most damaging of all. As already stated, no one is yet sure who wrote MyDoom and it is at least possible that we never will. Yet what is clear is that millions of pounds worth of damage and disruption – and the potential for many future cyber crimes – have been caused through the labours of probably just one person sitting alone at a computer terminal somewhere in the world.

This then is perhaps the most disturbing aspect of worms viruses; the sheer disproportionate effect that a computer programme can wreak over such distances and for such extended periods.

It is hard to think of another crime, either in cyber space or the real world, that can match the relative effect of a virus or worm. The impacts can go even beyond mere physical and even financial damage. There are few more frustrating feelings than knowing that your computer has been infected by a virus; the thought of all the mental energy and time you will have to expend just to fix the problem is deeply irritating. Even the process of having to delete infected email after tedious infected email from one's inbox can make the blood pressure soar. (The fact that the messages are usually written by people who appear to have no grasp of grammar or spelling just adds to the feeling of frustration.)

One can only sympathise with the sentiment of the IT network manager at MIT in Cambridge, Massachusetts, one of the pioneering centres of the computer revolution, after it was hit by the rapidly spreading Sobig.F virus in 2003. 'There is a special section of hell reserved for the guys that write these things,' Jeffrey Schiller told the media[1].

Meanwhile Jaron Lanier, one of the creators of virtual reality and a pioneering thinker about computers and the internet[2], is also loudly critical of what many virus writers do, even if he also blames large corporations such as Microsoft for unwittingly allowing the conditions in which viruses flourish. Lanier believes that the ultimate impact of what virus writers do to society cannot be overlooked. 'My feeling is that if an individual knowingly causes enormous amounts of wasted time for literally millions of people, it has to be thought of as a crime.

'Vandalism at that magnitude translates into an incremental impoverishment of society. And since wealth is what creates things like healthcare, it ultimately causes death.'

Such strong words from one of the internet revolution's true radicals and free thinkers indicates the depth of feeling that most people – even those in tune with the openness of the early hacker ethos – feel about viruses. But even though they arouse strong emotions, they are still not well understood by the general public.

Virus versus worm

The term computer virus is generally applied indiscriminately to all programmes that go and wreak havoc; many of the 'viruses' are in fact worms. MyDoom, for example, which we have earlier referred to as a virus, is in reality a worm. The distinction has implications for how they are handled and removed, even if the definition is becoming blurred in common parlance. The distinction is waning too because of the way that virus creators use so-called blended attacks incorporating different types of worms and viruses.

However, Matthew Ham explains the difference between the two.

'A worm is completely self-contained in general,' he says. 'A virus needs something to latch onto, be that a programme, a document or even the boot sector of a hard drive. A worm does not need that something. The worm is a programme of itself. Running that programme does not attach it to anything; it simply sends it somewhere else.'

He adds: 'The key way to disinfect a worm is to delete it. It's much more tricky with a virus; you have to remove it from whatever it has attached itself to.'

There are also an awful lot of them, both viruses and worms, and as we shall see them come in many different shapes and forms and live in various environments and sectors. (An increasingly popular term to describe both viruses and worms is 'malware', which covers all malicious programmes, including Trojans.) Overall, and depending on which definition one uses there have probably been somewhere between 40,000 and 60,000 created in the last 20 years, though some estimates put the figure even higher.

Though this sounds a huge number, only a relatively small number are regarded as particularly dangerous and active at any one time. For example, as of June 2004 there were reported to be around 300 viruses that were spotted lurking in cyberspace, active and to varying degrees potentially dangerous to the unwary computer user. The usual figure in the last few years has been around 200 at any given time.

Viruses and worms are said to be 'in the wild', an exotic expression that is used by the WildList organisation to denote viruses and worms that might be – in military parlance – a clear and present danger. The mission of the WildList organisation is to provide accurate, timely and comprehensive information about in the wild viruses to both users and product developers[3]. The WildList is monitored by a diverse group of more than 55 qualified volunteers, and is made available free of charge by the organisation.

The Virus Writers

By contrast those viruses that never made it out of computer laboratories are known as 'zoo' viruses. These may be of historical or technical interest to technology experts but they are generally no threat to the outside world. An extended definition of zoo viruses might include those that used to be in the wild but have since become 'caged', put in the zoo thanks to antivirus measures or simply because the sector in which they lived – typically old operating systems few people use any more – has largely vanished.

To this group can be added the new class of viruses and worms written by writers whose self-appointed function it is to show the theoretical capability of viruses without actually unleashing them into the wild to cause damage. Such writers, who are usually extremely skilled programmers, will typically send their viral progeny to antivirus companies and experts to show them what is possible. These 'proof of concept viruses' are not sent to AV firms entirely for altruistic reasons; the motivation appears to include, as mentioned, for the writers to show how smart they are and also to show the authorities the futility of endless patching of solutions for new malware. The virus writers, so the argument goes, will always be one step ahead.

Writers of benign or proof-of-concept viruses are sometimes referred to as the 'white hats' of the virus writing community, in contrast to the 'black hats', who release viruses in the wild and cause indiscriminate damage. It is a romantic concept, the distinction between the 'good' or 'white' virus writers and those who have gone over to the 'dark' or 'black' side. As we have seen earlier in this chapter, similar phraseology applies to the world of hacking. The reality, though, is that the line between black and white gets blurred and the motivations for virus writing are more complex and varied than they may at first glance appear. But before we consider why virus writers do what they do, we first need to look at how viruses began.

THE COMPUTER VIRUS ERA

The first PC virus is generally accepted to be a programme called Brain[4], which was written in Pakistan in 1986. Even now no one is quite sure of the true origins of this virus. It is thought to have been written by the owners of a small company called Brain Computer Services in Lahore, though there is some doubt about this; it could have been written to make it look as if was written by the company. One theory is that the writers – two brothers – wrote the virus as a form of advertising for their firm. Another theory is that the virus was intended to remind users that the firm had copyright to its own software. The true answer may never be known. But meanwhile the virus did spread, albeit slowly.

It was what is known as a 'boot sector' virus, meaning that it infected the boot sector of a computer. (In those days computers were started or 'booted up'.) After booting up the computer the user would load applications via a floppy disc. Any floppy containing a boot sector virus would try to write itself to the machine's boot sector. This meant the virus could take over control of the machine's fundamental core and allow it, for example, to lock the machine or drop characters off the screen. Thus the virus would lurk on a floppy disc and leap onto a machine's boot sector once its host disc had been inserted.

The first stealth virus

Brain was not only the first PC virus, it was a virus of contradictions too. The message that flashed up when the infection took hold was:

Welcome to the dungeon. Copyright 1986 Brain & Amjads, PVT, LTD. Virus shoe record V9.0 Dedicated to the dynamic

136

memory of millions of virus who are no longer with us today – Thank Goodness. BEWARE OF THE VIRUS> This programme is catching. Program follows after these messages.

The virus even contained the telephone numbers of the computer company! Yet while the virus writers seemed open about who they were, the virus was also at the same time the first 'stealth' virus. This meant that when a computer user tried to check if the boot sector was infected, the virus cleverly displayed the original uninfected boot sector and was thus able to hide its presence.

Despite this ingenuity – especially for such an early virus – Brain did not cause any deliberate damage, even if its presence inevitably slowed down the clunky PCs used at that time. It spread slowly, almost unheralded at first; though by 1988 the Brain virus had been discovered at various locations across America.

This was the true start of the computer virus era. Yet the realisation that such nightmarish programmes were now in the wild came as no great surprise to people in the know, even if it came as a shock to the steadily growing band of ordinary PC users.

Ever since 1949 when Hungarian scientist John von Neumann came up with the theory of self-replicating programmes – the foundation work of, for example, computer memory – the idea of viruses and worms had been a theoretical possibility. Some 30 years later technicians at one of the United States' most technologically advanced centres, the Xerox Palo Alto Research Centre in California, made use of a 'worm' programme whose task it was to burrow around its computer network looking for processors laying idle. In other words the first worm – the ancestor worm of later worms – was used to increase efficiency.

In 1981 and 1982, and little noted at the time, came the arrival of a virus affecting only Apple II machines and which was, like the later PC virus Brain, transferred by floppy discs. This virus, which originated in Texas, was called Elk Cloner and one of its tell-tale signatures was to display an irritating little rhyme on the user's screen. It read:

Elk Cloner: The Program with a personality
It will get on all your disks
It will infiltrate your chips
Yes it's Cloner!
It will stick to you like glue
It will modify ram too
Send in the Cloner!

Again, and like Brain, Elk Cloner did not try to destroy data, though it could inadvertently damage some discs it was trying to infect. Meanwhile in 1983 Fred Cohen, a research student at the University of California (UC), was working on a thesis on the theoretical existence of viruses. With the help of others he created one under 'laboratory' conditions in November 1983. A virus, according to Cohen's definition, could 'affect other computer programmes by modifying them in such a way as to include a (possibly evolved) copy of itself.'[5]

The term 'virus' was borrowed from the biological world and applied to these programmes in the early 1980s. The person credited with coining the term virus was UC academic Leonard Adleman, and the name stuck.

In many ways virus was a good choice of name. It was dramatic and certainly made people think about the impact of such programmes. Moreover the name fitted neatly into the idea – prevalent in some parts of science and technology – that the human brain works a bit like a computer and vice versa. So if a human being or a human brain could catch a virus, why not a computer too?

Viruses in the wild

In those early days there was a lot of talk about finding the cure for viruses or being able to inoculate or vaccinate against the threat. Specialist magazines even commissioned drawings showing hypodermic needles injecting circuit boards, just to emphasise the point. Now however such over-the-top comparisons have died out and there is a feeling among many in the industry that the likeness between human and computer viruses has been overplayed.

Matthew Ham, says: 'I think some people have taken [the parallels] to inordinate lengths and said that simply because you can do this with a living virus then you can do the same with a computer virus. It should really be taken just as an analogy.'

In any case Cohen's ground-breaking work – and to a lesser extent the existence of Elk Cloner – had prepared the computing industry for the eventual arrival of viruses in the wild.

This was just as well, because soon after Brain came a host of other viruses and 1987 was the year when this new phenomenon really took a grip on computing. One early virus was Lehigh, a destructive but not very infectious virus that never left the confines of Lehigh University in Pennsylvania, followed by Jerusalem and then the Christmas message worm that hit IBM's office computers (though nowhere else), much to its embarrassment.

Many of the early viruses were designed to spread through the use of floppy discs, which in those relatively early days of personal computing were habitually swapped from users to users, to exchange programmes and data. This highlights an obvious but sometimes overlooked point about the nature of viruses and how they spread. The writers of viruses design them to exploit whatever is the current favoured method of communication between computers. For example, when most people used floppy discs to transfer data, the viruses exploited that means of communication to spread.

Later, when users started to swap programmes and word documents, virus writers shifted their focus to enable viruses to spread with the use of programmes and documents, and via email. Now more and more users are using 'peer-to-peer' (p2p) networks – for example KaZaa – to swap music and other information. So it is no surprise to learn that many current viruses are exploiting p2p file sharing to spread themselves. There is also a major increase in the use of worms that attack and exploit networks, as many computer users are part of networks.

Matthew Ham sees a sense of history repeating itself. 'It's only very recently that it has gone back to where [virus and worm attacks] can be done through a network – which was where it started with the Morris worm. It's very much gone full circle.'

The Morris worm was indeed a major and deadly development in the history of viruses. This was not just because of what the worm did, and who and what it was able to attack; but also because of who the author of this powerful worm was.

BIRTH OF THE NETWORK WORM

Robert T Morris Junior, was an exceptionally bright 23-year-old student who, in common with a number of young men his age, was gripped by the idea of computers and software. Where Morris differed from many other enthusiasts however was that computing was in his blood; his father was Robert Morris Senior, chief scientist at the US National Computer Security Centre in Bethesda, Maryland, the arm of the top-secret National Security Agency devoted to protecting computers against outside attack. Morris Junior therefore grew up in an environment in which he not only understood the power and reach of computers, he also understood the enormous importance that was attached to keeping them secure.

In 1988 Morris Junior was a studying for a doctorate at Cornell University after taking his first degree at Harvard and seemed destined for a steady if unremarkable career in academia or perhaps, like his father, connected to the security industry. All that was about to change, however, when the ingenious young man decided to try out some programming code he had been developing. Morris Junior had found what seemed like a hole in Unix – the universal communications code of the telecommunication system, which allows one computer to send data to another – and like many true hackers of old decided to test the problem out.

On 2 November 1988, and using his computer attached to the still-fledgling internet, he released his code via his college network and went off to bed. (Morris actually released the worm from a computer at another university; he used remote control to do this from his computer at Cornell.)

He was tired out after days of almost obsessive work and had intended to check on the progress of his little project the following morning.

Unfortunately for the young student, the reaction was rather more than he had anticipated. Morris had expected that his code – creating what would become known as a worm – would stay living undetected within the internet. Instead, due to a programming error, the worm did not behave as expected and instead of 'living quietly' it began to rampage around the network like an angry gorilla. Morris had omitted to turn off the command that told the programme to install itself once on each computer and then search for another. Instead it kept reproducing itself like a virulent organism.

At that time there was no worldwide web as we understand it today (the protocols for that were still being developed and the web was still a couple of years away) but the fledgling internet that had started as the ARPANet in 1969 was growing fast and was thriving. Research centres, universities and of course government and military institutions all made use of this revolutionary information-sharing network.

Unfortunately for these users, Morris Junior's unruly worm – later dubbed simply the Internet Worm – was about to take advantage of the very same network. As the worm made its way across the ARPANet and burrowed into local networks, people quickly began to sense there was a serious problem looming. In what would go down as one of the most masterful understatements of all time, Andy Sudduth of Harvard University posted a message at 34 minutes past midnight on 3 November in which he said simply: 'There may be a virus loose on the internet.'

The words may have been simple and understated, but they would have sent a chill down the spine of anyone who had a knowledge of computer security. Until that point viruses and worms had largely spread by the use of floppy discs. As we have seen, virus writers naturally tailor their creations to the communication system currently in vogue. What Sudduth's message meant was that viruses and worms had now 'jumped' to another form of communication and would now start to colonise the network of networks – the internet. The network worm was born.

In fact, at that precise moment, and thanks to Morris' creation, the internet was coming apart. As the worm spread and replicated itself, Vax and Sun computers – which provided the backbone for much of the internet – across the United States were being overloaded with impossible tasks. This meant that anyone trying to get into these machines were blocked out – the computers simply could not cope.

Morris' worm had been far more 'successful' than he could possibly have imagined. Thanks to his programming, the worm was automatically copying itself through the internet, infecting the same computers over and over again and eventually forcing them to grind to a halt. Ultimately many of the systems administrators had little option but to cut off their machines from the internet, in an attempt to quarantine them from the infection.

The cost of purging the internet of the worm was put at millions of dollars. 'We run on $50,000 in government funds a day, and it's going to be three days before we can use our machines again,' said Laurel Simmons, facilities co-ordinator for the Artificial Intelligence Laboratory at MIT at the time. 'The Laboratory for Computer Science has a much bigger budget than we do. So you can imagine how much this is going to cost.'

Clifford Stoll was working at Harvard when the worm struck. 'There is not one system manager who is not tearing his hair out. It's causing enormous headaches,' he said[6].

Most of the infected computers were Digital Equipment Corp Vax machines or Sun 3 computers produced by Sun Microsystems, computers that made up around 75 per cent of all US national networks. Among its most high-profile victims were the Lawrence Livermore Laboratory in California; Harvard University, Naval Research Laboratory, Maryland; the National Aeronautical and Space Administration Research Centre in Mountain View California; Stanford University; The Jet Propulsion Laboratory; the San Diego Super Computer Centre and the Space and Naval Warfare Systems Center in San Diego.

In all a total of 6,000 computers – the entire core of the internet – were affected. Morris Junior's worm had not just penetrated the internet; it had brought it to its knees. This was a pretty impressive achievement for a 23-year-old student, even one with a father who himself had such unimpeachable computer credentials.

The news was not all bad. Due to slight differences between US and European networks at the time, computers in Europe escaped largely unscathed. Meanwhile Morris, who despite his fatigue had come back during the evening to check on his programme, so impatient was he to see what had happened, was horrified to see what he had done. The effects on the networks were so great he himself had trouble gaining access to remote computers to check on its progress. Surveying the scenes of devastation that his 'invention' had wreaked Morris Junior realised he had little choice but to turn himself in. He confessed what he had done to his father.

Morris' worm worked by exploiting a 'trapdoor' built into the electronic mail programme of the Unix computer system. The trapdoor had been built by Eric Allman, the programmer who designed the Sendmail programme for Unix. It was intended to allow him to maintain his work without the tiresome bother of asking the permission of an administrator. Apparently Allman forgot to remove the entry point before the system was distributed in 1985 and Morris found it. Morris was so excited about his discovery that he jumped on his desk and paced around while describing the entry point, according to Paul Graham, one of Morris' college friends.

Armed with 99 lines of code, Morris intended to use the weakness in the system to start his 'intellectual exercise' and, using his computer at college, had entered the programme into the local computer network.

Both father and son were, according to reports at the time of the incident, 'deeply involved in the study of computer security and intellectually entranced by the challenge of finding holes and "back doors" in computer programmes touted as burglar proof'[7].

For Robert Morris Senior that was evidently part of his job. For his son it was a hobby, an obsession, and one that got disastrously out of hand. Anne Morris, wife and mother to senior and junior respectively, said the two men were acutely aware of their similarities: 'Of course they are aware of it. How could they not be? Their interests and careers will dovetail so that there will be a continuum of Robert Morrises over the course of computer science.'

Could it be that that the internet was brought crashing down because a bright son wanted to impress his equally clever father?

Once Morris owned up to his father that he was the source of the Internet Worm, the student inevitably faced criminal charges. Nearly two years later in May 1990 Morris Junior was fined $10,000 under the Computer Fraud and Abuse Act, put on three years probation and given 400 hours community service[8]. (Morris has now resumed his place in the orthodox academic world of computing and is a highly respected professor in computing at MIT.)

It is generally accepted now that Morris Junior had no malicious intent when he released his worm into the wild. The worm itself had no destructive payload. It did not seek to delete data, for example; instead its sheer replicating power and presence did the damage.

This is quite a familiar tale with early viruses and even some today. The creator writes them thinking they are an interesting or amusing project, either to entertain friends with or perhaps (nowadays) to send to an antivirus company to show what can be done. Sometimes though these viruses can slip out of quarantine – either through accident or the actions of a 'friend' – and escape into the wild, with unpredictable consequences.

In Morris' case it appears he simply wanted to high-light known weaknesses in the Unix code that had not been put right. He certainly knew the Unix code well. The student, who incidentally had a reputation for com-puter practical jokes, had worked in AT&T's Bell Laboratories during his summer vacations. One of his projects there included rewriting communications secu-rity software for part of an informal network connecting most computers that run the Unix operating system, giving him a crucial understanding of how the internet worked at the time and the way it was secured.

A loss of innocence

The Morris worm incident was really a foretaste of what was to come with the arrival of the worldwide web and the possibility of using its tremendous information communications powers as a conduit for less welcome data. It also taught the more alert companies a valuable lesson; not to reply on operating systems that worked on just once basic code, for example Unix, but to have a varied series of code 'platforms'. Those firms that already used a variety of codes during the Morris worm episode were at least able to keep part of their system working.

Meanwhile for many later virus writers and hackers, Morris became an unlikely hero; unlikely because of his own academic leanings, because of his denial of causing the damage deliberately and, of course, because his father was not just a spook (someone working in the intelligence and security services), but a spook whose job it was to stop hackers and their kind.

To the hacking and virus community here was a man who had written a programme that had jammed, among others, a military network and done the unthinkable; he had rendered the system that was meant to survive a nuclear war impotent by attacking it from the inside.

Morris had embarrassed the technology establishment, wreaked millions of pounds worth of damage, and in the process set the target for future viruses. It would be a hard act to follow, but the age of internet viruses had begun. The internet had lost its innocence even before it had really begun.

Landmark viruses

In the years since the Morris worm there have been many attempts by virus writers to write ever newer and more powerful viruses. When one considers that perhaps more than 50,000 or even as many as 100,000 have been written and yet that only a few hundred at most ever have much impact, the strike rate of success is remarkably low. Indeed many would-be viruses prove completely ineffective and show a marked reluctance to infect anything at all. The result is as if someone has tried to breed a ferocious pitbull terrier and ended up with a dopey Labrador that just wants to lick your hand.

Matthew Ham, whose job involves 'road testing' viruses in laboratory conditions, says: 'A large proportion of viruses are simply so badly written that they will not replicate except possibly on the machine of the person who wrote them. I am constantly astounded at how difficult it is to replicate some of the viruses when we test them. So you wonder how they actually managed to make it into the wild.'

Some, of course, are well written and do make it into the wild to stunning effect. Indeed the history of viruses in the world is studded with landmark viruses as writers have found new ways of exploiting weaknesses and the behaviour of computer users.

One such huge virus was Melissa, which was launched in March 1999, some 11 years after the Morris worm, and to devastating effect.

Melissa was one of a breed of so-called macro viruses that were taking advantage of the huge growth in email traffic in the 1990s and also which took advantage of the fact that Word documents – sent for example as attachments – have the ability to have programmes written into them. (Technically Melissa is a 'script virus'[9] but they use similar language to macro viruses.)

Before macro viruses, writers tended to focus on the system's operating system. The favourite method of infecting a machine was to attach or append the virus to an executable programme; in other words you run the programme and you run the virus.

Macros however actually work within the programme. The writers know that a lot of people run Word, for example, so they send a person a document that has the virus in the format settings. These are tiny little 'programmes within the programmes' that run when someone opens a document.

Macro viruses during the late 1990s and early 2000s were the most prevalent viruses. Unlike other virus types, macro viruses are not specific to an operating system and spread with ease via email attachments, floppy disks, web downloads, file transfers and cooperative applications. Macro viruses are written in 'every man's programming language' – Visual Basic – and are relatively easy to create. They can infect at different points during a file's use, for example, when it is opened, saved, closed or deleted.

Like many viruses sent by email, the author of Melissa used social engineering to persuade recipients to open the attachment. We have already seen how many hackers have used social engineering to gain entry to closed computer systems. In the case of virus writers they use simple deception ploys to reassure the recipient that the email message can be trusted.

In this case the language use in Melissa emails made it seem as though the message was from a friend or colleague. Fooled by this simple ploy, many people did open the Melissa attachments – and soon found themselves infected. The email launched a programme that went to the address book in that user's Microsoft Outlook email organiser and emailed the first 50 addresses a replica of the original email. The impact was massive and swift. The virus spread swiftly around the planet and soon an estimated one million computers were infected. It was the fastest-spreading virus anyone had seen at that time.

As it happens, the damage that Melissa did to an individual's computer was not dramatic. But as is often the case with mass-impact viruses, the effect was greatest on servers and Internet

Service Providers (ISPs), which suddenly have to deal with a huge surge in email traffic. Later estimates put the cost at clearing up the damage of Melissa at around $80 million (about £50 million)[10].

At least in the case of Melissa retribution was swift. Within scarcely a week of the release of the virus the person responsible, a man called David L Smith, was arrested and later charged. Smith was an interesting virus writer in that he did not fit the stereotype of a virus writer. Smith, from New Jersey, was aged 31 and appeared to have a relatively successful career as a computer programmer. He did not seek to disguise his guilt either. Soon after he was tracked by police and expert trackers from the computer security industry, Smith admitted that the creation of Melissa – named in tribute to a stripper in Florida he knew – was a 'colossal mistake' He also claimed that he had tried to put in safeguards to stop the potential for widespread damage he ultimately caused[11].

Cyber sting

Clearly contrite, Smith was willing to do a deal with the criminal justice system; in return for a lighter sentence he would help police track down other virus writers he knew. This was a welcome moment of breakthrough for the antivirus industry. Many writers can go undetected for years or even indefinitely. Yet here was Smith, prepared to trap his virus-writing brethren to save his own skin. The authorities did not waste the opportunity.

Within weeks of his arrest Smith had embarked on a remarkable 'career' as an undercover investigator, using his intimate knowledge of virus writing and the virus-writing community to win other writers into his confidence. For nearly two years Smith operated in this twilight zone, on bail himself for his crimes but working hand in glove with the FBI and at its expense to crack open the closed world of virus writing.

By that time Smith himself had been sentenced by a court in New Jersey and been handed a 20-month gaol term, far lower than the 10 years he might have expected had he not co-operated with the FBI.

At Smith's sentencing prosecutor Christopher Christie told the court: 'Virus writers seem emboldened by technology and enjoy the thrill of watching the damage they reap.' He then added: 'But the case of Mr Smith and his Melissa virus should prove to others that it's a fool's game.' Fool's game or not, it was one that many virus writers were still determined to play.

The Smith cyber sting was ultimately to produce real results. From his online contacts and messages Smith was able to pass on contact details of a Dutch virus writer Jan DeWit, who was behind the Anna Kournikova virus in 2001. The virus exploited the popularity of the pin-up Russian tennis player Anna Kournikova and was hidden in an email which invited the receiver to open a picture of her called 'AnnaKournikova.jpg.vbs'. Upon opening, the virus copied itself to the Windows directory and then sent the file as an attachment to every address listed in an infected user's Microsoft Outlook address book. It also attempted to launch a browser directed to a Dutch computer shop's website on January 26 of every year.

Ranked as a medium risk virus by the anti-virus companies at the time of its launch the virus crashed email servers because of the high number of messages it generated. The information was passed on to the authorities in Holland and DeWit was later arrested, brought to trial and put on probation for his crimes. DeWit's sentence, however, by a Dutch court to just 150 hours of community service provoked dismay in the antivirus industry, who saw it as a pitifully small punishment for a young man who worked in a computer store and had a personal collection of more than 7,000 viruses, and thus must have been aware of the damage he could cause. The dismay turned to scorn when DeWit appealed – unsuccessfully as it turned out – against the sentence on the grounds that it could 'harm his career'.

Meanwhile in the popular holiday resort town of Llandudno in North Wales a young British DJ and web designer was growing increasingly cocky about his own exploits in the world of virus writing. Simon Vallor, who was 22, appeared proud that he had produced 3 viruses that, while not on the scale of a Melissa or even the Kournikova virus, had nevertheless made their mark on computers around the world. The three viruses Vallor had released were called Gokar, Admirer, and RedesiB.

Unfortunately for the DJ his pride in these creations was to be his undoing. He could not resist boasting about his achievements in a chatroom, a venue he doubtless felt was full of like-minded souls and sympathisers. It probably was – apart from one of them. This person turned out to be David L Smith in his new disguised role as an FBI informer.

Smith's information on Vallor was soon passed via the FBI to the police in Britain, and the virus writer was arrested and charged under the UK's 1990 Computer Misuse Act. Early in 2003 Vallor pleaded guilty to the offences and was sentenced to two years imprisonment at Southwark Crown Court in London, despite his claims that he had not intended to cause any damage.

Virulent viruses

The authorities were less fortunate in May 2000 when the notorious Love Bug (also known as VBS/LoveLetter) rampaged around the planet's computers. This virulent virus attacked 45 million computers and caused upwards of £6 billion worth of damage, but became so well known and so hyped by the media chiefly because of the high-profile identity of some of its victims. These included the United Kingdom's parliament, where the internal email system had to be closed down because it was infected, the CIA, State Department and Pentagon in the United States and the banking system in Belgium, which had to shut down its ATM system.

All the evidence for this virus – whose carrier email enticed recipients to open an attachment with the seductive words 'I LOVE YOU: A love letter for you' – pointed to a rather tatty apartment block in an unprepossessing part of the Filipino capital Manila. The prime suspect for the offence – though his computer curiously vanished after the virus was released – was a moderately talented 23-year-old computer student called Onel De Guzman. On the surface the evidence was strong. It was revealed that De Guzman had recently suffered the indignity of having a thesis rejected by his tutors. This thesis argued the case for a computer programme – curiously similar to Love Bug – that would allow an internet user to steal passwords and thus spend more free time on the internet.

There was just one snag for the authorities. The Philippines did not that at that time have any legislation outlawing what De Guzman had allegedly done. So while he was arrested and held for a while, he was never charged with the offence. (New legislation was quickly passed in June 2000 but could not be retroactive.) De Guzman was also careful never to admit sending it – though he conceded he may have had a hand in 'cooking' (ie compiling) it – and suggested hackers may have broken into his computer to send it into the wild.

This episode, and the laughably lenient sentence given to De Wit in Holland (see above Box), shows once again that the global fight against cyber crime is only effective as the weakest link in the chain of legislation outlawing it, and is dependent on judicial authorities to take the issue of digital security seriously.

Though De Guzman never admitted his role in the Love Bug outbreak, he did later explain why virus writers do what they do during an online chat with CNN in September 2000. When asked by the host what he thought a virus writer's 'motivation' was, De Guzman replied: 'They want to learn. They want to be creative.'[12]

Most of us might find such a response startlingly naïve in justifying why someone should cause millions or even billions of pounds of damage plus unfathomable misery for countless millions of ordinary computer users. Yet the Filipino's answer does shed some light on an important question. Just who are virus writers; and why do they do what they do?

A VIRUS WRITER'S IDENTIKIT

Virus writers, like hackers, stamp collectors, train spotters and other people with a common interest, tend to congregate together. Obviously they usually do this remotely (via the internet) rather than physically (using a church hall or the local library); but they still meet up. And like any enthusiasts of a particular hobby they like to show off to their fellow enthusiasts, with whom they will often share a competitive camaraderie.

Just as a stamp collector will be keen to show off his prized penny black to other collectors, the virus collector wants to show off his latest virus.

It is a curious and contradictory trait of virus writers that they meet in an environment – cyber space – where the discussion they are having is only possible because of the very communication system that they want to wreck. However, we have to be careful here in attributing the same motives to all virus writers. Many do not aim to destroy the internet and the email system, even if that ultimately could be the result of their actions.

In fact, those who have studied virus writers for many years have found it hard to produce easy identikit snapshots of a 'typical' virus writer. The stereotypical view, as mentioned earlier, is that of an adolescent male, probably a loner, who takes out his teenage angst on the world by creating viruses from the comfort of his bedroom.

Some writers do conform to at least part of this picture. An example is the author of the Sasser worm, which caused severe disruption to computers and networks in May 2004, including to coastguard services in Britain, hospitals in Hong Kong, post offices in Taiwan and railway networks in Australia. It did not move via email but used the internet to scan for computers with vulnerabilities, and then sent the programme direct to the computer.

The culprit who confessed to being the author of the destructive worm turned out to be a shy 18-year-old German boy who still lived with his parents in the small town of Waffensen in Lower Saxony. Sven Jaschan has been described as a loner, even though some antivirus experts suggest he may not have been working alone. In an interview with *Stern* magazine[13] Jaschan appeared to take 'credit' also for writing the common Netsky virus and said that most of his classmates knew that he was its author.

One of the most noteworthy things about Netsky, which is delivered in email attachments, was the number of mutations made to both the virus and its name. Its most virulent version Netsky-B was a modified version of NetSky-A, a computer virus that surfaced on 17 February 2004. Its final form to date is known as Netsky-V. Rated by the security companies as a medium-to high-grade threat it spread quickly and, though not nearly as virulent or destructive as MyDoom bug, it still infected hundreds of systems, including embarrassingly the computers of the computer communications company Lucent.

Most significantly from the point of view of motivation, Jaschan said the episode had boosted his esteem among his contemporaries. While denying he intended to cause any damage – an oddly familiar refrain among all virus writers who get caught – the teenager told *Stern*: 'It was just great how Netsky began to spread, and I was the hero of my class.' Yet while Jaschan conforms to the nerd-who-can't-get-a-girlfriend stereotype, there are plenty of others who do not; the previously mentioned 31-year-old David L Smith of Melissa infamy being one of them.

Script kiddies versus academics

A common way of defining virus writers is to divide them into two groups. The first contains the 'script kiddies' – such as Jaschan – who like writing and releasing code into the wild because they get a buzz from it and it gives them a sense of power. Such writers are not often particularly talented programmers – they tend to use the many virus-writing kits now available – and do not often have very developed social consciences. It is not so much that they intend harm, more that they are morally and emotionally illiterate (and often literally illiterate too) youngsters who simply just don't think about the consequences of their actions.

Someone who fits into this group is Simon Vallor from Wales in the UK, one of the young virus writers who was prosecuted thanks to David L Smith's undercover work.

In an interview with a local radio station before his conviction, Vallor describes how spending time on his computer and with viruses helped him escape from real life – especially after the death of his mother[14]. 'I started spending 20 hours a day on the computer. That was what my life revolved around – it was out of bed and onto the computer. It was escapism, to get away from everything that was happening around me. No one knew me online.'

The young DJ said he had learnt how to create viruses almost by accident. 'To start with it was just a programme experiment. I was just exploring the function. I didn't have a clue the virus was going to spread at all.'

The other group contains the 'academics'. In contrast these writers tend to be older and brighter than the script kiddies, and are often extremely talented programmers. Their motivation for writing viruses and worms might vary considerably. Some write viruses simply because they can, and want to highlight flaws in software. (They especially enjoy spotlighting flaws in Microsoft operating systems.) These writers will typically not release viruses directly into the wild. Though they may have a strong disdain for large corporations 'taking over' the internet, they are also socially attuned and more responsible and will usually send their creations to antivirus companies.

Breaking down categories

However, here the easy labelling of these two groups starts to break down. For not all the writers within the 'academic' category are socially responsible. Virus experts have told the authors that they believe some among this 'academic' group may be the most dangerous virus writers of all, combining genuine programming skills with a sense of grievance against the 'big bad corporate world' that is 'destroying' the internet.

While they may not release their viruses directly, they may 'leave' them in such places where they know younger wannabe writers will find them. A leading AV consultant told us: 'These "academics" are the most dangerous because these are the ones who come up with the code that is often released by the script kiddies.'

Morally this makes those virus authors as culpable as the kids who actually release them, even if the 'academics' might like to pretend to others – and perhaps themselves – that they have done nothing wrong.

Moreover not only is this virus-writing elite producing the most virulent viruses, they are far harder to catch; precisely because they are often one step removed from the actual offence of releasing a virus. Even if things go wrong and the virus leaves behind too many tell-tale 'fingerprints', these resourceful authors are not beaten. Remember the example of the MyDoomA virus cited earlier, and how a worm called DoomJuice followed it with the sole intention apparently of removing identifying traces from the earlier infection?

This convenient division between script kiddies and academics may not be enough to reflect the complexity of the world of virus writers. One self-proclaimed writer from Holland, a 16-year-old calling himself Blue Owl, believes there are four distinct groups of virus writers. He told *PC Magazine* in 2004[15] that the four groups are: 1) the creators and academics; 2) student researchers; 3) the script kiddies; and 4) the cyber terrorists.

Of these Blue Owl says the first group is the brightest, a group to which of course Blue Owl claims membership. He tells the magazine that for him writing a virus is like an act of creation. 'A virus is something that lives. In real life you can't make a kind of animal. You can in the computer. It's like playing God.'

On one point at least he is in agreement with many in the antivirus industry – that the viruses of most script kiddies 'suck'.

Another way of categorising virus writers is to consider simply whether their motives are intentionally bad – or merely misguided.

Matthew Ham, consultant for Virus Bulletin as previously mentioned, is certainly wary of being too dogmatic about categorising the writers, pointing out that it is not just people with an obvious anti-establishment grudge who take part. 'There is a wide variety of people who create viruses, wider than people assume. There are some very reasonably paid professionals who have been working in decent companies for many years.' He adds: 'There are as many reasons for writing viruses as there are for using computers.'

Ham does see a clear distinction however between the people who write because they want to be noticed – their 15 minutes of fame –

and those who have more sinister motives. 'Even from the start there seem to have been two branches of virus writers; the ones who were doing it to show that they were clever, and the ones who were doing it in a slightly more malicious way.'

He believes the level of malice is both increasing and changing; and that more and more virus writers are designing programmes to leave 'back doors' on computers that can be exploited by criminals later, even if such writers are still in the minority.

David Emm, Senior Technology Consultant of UK antivirus firm Kaspersky Lab, is also clear that there has been a worrying shift in the motives of virus writers in recent years. 'In the 1990s viruses could be placed alongside other acts of vandalism. More recently, we've seen wider intent. Mass-mailers since Melissa have clearly been written by people who knew their creations would have an impact on companies' ability to do business, by undermining their email systems. And viruses and worms have been used for financial fraud; phishing scams, for example, that try to get your personal banking details.'

Buying and selling

Even more worrying for the computer industry and those of us with computers is the suggestion that criminals are now starting to employ virus writers in a mirror image of the way that, for example, antivirus companies employ staff to help detect and protect against viruses.

Mikko Hyppönen, director of Anti-Virus Research at the F-Secure Corporation in Finland, is one who believes that some virus writing is becoming more organised. He paints a grim picture of virus writers being taken on by criminals, and even of virus writers putting themselves forward as hired guns to be bought by the highest bidders.

He says: 'Yes, criminal gangs are employing virus writers. We have also seen virus writers actively offering their services to criminals. Most of this discussion and recruiting and buying and selling of their services goes on in the underground economy, mostly on discussion websites running on servers in faraway places or difficult-to-find locations.

'You can find people buying and selling virus-writing services and distributed denial of service attacks; so you can simply buy an attack. You just tell them the target and pay them. Typically you pay them by using PayPal [an online payment system] or Western Union transfer.'[16] Hyppönen adds that the market for such attacks is a new phenomenon: 'It did not exist at the beginning of 2003.'

This alliance between the criminal mind and unscrupulous virus writers will only increase the vulnerability to attack not just of ordinary computer users and companies, but of the email system and the internet itself.

An example of the astonishing sophistication and speed with which viruses and worms work was dramatically demonstrated in 2003, at about the time that the new 'employment exchange' for virus writers for hire was starting. At 7.31am on 25 January of that year, Hyppönen was among many to spot the arrival of a new star worm in the firmament. Later called Slammer, this lightning-fast worm started to scan every available IP address – effectively the address for each computer with an internet connection – on the planet. This was then some 4.2 billion IP addresses; and Slammer took just 13 minutes to accomplish the task.

Hyppönen recalls: 'By a quarter to eight it had done everything it wanted to do. It had scanned – and then infected – every single machine that was vulnerable, that was connected to the public net. It is the equivalent of someone designing a phone robot that would call every single phone number on earth in 15 minutes.'

Not only was this worm fast, it was tiny, too. The entire code was just 376 bytes long; short enough, for example, to be contained in just three Short Message Service (SMS) text messages.

No one is sure who carried out this rapid and sophisticated attack, though it is possible they may have made use of 'proof-of-concept' code written by software researcher David Litchfield. Litchfield had exposed a flaw in Microsoft's SQL Server software – a flaw the worm exploited – during research work for a banking client. Litchfield had quite properly sought to make people aware of the vulnerability, yet by the time the attack took place many networks had been slow to react and were still at risk.

Initially suspicion fell on a Chinese hacking group, called the Honker Union of China, after it had published code similar to the Slammer worm. Yet there has been little hard evidence since to link this curious group to the Slammer outbreak.

The Honker Union is not the only gang of virus writers around; indeed, since the days of the first viruses, loose affiliations of writers have sprung up to swap information and of course to publicise themselves. For example, Blue Owl (mentioned earlier), claims membership of a group calling itself the Ready Rangers Liberation Front, an alliance of mostly European-based virus writers. In the past there have been other groups, notably 40 Hex and Phalcon/Skism. (Virus writers tend to go for exotic, not to say impenetrable, names; another example of them being desperate to show how clever they are.)

However, the best known today is the also improbably named group 29a[17]. This group is another with European roots, its fluctuating membership drawn mostly from Eastern Europe, Germany, Austria, Russia and also Spain. Its website is currently hosted in Slovakia and the message displayed on its homepage leaves the visitor in little doubt what they will find there, should they be brave enough to look inside. It reads:

*** *Warning* ***
This site contains viruses, Trojans and other
software that may damage computer systems.

If you don't like the stuff on this site feel free to
LEAVE at any moment.

Its name too, gives a buried clue either to its sinister motivation or, far more likely, to the group's ghoulish sense of humour at the world's expense. Translated into the hexadecimal counting system (as opposed to the decimal system we use) it reads 666, the number given in the New Testament's Book of Revelation to represent the Beast or Devil.

This is a group that certainly does write viruses, and very clever and effective ones too. Yet its moral 'get out' clause is that it may write them but it does not release them. Also contained on its website are the words: 'We code viruses for the fun of it, because it's our hobby, not because we want to harm other people or to get ourselves into trouble.'

For this group, which has been around since 1996, the 'fun' is to be had in the intellectual challenge of writing a virus no one has thought of before, and that exploits previously undetected flaws in software. A good example of this was in June 2004, when members of the group announced they had succeeded in writing a virus that would spread between mobile phones using the wireless Bluetooth technology.

This next level of viruses had long been anticipated, but 29a got there first. Of course, as with their previous creations, they themselves will not release the virus into the wild. But experts fear that, like other 29a viruses, it may be published in one of their annual 'ezines' (online magazines) – and will eventually fall into the hands of the script kiddies, who will try to pass it off as their own.

Mikka Hyppönen says: 'I am fairly sure – I hope I am wrong – but I am sure that their next edition of their magazine will include the new mobile phone virus. So far it is not in the hands of the script kiddies. But when the magazine comes out – and if it is included in there – it will fall into their hands and then it will be out in the wild. And that is very serious when that happens.'

Therefore 29a is a good example of the 'academic' virus writers, discussed earlier, who write powerful viruses and who do not directly cause harm by distributing them; but who often allow them to be published and thus can be sure they will be released into the wild – by someone else. Presumably maintaining an arm's length from the physical distribution of the viruses enables 29a to salve its consciences even while it dreams up yet more ingenious viruses.

Soon after it came up with the first proof-of-concept of a mobile phone virus, another member of their group published the first portable PC or hand-held PC virus, malware that infects the Windows CE operating system used to run such devices. The creator is a 29a member, known as Ratter, from the Czech Republic and the virus – published in July 2004 and not yet in the wild – is known as WinCE/Duts.A.

Yet as potentially harmful as the 'academic' groups of virus writers are, there is a new and possibly even more worrying development in the world of the cyber security and one that is starting to affect many individual internet users on a daily basis. In the digital age it threatens to become one of the biggest crimes that we have yet seen. Few of us, it seems, are immune to identity theft.

CHAPTER SIX
Identity Theft

As the Western world has begun to rely more and more on technology, electronic data and digital storage, so the criminal has learnt to adapt. In an information age, information is money. The criminal has learnt that if they can manipulate and control information they can make money. At the same time, information has begun to define our identity – who we are. We are no longer simply Mr or Mrs Jo Brown of Acacia Avenue but are comprised of various bytes of data stored on numerous databases by many different organisations. Whoever gets access to and control of that information can effectively become us. The digital world has simply made identity (ID) theft that much easier for criminals; the digital citizens of Western society are victims of their own success.

The news is not all bad. Society is continually looking for better ways to safeguard personal information, and this process will continue in the future. More and more companies will be offering – for a fee – to be able to 'verify' that we are who we say we are in some kind of online 'validation' scheme. This is a trend that is already starting with insurance companies in the United States.

There is however an inherent problem in our attempts to improve digital security. The more that we come to rely on certification schemes to check the identity of people, the more such schemes are attractive to criminals as a way of ensuring they can operate with impunity. For, while a criminal without digital 'proof' of who they are may not be able to con anyone out of money, a criminal who can gain access to such proof will be trusted without question. When this happens the digital shield that we try to place around ourselves will become a weapon that can be turned upon ourselves. Criminals with the right technological know-how will still be able to 'become' us.

CYBER IDENTITIES

There are a number of ways that we can have our identities stolen. Criminals may gain access to one of the many databases that contain a person's details – either through hacking or through inside contacts – and then use this information to impersonate the person.

Another way is through a criminal gathering all the available published data they can find on an individual, for example from the internet, and using this to assume the identity. It is worryingly easy to leave our 'digital footprints' around the internet; our full name, address, date of birth, email addresses are just basic examples. Add to that the possibility that we might have our CV on a website or details of our parents' names or clues to our hobbies and interests, and one can see how criminals can begin to draw a convincing cyber picture of us from seemingly innocent data.

A third technique is where criminals use sophisticated technology to raid an individual's computer and steal personal and financial information from them – often without their knowledge.

Yet another occurs when criminals impersonate official organisations and deceive individuals into handing over private information. Once the criminals have gained the information, they can then use this to make money, usually very quickly and often very safely. One method is to use a person's personal information to exploit their existing bank account or credit card details, for example, and spend existing funds.

Another technique is for the criminals to use this personal information to create new accounts, cards or loans in the victim's names. This last tactic is being used more and more. In a recent survey the US company ID Analytics looked at thousands of accounts opened with financial institutions in the US that were in the 'bad debt' portfolio and discovered that, of these, 70 per cent were actually fake accounts[1].

One of the most alarming developments in this area is what might be called a double ID theft, in which the criminal impersonates a company in order to rob the victim of their personal details – and their money. The online version of this is known as 'phishing', which we have already briefly looked at in previous chapters.

PHISHING FOR MONEY

The concept of phishing – which first stormed the internet in 2003 – is a simple one. Cyber criminals go out 'fishing' ('phishing' is just a geek 'translation' of 'fishing') on the internet and via email for crucial bits of financial information about individuals. To go fishing one needs a bait; the 'bait' that the cyber phishers offer is to pose as banks or financial institutions – and increasingly other organisations too – and email their potential victims. These victims will be customers of the impersonated bank or financial institution, and they will follow the instructions from the email to go to the organisation's website, where they will be asked to confirm their passwords and account details. In reality of course it is not the bank's website but a dummy one made to look like the real thing. Once the 'phish' or victim has handed over their details the criminals then simply unload the unfortunate's accounts for every penny they have.

That is how phishing works in theory. In practice the criminals have a number of hurdles to overcome. First how do they find the customers of the organisation they have chosen to impersonate? For example if the criminals choose to pretend to be Citibank, how do they reach Citibank clients? The answer is that they usually use spammers – mass email marketers who sent out vast numbers of unwanted emails known as spam. The spammers send out hundreds of thousands of fake Citibank messages, in the knowledge that while many of them will go to non-Citibank clients – who will presumably bin them – enough emails will reach genuine customers.

Another key problem for the fraudsters is how to persuade the customer that the actions they are being asked to perform are normal and safe. There are two ways the phishers try to achieve this. The first is using technology. Their aim is to make the email and the website as authentic as possible. The second is by social engineering; delivering the right kind of reassuring message in the right way to ensure that your victim trusts you.

This impersonation of businesses – known as corporate identity fraud – was already well known in the offline world before the arrival of phishing. According to officers from the UK's National Criminal Intelligence Service (NCIS)[2] it had already reached sophisticated levels.

'[Criminals] will print business cards, obtain stationery and even set up fake departments,' said one NCIS officer who asked not to be named for security reasons.

'We have found people masquerading as high-street banks, where every detail on the cards and the letters they are using is correct apart from the direct line and mobile phone numbers that they supply. The internet has helped them enormously. Now they can even copy the websites so the contact website address that they provide only adds to the impression of reality they create.'

In the phishing cases early attempts by the criminals were often unsuccessful because the websites and emails did not look convincing and because the use of language was poor. While their targets are usually Western and English speaking, many phishers are from Eastern Europe and Russia. Therefore the phishers' poor grasp of language often let them down; none but the most careless of individuals were taken in by them. But the phishers began to improve their language skills – it is thought they employed native English speakers to write their messages and websites – to increase their chances of success.

Sandra Quinn is corporate communications director for the UK's Association for Payment Clearing Services (APACS)[3], the influential trade body for financial institutions on such issues as credit card transactions, and an organisation that has closely observed the phishing phenomenon since it burst onto the scene.

'At the beginning it was very easy to spot because they used a transatlantic language and the sites were a bit scruffy,' she agrees. 'But all of that has changed over the last nine months because they have become very sophisticated and the language is very good – and so is the message. Every month they are becoming much more convincing and much more numerous. At one stage there were two or three hits a month – now we are finding that there are two or three a month in the UK and forty a month worldwide.'

As well as the language, the social engineering used by the conmen is becoming increasingly sophisticated, and is even turning growing public concern over the frauds to their advantage. 'We are also now seeing fake websites that have "warnings" on them, telling people to be wary of fraud and emails,' she says.

Sandra Quinn of APACS (see above box) says that the early targets included Britain's 'big four' clearing banks – Barclays, Royal Bank of Scotland, Lloyds TSB and HSBC – quickly followed by other leading British institutions such as the Nationwide, Halifax and Egg.

'I think the reason why they went for [the UK] is because we have a reputation for banking and because of the English language. There were attempts to hit the French banking system but the language was so bad that the French people, who are very sensitive to bad

French, spotted them instantly. I understand that they have now improved the language and the emails in general, which is proof of organisation and "market awareness".'

The criminals behind phishing make their money from small percentages of the people they contact, so they rely on high-volume approaches to 'fish' for their victims. Sandra Quinn of APACS says the phishers may send out as many as 200,000 emails per one hit in an attempt to find someone vulnerable. Although the number of victims is comparatively low, the sums the criminals make can still be impressive.

'In each wave of attacks about 5 per cent of those contacted have an online account for that bank, of those a small handful reply and a smaller percentage lose money,' says Quinn. 'Of those people who do reply we have heard a lot of stories of people who have gone onto the website and then they have become suspicious and logged off; though there are people who have contacted us who have got suspicious after they have filled in their details.'

She says typical losses for individuals vary from £2,000 to £3,000, though the sums involved can sometimes be higher. These are significant pickings especially for criminals who are – in many of the cases – based in Eastern Europe or parts of the former Soviet Union.

Quinn's observation that phishing involves increasingly organised gangs fits with the views of the UK's National Hi-Tech Crime Unit (NHTCU) (see Chapter 3), who have been liaising with law enforcement agencies across Europe in relation to organised phishing gangs. This is where a specialist police unit such as the NHTCU plays an important role; because of its remit and international links it can take action against foreign-hosted websites and foreign criminals in a way that UK-based banks cannot.

An example of the action taken by police was on 5 May 2004, when officers from the unit arrested 12 people in London and the south east of England[4]. The suspects were detained in connection with alleged money laundering on behalf of phishing gangs.

Money laundering often goes hand in hand with hi-tech crime. One of the 'obstacles' for the phishers, for example, is how to move the money they have plundered from their frauds out of the country where the crime took place. Regulations aimed at controlling the flow of money connected with organised crime and terrorism have made it hard for the phishers to move the money directly out of, for example, the United Kingdom.

The gangs therefore employ other people in the host country to open bank accounts where the money can be laundered and then sent on to the syndicates back home, minus a 'commission' for the launderers. Typically this commission is 7 per cent.

In this case the 12 arrested were 6 men and 6 women from countries including Estonia, Latvia, Russia, Ukraine and Lithuania. They were suspected of working on behalf of what the police describe as 'Russian organised crime'.

Significantly a number of other agencies helped the NHTCU in the arrests, including the UK's National Crime Squad, the FBI and the US Secret Service. At the time of the detentions the NHTCU's deputy head, Detective Superintendent Mick Deats, said organised crime had been targeting Russian speakers to help them launder their money.

'We believe this gang has sent hundreds of thousands of pounds back to Russia. It has targeted a large number of high-street and internet banks, and, because it is unable to break into the banks' systems itself, it is resorting to duping account holders into parting with their details.'

He added: 'This is a sophisticated operation involving false identities, and only by working together with the banking industry and other law enforcement agencies has this [arrest] been possible.'[5]

Just a few days earlier the unit had also arrested a 21-year-old Briton from Lytham St Anne's, Lancashire, in the north-west of England, on suspicion of carrying out phishing attacks against smile, the internet banking arm of the Co-operative Bank. However the detectives stressed that they did not believe the man arrested was linked to any organised gang but was suspected of being what they termed a 'copycat' phisher, an individual who imitated the actions of the phishing gangs.

The prevalence of phishing attacks has now begun to encourage banks and other financial organisations to abandon their customary secrecy and caution. 'From our point of view it has shown that there is a need to share data information between us and other organisations,' says Quinn. 'As a result of this some of the banks have set limits into the systems on how much money people can move around.'

The cost of phishing

For the financial world phishing is damaging in two ways. One is that such scams can undermine customer's trust in online banking and, as banks have moved away from real world branches and more towards web-based services, any long-term and serious dent in consumer confidence in the internet could be disastrous. Phishing scams are very public and cannot simple be discreetly handled behind closed doors.

The second is the direct cost of the attacks. Although the people whose money is physically taken are the customers, the banks currently indemnify their clients against any losses online – rather as happens with most credit card fraud. As a spokesman for Barclays bank explains: 'None of our customers has lost any thing because of these scams. All of our customers are covered against fraud by an online guarantee that we implemented when we started online banking.'

Without such guarantees, of course, trust in online banking could vanish overnight. Late in 2004 some banking organisations in the UK hinted that they were losing patience with the growing losses as a result of phishing attacks. It was suggested in media reports that there could be cases where customers were so negligent in checking whether they were being defrauded or not that they could be in breach of their terms and conditions as a customer. This in turn could mean the bank would not compensate them for their losses.

Such a step by banks around the world could of course have a massive impact on the future of internet banking. And it remains to be seen whether financial institutions will really chose to go down this risky route.

The frustration of banks can be explained by the figures. The authors were told by security sources that by the summer of 2004, phishing scams had cost financial institutions in the UK alone a total of £60 million in compensation to defrauded customers; far more than has been publicly admitted.

Criminals have learnt that trying to attack directly the well-protected bank websites and databases is difficult, time consuming and ultimately likely to end in failure. It is far easier to target the weakest link in the banking chain; the customer. Criminal gangs rely, as they have always done, on the assumption made by most people that crime happens to others, not to them. As a result they are not always sufficiently vigilant when it comes to divulging sensitive information.

As Sandra Quinn of APACS observes: 'In a sense there is nothing new in this. Just for an exercise a computer company once asked people in the street for personal information like their mother's maiden name and the name of family pets and other personal information that people often use as passwords. Nine out of ten people supplied it.'

In another example, a computer security company offered city office workers chocolates in return for the passwords on their computers – and 70 per cent of them handed them over.

Banks are not the only targets of phishing. The police expect other prominent online companies – for example, large online retailers such as supermarkets – to become targets in the coming months and years.

Bogus ids

Online identity theft scams also work on a lower scale, where perhaps just a small business or individual is being impersonated. At the start of the book we mentioned the case of photographic student Matt Glen, who was ripped off by a conman who had taken over the online identity of the seller of a camera on eBay.

Glen was not alone. He later discovered that a friend of his had similarly been conned by someone posing as an eBay seller. 'A friend called Johnny told me that he had tried to buy a digital video camera over the internet from a man in Spain for £700; it should have been £1,500,' says Glen. 'The man used a fake passport to prove his ID at the Western Union office and Johnny was able to prove that, so they gave him his money back.'

The cyber criminal's Swiss Army knife

Meanwhile in August 2004 evidence emerged of yet another online scam aimed at obtaining bank details and passwords. Interestingly this technique combines different elements of internet crime; spamming, the use of malware and identity theft. It is a clear sign, as discussed in the previous chapter, that virus, worm or Trojan programme writers are combining forces with more conventional criminals.

In this fraud, thousands of spam messages are sent out thanking the recipient for the 'order' they have made for computer goods, web hosting or something similar. Of course the orders are entirely fictitious. But the recipient is encouraged to go to a website – typically hosted in China or the United States – to get more details of the order. Should the unwary visit such a site they will probably find just a site 'under construction' and immediately leave. However, in the short time they are on the site a Trojan programme (a piece of malware) will rapidly download itself onto the victim's machine; that is, if it is not protected with up-to-date antivirus software, the latest operating system security patches and a firewall.

This particular Trojan is programmed in such a way that the next time the victim goes to their banking website it will record details such as their account password or PIN number. This is done by a process known as 'keystroke logging' (see below Box). These details are then passed from the Trojan via the internet to the criminals behind the scam, who use the data to empty the victim's account of money.

Just to rub salt into the wound, the malware also compromises the victim's computer in such a way that it can be used as a 'proxy' computer to send endless streams of spam to other hapless users. Detective Chief Superintendent Len Hynds, head of the NHTCU, describes the multi-faceted attack as the 'Swiss Army knife of the cyber criminal.'

MALWARE DOWNLOADS

One unwitting victim of online identity theft using automated malware technology is Des Drury, the 61-year-old owner of a chain of bakery stores in Liverpool. Criminals stole money from his Barclays account twice – once practically from under his nose as he was logged onto his banking website. 'The first time for £5,000 and the second time for £3,500,' Drury recalls ruefully.

'The first time it happened I had gone into the bank to make a deposit. I always ask for a balance when I make a deposit. I noticed that £5,000 was missing so I asked for a printout. It said that I had paid out the money as rent,' says Drury. There was one small problem; he did not have anything to do with the properties mentioned in the print out.

'Then I noticed that by the side of transaction it said OLB, which means Online Banking and I pointed that out. It was then that they suddenly took some notice and they called their fraud and security people in. They asked me if I had opened any unusual emails because there's this thing called "phishing" and I told them I haven't opened anything.'

In the second fraud says Drury, the criminals were 'dead cheeky'. He explains: 'I logged onto the Barclays website to check my account and I noticed that the computer was running a lot slower than normal. They have told me now that that's a sign of someone else using your machine.

'Anyway around about 11 am it was running really slow. And then I saw that they had moved £3,500 from the deposit account and put it in my current account; and then they moved it to another Barclays account down in London!' Although Drury says the man who stole his money was eventually caught and that Barclays compensated him for his losses, he is now wary about using his computer.

In Drury's case it seems he was not the victim of a phishing attack but had somehow inadvertently downloaded a Trojan programme from the internet.

Once a Trojan programme is on the computer (usually from being unknowingly downloaded via the internet) it is programmed to search for keywords such as 'Barclays' and be given the ability to move automatically to the next step. If the programme's scans find one of the key words – the name of a bank – it will switch to its next task, which is to search on the internet and download a keystroke logging programme. This is software that records the keystrokes a person uses on a keyboard. Basic key loggers are often offered for sale in spam messages and are marketed as a means of people keeping track of what their partner does on their computer and where they visit on the internet.

The reason that the 'search' function and the 'key logger' function of the Trojan are kept separate is so that the downloads required to make the Trojan work are kept as small as possible. This reduces the chance of a user spotting that something is wrong as the Trojan is surreptitiously downloaded from the internet onto the computer.

Once the key logger is on the system it will normally be programmed to catch the first 200 bytes of data written after a particular trigger point (for example, the name of a bank name). In other words if the computer user types the word 'Barclays' then the Trojan programme will record the next 200 bytes of whatever is typed in. The hope for the criminal is that this data will include the victim's password or PIN numbers for their account. This potentially vital and secret information is then sent from the computer to be stored safely on another machine under the control of the criminal.

As a security measure a bank will often only ask for part of a password or part of a PIN number. However, the Trojan programme can also get around this defence ploy. The key logger will keep on sending out the trapped data so the password or PIN number can be 'assembled'. Around 99 per cent of people use a memorable word as their password and a word that will make some sort of sense, so assembling it when one has all of the characters is not difficult.

Another security ploy often required by banks and other organisations is that people use a mixture of letters and numbers for their password. Once again this can usually be overcome by the Trojan and by the criminal assembling the confidential password. Most people put the numbers at the end or the beginning of the word or letters, and they will usually follow a numerical order, making the assembly of the password quite straightforward. The same is true with PIN numbers. Given that a PIN number is four digits and that the user is asked for three numbers at their log-in, it is not too difficult to harvest the remaining number.

Dummy favourites

There are other ways in which one's digital identity can be stolen or borrowed online by different forms of malware. For example, a virus or a Trojan might infect a machine's web browser and corrupt the user's 'favourites' or bookmark list. When the user wants to go to their online banking site they look down the favourites list and hit the one for NatWest bank (or whichever company it is) as usual. The user is then taken to their customary NatWest site – or at least they think they are. In fact the malware has changed the destination of the link and instead directs the user to a bogus site set up by the criminals.

The really clever part is that when the user calls up a particular page from the site they actually do call up the real NatWest pages, so the experience seems authentic. What they do not know is that as they type in their passwords, account numbers and other details the criminals hold on to this information for use at a later date. The only clue for a person that this is happening is that the pages download a little slower than usual.

Another growing trend is the use of so-called browser attacks to obtain a victim's private information. A browser attack is where someone alights on a seemingly harmless website, and the website automatically downloads malware via the user's browser – for example Internet Explorer. This malware can then be used to search for and steal information from the user's computer.

Another ingenious variation on the automatic ID theft menu is the use of bogus but realistic-looking dummy websites that lurk in cyber space close to the location of the site they are mimicking. These are the spider's webs that the victim – the fly – must avoid as they make their way around the internet.

Andrew Durant, head of the Fraud Investigation and Recovery Services Team at accountants BDO Stoy Hayward, describes how these double identity frauds work. 'An online shopper looking for a particular website may inadvertently log onto a website that has been set up [with an almost identical website address] by a fraudster to look like the website.

'The shopper browses the copied website and finds the products he or she is looking for. They are then asked to give their name, address and credit card details. The fraudster then uses these to obtain goods on other sites or over the telephone.

'Furthermore, the details can be used to clone credit cards that can be used. This all only comes to light when the individual receives their credit card statement and is shocked by what they see.'

MINING THE DEEP WEB

The above examples of cyber identity theft involve the use of relatively sophisticated technology by criminals to harvest someone's data so they can assume their identity. Such examples often entail an initial impersonation by the criminal, posing as a bank or bona fide commercial website to obtain the data.

However, criminals also use the internet for what might be considered to be more 'conventional' identity theft. As has already been stated, many details about us are stored – quite innocently and properly – in all kinds of places. One of these locations is the internet. These may be easily accessible on the worldwide web and locatable by search engines such as Google, or they might be contained in what is sometimes called the 'deep web'.

The deep web is simply those parts of the internet that are not searchable by external search engines and where one usually needs some form of subscription or membership – sometimes free – to look around. A good example would be the excellent Friends Reunited website[6], which has millions of members. Its many pages and databases are not accessible by search engines but are easily scoured once one has signed in. Another example of course is a site such as 192.com in the UK. Here one can search electoral roll and telephone numbers online for a fee.

Huge amounts of data can be found on individuals in similar databases and websites all around the world. This is one of the joys of the internet; that people share and swap details about each other from one side of the planet to another at little or no cost and within seconds. The tragedy is that, on occasions, criminals exploit such details for their own purposes. Whether from websites, open searches, electoral roll checks or many other sources, identity theft criminals hunt for valuable data on individuals, mining the internet much as miners sift for gold nuggets. With these nuggets of information the criminal can built up sufficiently convincing pictures of individuals to assume their identities and obtain or use credit cards, loans and even bank accounts.

The sheer number of databases in which an individual's details may appear is bewildering. The lobby group Privacy International[7] has compiled a list of categories under which there are UK databases containing our details. The list, which runs to 41 examples, covers all parts of our daily lives, from corporations such as bank, market intelligence and insurance databases, government institutions such as the Child Support Agency, the national census database and the NHS central register; to utilities such as electricity and finally supermarket loyalty cards and TV licensing. Similar lists will apply in other countries.

Meanwhile Simon Davies, director of Privacy International, says that in the early 1990s the company worked out that an economically active adult in the developed world was located, on average, in 200 major databases. Recent research conducted by Privacy International reveals that the figure has now soared to around 700. Naturally some databases are far more secure than others, and criminals might only gain access to information on them through hacking or corrupting someone who works for a company holding the data. Other databases however are readily available whether for free or for the payment of a small fee.

Big business

Two recent large-scale cases in the US highlight both the growing prevalence of ID theft there and elsewhere in the developed world. One was the theft of more than 40,000 credit card numbers in the US belonging to customers of the popular BJ's Wholesale Club. The numbers were stolen from the company's database some time in late 2003 and early 2004.

In a separate case earlier in November 2002, the FBI charged three men with what was they then called the biggest ID theft case in history. The three men, including Philip Cummings, a Briton, were arrested in connection with the theft of the personal identities of more than 30,000 people. It was claimed that Cummings, who worked for Teledata Communications, which supplied software to link the systems of banks and credit reference agencies from mid-1999 until March 2000, used his position to steal thousands of credit reports on individuals. He then passed these on to the other two men for $30 a time. The information in the reports was used by others to steal and create identities and to steal from bank accounts using credit cards.

Losses from the scam were believed to be more than $50 million and it is thought a network of at least twenty ID fraudsters was involved in using the illegally gained information. Cummings pleaded guilty to conspiracy and fraud charges in September 2004.

Such examples show how ID theft has become big business. The cases also explain why ID theft is a major concern for the FBI. John Gillies, of the Financial Crimes Section in the FBI's Criminal Investigative Division, puts the amount of money involved in ID theft in the US at more than $50 billion. Not all of that is technology based, but much of it is and this is the part of the ID theft that is growing 'exponentially', he claims. Partly, says Gillies, this is because it's 'easier to get the information [the criminals] need that way'.

Gillies also confirms that not just Russian gangs are involved but Italian organised crime too. He also hints at even more worrying trends. 'Terrorist organisations are involved in identity theft, and not just for financial reason, but I can't comment on that,' he says.

Piecing it together

An example of how gangs can piece together identities and then use them to commit fraud was uncovered by the National Hi-Tech Crime Unit (NHTCU) in 2003. In Operation Pestle the unit was faced with a group of individuals who were using the internet to assume the identities of dead people.

Officers discovered that the gang was making use of house auction websites to find out details on the recently deceased. Armed with this information the group was able to forge documents to open bank accounts and obtain loans from financial institutions such as

Lloyds TSB, the Halifax and the Co-operative Bank. In all the gang defrauded the institutions out of £350,000 over a period of two years; and were continuing to plan ID frauds even while they were on bail after being arrested for the initial frauds.

The six men, all with addresses in or near London, and who were all gaoled in November 2003, used the money to buy houses in Britain and Nigeria, expensive cars and jewellery. The police used powers under the UK's Proceeds of Crime Act 2002 to seize a Porsche car from the convicted men as well as cash.

The NHTCU's senior analyst Helen Saunders, who worked on the case, explains how the ID theft gang operated. 'They were researching people's ID on the internet,' using sources such as 192.com and phone directories to research their new identities. Then, she continues, 'they were putting mail redirections in place in order to gain false documentation. They would get a bank account, then two weeks later phone up saying they wanted a £10,000 loan to buy a car.'

419 fraud

In a category all of its own is the crime known simply as '419' fraud and linked forever in most people's minds with one African country: Nigeria. The name '419' comes from the section of the penal code in Nigeria that outlaws the fraud that the conmen operate.

419 is what is called an advance fee fraud (AFF), in which the offer of great riches is made by the conman, if the victim pays a small upfront 'fee' to help the transfer of the monies. Strictly speaking this is not a crime of ID fraud as the criminals do not steal their victim's identity (though they do impersonate others during the course of the crime). Nor is it simply just an internet crime, as the scam existed in letter and fax form before the days of email. However there is little doubt that the arrival of the internet saw a huge explosion in the prevalence of this crime and it deserves a mention in its own right. In any case one of the most common 419 scams now involves the creation of official-looking websites that masquerade as banks or other financial institutions.

In essence the 419 fraud is very simple; the conmen pretend to the victim that they have a huge amount of money locked up for some technical reason in a foreign account or country, and that they desperately need the help of an outsider to gain access to the money. They promise the victim a significant share of the spoils. All the victim has to do is to incur some modest expenses upfront to secure the money. Needless to say that if the victim does pay the upfront fee they never see any money in return.

The 419 frauds were first seen in the mid-1980s when oil prices were weak and the national earnings of this oil- and gas-abundant West African country were correspondingly low. Typically the fraudsters will pose as civil servants, oil company staff, bankers and even in some cases as Nigerian princes.

The conmen exploit a number of factors to make their frauds credible. One is that Nigerians speak English and thus are able to converse in the international language of business with people all over the Western world. Secondly the oil boom of the past had attracted to Nigeria many people who were looking for get-rich-quick schemes; in the 1980s there was a sense that Nigeria was a place where one could make large amounts of easy money.

In one respect they were right; though the people making the money were not the outsiders, but Nigerian and other conmen making money from gullible and greedy foreigners.

A feature of the 419 scams is that they use topical events to reinforce their messages and to convince recipients that that they are merely the unfortunate victims of international politics. Another feature of the frauds scams is that once the criminals find a willing victim they will harass and prey upon them until they have cleaned them out, or before the victim finally tells the authorities.

These frauds have been taken very seriously by the US. The US Secret Service is just one of the organisations charged with dealing with the 419 frauds, together with the Department of Commerce. During the 1990s the AFF scams were seen as potentially a serious danger to US financial stability and the growth of the internet and number of internet users has simply encouraged the continuation of the frauds. Not only are there more and more potential victims online, it is also cheaper for the fraudsters to reach them by email than by other forms of communication such as fax or letter, though the 'return rate' on 419 faxes is around 1 per cent, roughly the same rate as for emails[8]. (Not that the 419-ers often pay for either stamps or faxes; they prefer to bribe or coerce postal and telecommunications services from local officials.)

The scale of the 419 frauds is hard to estimate. The US Secret Services says it receives around 13,000 complaints a month from people who have received 419 communications, the vast majority of which – 80 per cent – now arrive by email. The financial cost to US victims over the past three years to 2004 is put at some $100 million, though given the embarrassed reluctance of many victims to come forward to the authorities, this is almost certainly just a fraction of the true financial losses. The National Criminal Intelligence Service (NCIS) in the UK alone dealt with 150 cases in 2003, each with an average loss of £30,000. This does not take into account victims who are either dealt with by local forces or who never come forward. Some estimates put the total global loss at the hands of the 419 frauds at $4 billion but it must be stressed that such figures are almost impossible to verify.

The Nigerian authorities, understandably worried that their nation might become synonymous with fraud, have cracked down on the operation of the 419 scams and many of the conmen have now moved to other African nations. In particular a number have gone to South Africa to take advantage of the good telecommunications there; from that country they send bulk emails around the world to potential victims.

One multiple victim interviewed by the authors is Heinrich Reents, a 70-year-old German industrialist and university professor with perhaps more experience of 419 than anyone. A 419 gang has relieved him of a total of £2 million over the last decade in the course of 15 separate scams. Curiously, he still seems prepared to lose even more.

Every day he receives around 30 faxes, numerous phone calls and hundreds of emails from the gang, whose behaviour can only be described as like a hunting pack, determined to drag him down.

An intelligent and caring man, Reents has been fleeced by the gang because of an ambition to build a foundation for the advancement of science in Nigeria. Knowing of Reents' ambitions, he has been approached on many occasions and told that the funding for his project has been found in Nigeria itself; all he has to do is to pay for the bribes and the paperwork to free it up (at around £50,000–100,000) a time. The bill has now reached over £2 million.

Reents has around eight thousand documents and a list of around one thousand phone numbers that he is sure belong to 419 gang members.

Despite his complete failure to receive any funds, when interviewed by the authors Reents retained a strong belief that he would eventually get money for his foundation. He explained: 'I want to set up an educational foundation for the children in Nigeria and I want to use this money to do it. I think that this is the right thing to do and that it is the solution to the problems that force them into this type of fraud.

'I know that [the money] exists ˙because I have spoken to the children of the Abacha family and I know them very well. I know that the problem is that there are people standing between them and me who see this as the opportunity to make money and that is what they are doing. Releasing this money is only a matter of time.'

The 419 gangs do not always hide behind emails and faxes but instead on occasions meet their potential victims face to face in an attempt to impress them that they are genuine.

An example of the smooth frontmen used by 419 gangs is Chubuwunga Ndukuba (probably not his real name), a 35-year-old Nigerian who operated in London in the late 1990s and early 2000s. Ndukuba lived the life of the successful businessman. He stayed in a flat near Harrods store in the exclusive Knightsbridge area of the city, drove a blue, soft-top Rolls Royce, wore designer suits and was a regular at the bars at the Dorchester and Intercontinental hotels. In a sense Ndukuba was a businessman; though his business was fraud and he was a frontman for a determined and very successful 419 gang. Using charm, good manners and a forceful personality, Ndukuba's job was to persuade the gang's often wealthy clients that the gang's operation was genuine. As backup, grand accommodation was hired on short-term rents to impress the victims of the gang's wealth and good connections.

When eventually Ndukuba was arrested and convicted in London, the Nigerian was especially distraught at the loss of his Rolls, which was confiscated by the authorities. In 2001 he received a four-year gaol sentence.

Despite these limited successes against the 419ers, they remain an ever-present and significant threat to the unwary.

CHAPTER SEVEN
The Bot Herds

Imagine the vast open plains of the African savannah; fertile lands where animals of all descriptions roam freely, happily going about their normal everyday existence. Then imagine that on the horizon lurk large herds of predators, waiting silently and unseen to attack the unsuspecting prey in front of them.

Now suppose that these herds are under the control of a handful of malevolent herdsmen, evil controllers who can manipulate the predators herds at will, and at whose command the attackers will launch an immediate attack. The victims will be singled out for one of two reasons; either because someone has employed the herdsman to eliminate them – or simply because the herdsman does not like that particular animal.

Such an unpleasant scenario is perhaps best suited to the reels of a second-rate science fiction movie. Yet what is described above is happening now; not on the plains of Africa but in cyber space. In place of the packs of predator animals there are what are known in the jargon as 'bot herds' – herds of robotic software – or 'bot armies' (already met briefly in Chapter 1). The 'herdsmen' exist too. Known by some as 'bot shepherds', these shadowy characters are orchestrating attacks by the bot herds all around the world, variously motivated by hatred, money and ideology.

The victims? They are the ordinary personal and corporate computer user, individuals and businesses who own and run websites and networks and who have not protected themselves from online attack. Especially at risk is anyone who seeks to make a living from a website.

FLOODING THE PIPES

The existence of the bot herds is now regarded as one of the biggest threats facing the internet today. Among those whose job it is to worry about cyber crime, the activity of these malevolent electronic hoards is one of those issues most likely to keep them awake at night.

In particular it is the use of bots for what is known as a 'denial of service' (DoS) attack or a 'distributed denial of service' (DDoS) attack (both mentioned in Chapter 1) that is the most worrying development. To recap, the general form of attack is called a denial of service (DoS), while an attack from many computers – ie 'distributed' across a wide area of the internet using a 'bot army' – is called a distributed denial of service (DDoS) attack. A DoS attack, as its name suggests, occurs when aggressors use various techniques to overload a website, server or network with so much internet traffic that it can no longer work as intended. Typically this is done by bombarding the website, server or network with so much useless information and digital clutter that it becomes overwhelmed and has to be taken down by its administrators.

A physical analogy is what happens to a drainage system during a torrential downpour. Drainage systems are designed to take certain volumes of water through them, depending on the structure of the system and on how thick the drainage pipes are. During normal rainfall and even heavy showers the drainage copes, and the water is able to run away. The system functions. But if there is an exceptional downpour the system is flooded with too much water, the drainage becomes blocked and ceases to work. The result is an unseemly mess, floods and almost certainly financial loss.

The physical conduits through which data travels via networks, including the internet, are also often referred to as 'pipes'; so the analogy is an apt one. In many cases the 'pipes' used by many websites, servers and even Internet Service Providers (ISPs) are quite narrow, which means there is a limit to how much data can be processed at any one time before the system overloads. All it takes is someone or something to flood the pipes with too much data and the website, server or ISP could potentially crash. If this website happens to be a firm's only means of doing business then this can turn out to be very costly – and potentially disastrous.

Such information floods do not often occur naturally on the internet, though they are not unheard of. For example, if it becomes known that a website is publishing a particularly juicy bit of salacious gossip about someone famous and too many people try to read it at once, then this can overload the data pipes and crash the site. Far more usual, however, is the likelihood that someone will flood a data pipe deliberately; by using the bot herds to effect a DDoS attack on the chosen victim.

The potential scale and damage of such attacks is vast. According to the US Cooperative Association for Internet Data Analysis there are around 4,000 denial of service attacks on the internet each week[1].

Andy Blyth, a senior lecturer at the highly regarded School of Computing at the University of Glamorgan, and one of the UK's leading experts on the phenomenon, says only now is society beginning to appreciate the true nature of the threat.

'The bots are now getting more intelligent – now they are starting to look for patterns. We see bot herds that can take account of the fact, for example, that the US has only just woken up.' He adds: 'This thing can only get worse.'

In February 2004 the chief technical officer of US computer security firm TruSecure (now CyberTrust) Dr Peter Tippett, another respected observer of the scene, warned about the proliferation of bot herds and said that people who controlled them would have colossal amounts of computing potential at their fingertips. 'They have got more computing and network power than imaginable,' he declared.

Dr Tippett then went on to make what must have, to many, seemed like an extraordinary claim; that the herds could potentially knock out a nation's internet infrastructure with one of its data floods.

'Now there are more than a hundred thousand computers under the control of one, two or maybe five people; they can make these computers do anything they want, they could take out whole countries if they wanted to,' he said.

Technically speaking there is no such thing as a nation state on the internet; because of the inter-connectedness of global data connections they do not work along neat national boundaries. But as John Regnault, head of security at BT, and one of the world's four key Carrier Service Providers (CSP) – the backbone of the web – explains, that does not mean a country cannot be denied an internet service.

'There are various ways of looking at the network,' he says. 'You can't take out a country but you can take out a big company perhaps like an Aol or an MCI, and in some countries there are some [smaller] companies that are the largest ISPs.'

He adds: 'The amount of traffic [the attackers] can pile up is awesome. If it comes together then it can be gigabits and they do make sure that it doesn't come together before it hits the final router. If they make the attack big enough then it will start to overload the network.'

Therefore if just one or two ISPs dominate a nation's internet access and they are targeted or even just used by a powerful-enough DDoS attack, then that country can be taken offline.

Turning off a country

Extraordinary or not, the authors can reveal that within a few months of Dr Tippett's claim, such an event did occur – and that in effect a country's internet service was taken offline as a result of a DDoS attack carried out by bot herds.

The authors understand that this is what happened in Poland in the late Spring of 2004 and that a huge attack by waves of bot herds caused much of that country's internet to crash. The incident is still cloaked in mystery and secrecy. It is almost certain that Poland was not the target of the attack; and in fact the country was the probable source of the attack. As a result, the bot herds stampeded through Poland's routers, which had the same impact as if the country's ISPs had been the target.

A senior security source, with strong international connections, has told the authors: 'You can't say it was that country that was doing the attacking – what had happened is that they had used it as a zombie [for their own purposes]. It was a nightmare. They had taken over so many individual machines around the world; and they were pointed through that country.'

Another well-placed source confirms that Poland was the country 'turned off' during the attack.

Meanwhile Andy Blyth believes it may only be a matter of time before a country and its information infrastructure becomes the deliberate target of a massive and sustained bot herd attack. At the moment the criminal use of them is quite measured and they are being used in extortion attempts. 'But there's nothing to stop them from thinking "Let's use them against a country or on the critical control systems of a country and see what happens,"' he says.

ROBOTIC SOFTWARE

So what exactly are bots – and how do they work? The word 'bot' is short for robotic software. Bots are pieces of software programmed in such a way that they act automatically on their own, without the need for further human intervention. Robotic software has been around for some time, and many of us will consciously or subconsciously be aware of bots used for the most benign of purposes. The 'spiders' that large search engines use to 'crawl' over web pages to look for and collect links are one form of bot, for example.

Often a bot has some 'artificial intelligence' implanted within it so that it can react differently according to various circumstances, though ultimately of course the full scope of their actions and limitations is determined by the human who writes the original programme.

In the context of DoS attacks, the bot is simply a form of Trojan programme (ie malicious) that sits on your computer. These bots are sent out by the 'bot herdsman' to sit on people's computers until such time as they are ready to be used or 'harvested'. Typically they are not sent by email but roam the networks and are programmed to seek out machines that lack firewall and antivirus detection and so cannot detect them.

Once a bot has found a suitable host computer it can hide there undetected for weeks or months until it is needed for an attack. When a computer has been compromised in this way it is sometimes referred to as a 'zombie' machine, meaning the computer has been taken over by someone else for a new and malicious purpose. (Confusingly some of the earlier bots were called zombies, but it is now generally agreed terminology that the bot is the agent of the attack and zombie is the state created in a compromised computer.)

One of the weirdest elements to what is already a fairly weird scenario is that sometimes – in fact, very often – the owner of the infected computer will be blissfully unaware that there is a problem with the machine. They will have no idea that theirs is now a zombie computer as it will function quite normally in most respects. Even when the machine eventually gets 'called to action' and becomes part of a huge attack, the owner may still remain unaware that anything is wrong.

This characteristic makes this branch of cyber crime unique amongst crimes; a person can in effect 'enter' your house via the internet, alter a piece of your property (your computer) and then use it to commit a crime, possibly on the other side of the world; all without you being aware of what is going on. This can also raise some curious questions of legal culpability, as we shall see later.

Flooding the network

The bots cause damage by sheer weight of numbers. One of these bots acting alone cannot cause much damage if it is 'launched' against a victim. But put dozens, hundreds and now potentially hundreds of thousands together and the effect can be devastating.

They work destructively using what the internet is all about; focusing the combined power of networks. The internet as we know is a network of networks, a group of computers harnessed together. The combined power of so many computers working together can be an enormously useful tool for good – if it is controlled properly. For example many people will be aware of excellent projects in areas such as cancer research where the unused capacity of many home computers is transformed into what is in effect one giant super computer to crunch out solutions to complex equations[2].

Bots use the same potential – only they do it for malign purposes. They connect with each other, harnessing the processing power, but instead of that power being deployed to crunch data it is directed to generate millions of meaningless computer messages. These garbage messages are then used to flood the target network and slow it down, or bring it to a halt by exhausting the potential of the computers on the network to deal with it.

As Andy Blyth puts it: 'The analogy we use for these things is the butterfly flapping its wings somewhere in the world that has an effect on the other side of the world. Only this is 20,000 butterflies that all turn towards you and flap their wings at the same time.'

Bot wars

The development of the bots and bot herds started out, as often happens in the world of computing and the internet, as a kind of intellectual game. As the practical use of software robots began to be recognised, young whizz-kids wanted to find out the limitations and possibilities of this new form of software. Soon they realised that the bots could be harnessed together into groups, and it was not long before young hackers were playing games against each other using 'herds' of bots. It was just like playing another computer game; though this time the stage was the whole of the internet. Eventually they began to understand the potential of what they were playing with.

As Dr Tippett says: 'Right now they are using all these computers to fight each other, play games and show that they have power.'

Or as Andy Blyth puts it: 'Historically [bot herds] were created by a bunch of techno-geeks who just wanted to see whether it could be done.'

It was not hard, however, to see the criminal potential of bot herds. Instead of knocking out your opponent's website in some cyber game, why not take down the website or network belonging to a business? Better still, why not take down the company's website then get in touch with the firm and demand money in return for leaving the website unharmed in future? This was precisely what happened; the beginning of denial of service extortion attacks.

The arrival of these attacks had long been feared by computer security experts who had understood the potential of the technology, and by 2003 the cyber assaults had started to happen on a significant scale. Again, as so often in the history of technology, the hackers and geeks had paved the way; now it was the turn of the criminals to exploit the new technology for their own ends.

Andy Blyth sums up the transition. 'The techno-geeks thought that there were interesting technological challenges in getting them to work; now organised crime is getting involved, chiefly targeting the online gambling industry.'

Cyber blackmail

Betting sites are a prime target for denial of service extortion for two main reasons. One is that they have – or are perceived as having – a regular and healthy cash flow so in theory they have 'ready money' to pay out to the criminals. Secondly, these businesses, which have increased dramatically in number in the first decade of this century, rely almost exclusively on their websites to make money. If their site goes offline, they have no income stream. And with plenty of other sites to choose from, disgruntled customers may not come back to them even when they do eventually get back online.

'It's an easy sum for them to do – they make £1 million a day, if they are offline for a week they lose £7 million,' says Blyth. If you are taken out by a herd could you afford to lose that amount of money; but more importantly could you afford to lose your clientele?'

Phil Swinburne, the former head of the Metropolitan Police Computer Crime Unit, agrees that DoS threats are growing in significance and says it can be a very lucrative source of crime for criminals.

'It's just blackmail with the demands being made electronically. But if you hit 3,500 sites that need to be on the web for £60 a week, then you are making over £200,000 for a week's work – which is not bad.'

It is thought criminals targeted offshore websites used by gamblers in the US before American Football's Super Bowl contest in January 2004[3].

The seriousness with which such extortion attempts are being taken was shown by a dramatic police operation in 2004 against suspects based in Russia and other parts of the former Soviet Union.

On 20 July 2004 police in Russia arrested the three suspected ringleaders of a gang said to be behind the attempted extortion of

British online betting firms[4]. Since November 2003 cyber criminals had been taking down UK gambling websites with DoS attacks by blasting huge amounts of traffic at them. According to the police, the firms lost millions of pounds of business as a result of the attacks.

The criminals were then sending emails to the bookmakers demanding between £20,000 to £30,000 'protection' money in return for leaving the sites alone for a year, after which time they would expect a similar sum.

In particular the gang was threatening to take the betting firms offline just before major sporting events, always the most lucrative time for such companies. These events included the Grand National horse race at Aintree in Liverpool and the Euro 2004 football championships staged in Portugal.

The first crack in the gang's chain came when police in Latvia arrested ten people in the capital Riga, accused of helping to launder the money made from the racket. As a result of this a combination of numerous police forces – British, Russian, Latvian, Estonian and American among them – were able to piece together the money trail. This led all the way to Russia.

The three Russians were arrested after raids in St Petersburg and the Saratov and Stavropol regions of south-west Russia, raids co-ordinated by the Investigation Department of Russia's Investigative Committee – attached to the Ministry of Internal Affairs (MVD) – and the MVD's computer crimes specialist department.

The large number of different law enforcement agencies from different countries involved in the investigation not only shows how important DoS attacks are regarded, it is also a clear sign of the best – and perhaps only – way of thwarting such attacks: international co-operation. The lead investigation team in the UK, for example, was the National Hi-Tech Crime Unit (NHTCU), but officers from the country's Customs and Excise department were also involved, liaising with counterparts in Russia, the Baltic states and the Central Asian Republics. Others included in the hunt for the DoS gang were police officers in Australia and Canada, plus security teams from businesses both in the UK and elsewhere.

The head of the NHTCU is clearly delighted with the teamwork that had taken place. Detective Chief Superintendent Len Hynds says: 'The success of this operation is built on the foundation of international partnerships between law enforcement and business. The more we work together in the fight against organised crime, the safer the UK will be for business.'

He adds: 'Thanks to the response of all the parties involved, we have helped to dismantle a determined group of organised criminals. The clear message we are sending is that if you attack firms based in the UK, we will find you and stop you.'

Below is an extortion demand used by the cyber criminals:

Hello dear friends.

Your page .... is under our attack. We'll continue attack until you pay us $10.000

This money is a small help for our team. We think that it's not large money for you, because you earn much more.

As soon as you'll contact us, we'll stop attack & inform you about data of money transfer (Western Union).

After a stop attack we guarantee, that the we'll never attack your site in the future.

If you don't pay us that we'll continue attack, & you'll lose many clients and reputation.

Think above problems of attack and this small sum.

Best regards, your friends.

Though gambling sites have been a favourite target for extortionists, it is unlikely that they will remain the only victims of DoS attacks. David M Kennedy is director of Research Services at CyberTrust Corporation and a former army computer expert. Part of his job is to assess likely future threats, and he believes he knows whom the extortionists will target now.

'After the casinos I expect them to go after porn,' he says. 'If you look at where the money is on the internet, porn is in the same neighbourhood with respect to who's running the operation, how robust their operation is, how much technical support they have.'

'Citibank is not a very good target for these people because it's not very likely that Citibank is going to succumb to an extortion attempt. But looking at the other places on the internet where there's a lot of money, where a business relies on its internet connectivity in order to function, it strikes me that porn is a lucrative target.'

Andy Blyth too sees a wider range of targets in the future. 'If you look at some of the online auction sites, they have got to be targets. If you just take eBay; its membership is bigger than the online presence of many countries.'

Ideological revenge
Not all DoS attacks are used to make money. Some are launched for what might loosely be called 'ideological' reasons against firms seen as undermining the ethos of the internet and computing. We are back here with the echoes of the old hacker ethic, namely that people should have free and unrestricted access to computers (and the internet) and that the machines should not become simply the tools of commerce.

The chief 'enemy' in this respect is of course Microsoft, which has easily replaced IBM as the company that the techno-geeks love to hate. Twice in August 2003 the giant corporation's website was successfully, if briefly, attacked by separate distributed denial of service (DDoS) attacks[5]. The attacks were thought to have come from different sources, though each used a bank of 'zombie' computers around the world to direct the bot herds at the site. Microsoft was attacked again in February 2004, this time by an internet worm called MyDoomB, which had quickly followed the MyDoomA worm (see Chapter 5). The DoS attack was an 'add on' feature of the worm and was both predicted and easily thwarted by Microsoft.

Not so fortunate however was the software company SCO, from Utah, which sells the UNIX operating system. Its website was knocked out in the same month by a DoS launched by the MyDoomA worm. Though no one can be sure, it is thought that this attack may have been inspired by 'revenge' on the part of a fan of the open-source (ie non copyright) rival OS code Linux. SCO has been involved in legal action against some users of Linux code, claiming that it has incorporated some Unix source code – to which the Utah firm claims copyright – into their Linux operating systems.

Hactivists

Such attacks are not just aimed at business but at national and international institutions too. A taste of what might become more widespread in this respect in the future occurred during the Kosovo conflict in 1999. NATO and US government computers and websites were deluged with email bombs and hit with DoS attacks by anti-war protestors angry at the NATO bombing of targets in the former Yugoslavia[6].

The attacks became even more virulent after the accidental bombing of the Chinese Embassy in Belgrade, when numerous hackers in China – incidentally the home of many bot herds – launched massive cyber attacks aimed at the US and NATO. At one point the US site www.whitehouse.gov was taken down and stayed down for three days.

Chinese hackers also took over web servers and left messages such as: 'You have owed Chinese people a bloody debt which you must pay for! We will not stop attacking until the war stops!' on US websites. Those responsible for such attacks have been dubbed 'hactivists' – a combination of hacker and activist.

Denial of service attacks can also operate on a more personal scale, as shown by an example in the UK in 2004. A teenager who had been sacked by insurance company Domestic and General tried to get revenge by allegedly launching five million emails at the firm's website in a sustained three-day denial of service attack. The website inevitably wilted under the strain and went down, costing the firm a reported £18,000.

The 17-year-old, who cannot be named because he is a minor, was quoted by newspapers as saying: 'All the emails were harmless; just classic lines from films. I only had to pay for my internet connection. Everything else was free. I just wanted to cause them a bit of inconvenience.' He was later questioned by the police[7].

A rather different kind of cyber attack was carried out by an Australian called Vitek Boden in Queensland, Australia, in 2000. Boden was an out-of-work engineer who saw a way of getting work at the sewage pumping station at Pacific Paradise, north of Maroochydore. His chosen method of picking up some consultancy work was to use a computer and radio transmitter to take control over the works and release raw sewage into public waterways. Despite no fewer than 46 attacks Boden failed to get any work; but did succeed in getting prosecuted for polluting the area.

This curious case may have remained a quirky one-off, but then US security experts got to hear about it. Suddenly the alarm bells went off. If one lone engineer could take over and manipulate a public utility with such ease, what could a dedicated group achieve? What if, feared the experts, terrorists chose to subvert the utility infrastructure in a whole country such as the US, UK, France or Australia[8]?

The link with bot herds and DoS attacks is clear. As described in Chapter 3, the utilities of most Western countries are increasingly reliant on information networks, without which they would not function properly. In the hands of a determined terrorist aided by a greedy or malevolent bot herdsman, what could such an attack do to a country's water, gas or electricity supplies?

Andy Blyth says: 'From a terrorist point of view [DoS attacks] are potentially very attractive. From the point of view of generation [gathering enough bots] they are not far off the point when damage could be done by the taking out of parts of the critical infrastructure. Disrupting a communications network like the internet will become more and more attractive to them as more and more systems are connected and the dependencies increase.'

He adds: 'What starts to be worrying is that people are beginning to map out networks and find out where the bottle necks are. If you think about it, if I am trying to find the bottle necks then I could easily work out a way to do something like take UK Plc offline, and that would have quite significant results for the UK.'

In 1998 Tamil guerrillas attacked Sri Lankan embassies around the world with 800 emails a day over a 2-week period. Their messages read 'We are the Internet Black Tigers and we're doing this to disrupt your communications.' It was probably the first concerted terrorist attack on a nation state's computer system, though few believe it will be the last.

One of the main areas of vulnerability is perceived to be an obscure part of the Industrial Automation system of utilities, known as a SCADA (Supervisory Control and Data Acquisition)[9]. This is the control system that collects and stores data from the outlying parts of, for example, gas, water and sewage systems. SCADAs may seem arcane but there are an estimated three million of them in the US alone and they stand at the heart of the networks that run the water, fuel, sewage and electricity systems we all rely on. If they were brought down by a DDoS attack, the consequences could be alarming.

Zombies for hire

One reason why security experts are so alarmed at the potential for bot herds and DoS attacks is that they no longer reside in the hands of a few talented hackers. One of the most disturbing developments in this field is that bot herds are, quite literally, for hire.

David Kennedy of CyberTrust explains; 'A year ago distributed denial of service was subtle – it's not subtle anymore. There are a couple of new sites that have now been set up where they offer you a price list for doing things. The sites are written in English and they spell it out: DDoS for hire.'

He adds: 'It's an underground culture where you can buy the tools of the trade. You can rent a zombie for a week. They used to rent them for spam but the margin is not as good as it is for DDoS. Now for $1 dollar a week you can rent a zombie.'

This chilling picture is one recognised, too, by BT's head of security John Regnault. 'The problem that we see is that there appears to be some industrialisation of the DoS attack,' he says. The trade in bot armies at the moment is very real; they are exchanging bots for valid credit card numbers that have been lifted, and for cash.

'There is a definite trade in compromised hosts and the sites where it's happening from are easy to find. People are even offering money to people to compromise their own machines.'

Sometimes the controllers of the bots send out emails touting for business. One message from a Russian site and received by the authors reads: 'Do you want to get rid of your competitors? Or black-mail your boss because he didn't pay you? We can help!'

The ease with which someone can find the technology for DoS attacks was shown by the earlier case of the teenager who launched a DoS attack on his former employers. According to reports the youngster simply downloaded an email 'bomber' that he used to attack the company's website with five million messages.

That of course was a relatively unsophisticated attack. The fear is that very able bot shepherds may be for hire and be happy to lend their services (and their bot herds) to far more powerful attacks. The ultimate nightmare for security experts is that terrorists, who have the motivation, and criminal bot masters, who have the expertise, might combine to create devastating attacks on the world's digitally linked infrastructures. They could wreak enormous damage on a country's economy, partly because of an over-reliance on the part of the West on this often unproven digital means of running national infrastructures.

Worryingly, Dave Thomas of the FBI confirms there are signs that terrorists have spotted the potential of such technology.

'We have seen Islamic fundamentalists involved in the bot networks but for what purpose or why they want to use them we do not know,' he told the authors. 'They could be for the same reasons that everybody else wants bot networks; they could want to use them for denial of service certainly or they could use them for financial gain. We have seen an interest in it but we don't know to what extent that interest is yet.'

On the trail

Despite the NHTCU's success over the Russian DoS attacks on UK gambling sites, law enforcement agencies have found it extremely hard to track down the so-far elusive bot shepherds.

Partly, it seems, this is because they are so wary, even about who uses their services for hire. According to David Kennedy the bot shepherds keep a watchful eye on their flock even when they have hired them out, and are always wary of possible infiltration by law enforcement agencies.

'They'll rent you a hundred of these Trojan computers, these zombies, for $100 and then they'll monitor those computers to see that you use them for something harmful,' he says.

'If you're trying to penetrate and get to know these people better then you actually have to do something bad; because they'll be watching for you to do something bad. And if you don't do something bad they immediately suspect that you're some sort of law enforcement presence. If [the zombies] are not being used then they pull up stakes and disappear.'

The shepherds are especially careful at hiding what is often the most vulnerable link in their operation; the money trail. Often the criminals will use zombie computers to launder the money they have made from their criminal activities. They might for example open accounts with the online payment systems PayPal or e-gold, or switch money using a Western Union account. Again, this can be done without the owner of the affected computer being aware that their machine is being used. Moreover the criminals will not use just one account but a number of them to make it even harder for the investigators to follow the trail.

According to David Kennedy, 'They use layers of [accounts] so to peel back each one and find who's actually behind it all is a challenge; it's not something that can be done on a one-shot basis.'

He explains how the process works in practice. 'Once they control my neighbour's computer they can use it to set up a Western Union account that they'll use to launder this money from. Then they'll pick another neighbour and set up a PayPal account there. In order to get the money withdrawn they will go through multiple layers of my neighbours' computers. So law enforcement has to get hold of my neighbour's computer to see where he's making his payments from, get his financial records if they are using his credit cards for all of this, and then track it back a step at a time.'

Kennedy says the constant changes of pathways and tracks makes it difficult and especially time consuming to follow the trail. Then if law enforcement agencies do find a trail they might come across a zombie computer that is linked not to a criminal or any known person but just to a credit card stolen on the other side of the world.

Stolen credit cards are an important part of the operation of bots and bot herds, which is why there appears to be a regular trade in them around the 'bot community'. The cards are used, for example, to buy time on what are called Domain Name System (or Service) (DNS) servers. These servers are the meeting point of the human perception of the web with its digital reality; humans relate to words better than numbers, which is why the domain names we use on the internet – for example www.google.com – are in word form even though their 'true' address is a string of numbers, known as an Internet Protocol (IP) address. It is the job of the DNS server to translate the domain name into the correct IP address that corresponds to it.

The bots that sit unseen on infected computers are constantly scanning that machine to see its strengths and weaknesses and crucially to see what 'ports' are open and which are blocked. (A 'port' is the word used to describe the various communication channels through which a computer will communicate with the outside world once it is connected to the internet.) Each port has its own number – for example the Simple Mail Transfer Protocol (SMTP) mail server, whose function is to send emails from a PC, uses port 25, while File Transfer Protocol (FTP), a method often used for uploading files from PCs to be used on websites, uses port 21. The bot will then report back to the DNS server, passing on any necessary information and at the same time 'reporting for duty' to the bot shepherd.

Bot shepherds are becoming more and more aware that the activities of their herds are being tracked by the authorities, and are now becoming more subtle about how their bots report in. The result is an elaborate cat and mouse game between the authorities and the bots.

The bots do not want to create any pattern that can be recognised by the authorities, so often they will report in randomly as and when they come online.

Usually they will use the Internet Relay Chat (IRC) communication port, as this is quite a normal action for an online computer and will not attract the attention of anyone monitoring the internet. It thus allows the bot's activities to hide in the background of normal everyday internet business, making it very difficult for the authorities to differentiate their traffic from normal traffic.

Understanding the flows of traffic on the Net is crucial for the security industry and law enforcement. The only way to recognise that an attack is coming is to spot an information swell in the background 'noise' of the internet that is subtly different from the background itself; a sort of tidal wave that is gathering its own momentum.

Among the people hunting for signs of waves of unusual activity are the teams at Symantec's Security Operations Centres, whom we met in Chapter 2. By analysing the traffic and the slight variations, the teams hope to be able to forecast when bot attacks are about to occur. Graeme Pinkney, who runs the centre at Winchester, England, says, 'In most cases we have been able to predict the emerging threat by analysing both prevalent activity and the background noise.

'From our system we can watch the harvesting of bots three months before they are used. We can also predict what's going to happen over a 12-hour period from the patterns that start to emerge, so that we are in a position to issue warnings to our customers.'

The lost bots

Cat and mouse games between the authorities and the bots do not stop with bot shepherds programming their bots to report home randomly. Recently the bot hunters – the police and especially private industry experts – have been investigating ways effectively to turn off the bots.

When signals from bots are sent to the DNS server that controls them, they receive a neutral signal in reply; normally a string of zeros. This is a message from the bot shepherd telling them to stay in sleeper mode, undetected. However when the person controlling the bots wants to launch an attack he changes the neutral signal of a string of zeros to a positive one using numbers. This is attack mode.

The ploy being considered by the authorities is to find the servers that the bots are using, take over the control programme and set the signal to neutral indefinitely – sending the bots to sleep for ever.

This possibility has led to the rather eerie phenomenon of bot shepherds sweeping the internet with scanning programmes in an attempt to locate their lost 'herds' of bots; the cyber version of Little Bo Peep losing her sheep.

There is now a endless battle of ploy and counter ploy by the authorities and the herdsmen as each seeks to wrestle control of the herds away from the other. For example the bots might be programmed by the herdsmen to check a number of different DNS servers rather than just one. This would make sure that any servers now controlled by the authorities would not gain control over the bots; the bots would simply continue looking from server to server until they found one with the attack mode signal.

The authorities can counter this by sending a signal from a server to the bots, instructing them that once they had hit the first server in the list they are not to go on looking for any more. Again the shepherds can respond, this time by programming the bots to seek out servers randomly. Eventually enough of them would find an attack mode signal to start an assault. Thus the never-ending 'game' continues.

Particularly worrying for the authorities is the development of intelligent bots. These are capable of determining where they are in the world; and they know the significance of the various time zones.

For example, if you instruct the bots to attack a target in California they will know where they are in the world and will know at what time they will have to start their attack to bring the traffic to bear at the same time as the other bots; a co-ordinated traffic control system.

This 'intelligence' allows the bots to be scattered all over the world. They are buried in different time zones and range across a number of international boundaries and jurisdictions. This helps protect the bot herds from discovery or counter-attack; in effect the bot herds can find sanctuary in poorly policed territories.

For example in some countries in the former Eastern Bloc there are no laws that cover the hiding of bots on machines so it is not illegal, and the bot shepherds take advantage of that. One of the countries where many bot nets are thought to reside is China; another is South Korea, a country with a massive use of broadband, meaning the herds have plenty of bandwidth (space) in which to roam.

South Korea seems to have been a target of a systematic bot assault, possibly politically motivated. In the summer of 2004 government computer systems came under sustained cyber attack, almost certainly from computers based in China. The suspicion was that the attacks were mounted either by elements in China or possibly by forces in North Korea using Chinese-based computers as cover. The South Koreans believe that the North Koreans have trained a small army of hackers to launch cyber attacks on them and other Western nations. Computers at a total of ten government agencies were attacked in South Korea, including the country's defence and security agencies. Universities and sections of the media were also singled out for attack.

The potential dangers of such attacks are obvious. Andy Blyth says: 'The herds are deliberately scattered all over the world so they cannot be found very easily.' He also describes how shepherds protect their herds by controlling more than one at a time and by not putting all their bots in one giant herd. 'The standard herd size is 20,000–40,000 bots – though some are larger – and most bot-shepherds will control around six herds. The reason for the size of the herds is simple; it's a protection measure.'

Blyth explains: 'Because they are controlled via an IRC channel, if you can find the IRC channel then you can turn a whole herd off. You can do the same if you find the DNS server. So if you put all of your bots through one channel then you can risk losing the lot.'

Patch it

One major obstacle for law enforcement agencies in tackling bot herds is, ironically, anti-hacking laws themselves. If you cannot nullify bots from taking over a server, then the next best thing is to get into the zombie computers and turn the bots off at source. Yet to do this would almost certainly breach anti-hacking laws in Western countries, for example legislation such as the Computer Misuse Act in the United Kingdom.

As Blyth points out: 'If you go onto a person's computer and install a patch without their permission then you are effectively accessing their computer without their permission – which is illegal.'

More advanced operating systems such as Windows XP allow automatic patching updates that will protect against known bots.

Unfortunately many people with this facility on their machines do not take advantage of it. And with older OSs such as Windows 98 there is no such automatic updating. Such obstacles are frustrating for the law enforcement agencies.

'Because of the situation with the bots what the police want to do is to get a message out to people to patch their systems,' says Blyth. 'It's something that the antivirus people are already getting used to.'

Dirty tricks
Of course, these legal problems do not mean that law enforcement agencies around the world are not looking for new and more effective ways to stop the bot herds. A member of one Western private security team, who asked not to be identified, confirmed the team had been commissioned by the police in one country to find ways of launching counter-attacks.

'We have been asked to conduct some research into how do we turn the bot herds off,' said the source. 'Some of the things that we have been looking into are dependent on some of the changes that are being made to bots at the moment, such as their ability to upload new software – ie to change themselves.'

'We are also looking at ways that will help us to identify the DNS servers that they are reporting to so that we can take over the servers and thus the herd. We could then turn on the upload software command and cause the bot to self-destruct.'

This raises the possibility that in some countries – if the stakes are high enough – the police would be tempted to endorse a 'dirty tricks' campaign against bot herds. In other words it – or more likely people loosely working on the police's behalf – would be encouraged to take out bot herds even if the methods being used were against national laws.

The security expert outlined some of the other approaches that authorities could adopt. 'We could send out a message or we could ask Microsoft or one of the companies involved to send out a message to people telling them to go to a website and upgrade their computers. A lot of people are just not going to bother. And if it is picked up then the civil liberties people are going to start screaming about "Big Brother".'

He continues: 'An alternative is that via the police we could send a message to the people with infected machines telling them that their machine had been detected attacking another machine and causing damage – and that they could be liable if they didn't repair it. But that could also have Big Brother ramifications too.'

The protests that could follow tough measures taken against bot attacks was shown in 1998, when a group of American protestors launched a cyber attack against the Pentagon. The group – called Electronic Disturbance Theater (EDT) – objected to the US government's backing of the Mexican administration, which was taking tough measures against that country's Zapatista rebels. On September 9 EDT launched what it called FloodNet; essentially a DoS attack on a Pentagon website. However, the attack had been well advertised, and the Pentagon was ready with its own DoS counter-attack. In simple terms EDT's servers were overloaded with requests for data-heavy files that flooded and crashed the system; a class denial of service attack. FloodNet was halted in its tracks. In retaliation EDT threatened legal action, claiming that under US law the military was not allowed to become involved in domestic law enforcement.

Duty of care

There are also potentially worrying legal issues for consumers and small companies if their computers get taken over by bots or viruses. If a person's computer is used by another to commit a crime, are they liable for what their machine has done even if they did not know what was happening? This is no mere academic question. For if tens of thousands of computer owners are having their machines compromised and used for criminal acts, might not the victims have some claim for legal action against the owners for negligence? Or could they even face criminal charges? It is the same principle whether your computer is taken over by a bot or is a conduit for viruses that then go on to infect other machines.

Simon Stoker of Tarlo Lyons – a London law firm that specialises in technology law – says the legal situation is grey and will need to be clarified by inevitable test cases. 'It all comes down to do you owe a duty of care to other people. If you don't use antivirus software and transmit viruses, are you at fault?' he says. 'If you're a commercial organisation you should make appropriate checks; though if you are a consumer at home then things are less clear.'

Stoker says the law will probably turn on what an individual knew or should have known was happening, and then what they did to prevent it and how quickly.

'If you are aware of the potential of something to happen or that something is happening then you should act quickly to stop it. If you don't then you are negligent. If you don't use virus scanning then there may be a significant risk to others; but that has not yet been fleshed out legally.'

Stoker's view is that if would be helpful if people were aware that they could potentially be liable, as this might encourage greater vigilance from individuals.

The call for greater public awareness is echoed by Andy Blyth. 'The key issue regarding bots is that you have to get users to be responsible for their machines – and that is a huge problem.'

He says that people behind the DoS attacks deliberately target those who have not tried to protect their machines. 'They know that there are some home users who are not even aware that they need to patch their computers.

'So [the attackers] go to sites like Microsoft, which list the patches you need to fix certain vulnerabilities, and then they search for the computers that have not been patched.'

But Blyth also believes that Internet Service Providers could do more to prevent the activities of bot herds. One technical answer he says is to block a particular set of communication ports – called Bios ports – via the devices they use to route internet traffic, known as routers.

Yet no matter how vigilant the authorities are at tracking the extortionists, it seems criminals are always adept at coming up with new ways of forcing money out of people.

A new scam came to light in July 2004, when a senior computer security expert in the UK received an extraordinary email. The recipient was Richard Starnes, president of the security professionals association ISSA UK, and director of incident response at Cable & Wireless. He describes what the email, which appeared to come from Romania or possibly Bulgaria, said. It read:

> *We've placed several images of child pornography on your system and will report you to the police unless you pay us £50.*

> *Given what a tragedy the discovery of child porn can be to your life and career, £50 seems to be a small price to pay for instructions on how to remove this material.*

Of course there was no pornography placed on the computer, and being a professional in IT security Starnes was able to ignore the 'threat'. But inevitably some people who receive such emails will believe they could be vulnerable and pay the relatively small sum of £50 for the sake of their peace of mind.

Starnes himself believes the new technique shows a recognition by criminals that they have concentrated enough on gambling sites and need new targets. 'Organised crime is a business; they've had an idea of how to change their market,' he says.

Spam, the electronic plague

If bot herds and bot shepherds are new and exotic, then another not dissimilar internet phenomenon is drearily familiar to us all: 'spam', the sending of unsolicited email messages. A great deal of spam is sent out by people who control bot networks and who take over other people's computers with the express purpose of using them to send out streams of unwanted emails.

Of all the many problems of crime confronting the web, none is perhaps as frustrating and irritating as that of spam. Many fear that the unnecessary work – and offence – caused by spam could even threaten the future of the internet if it alienates too many people from using it.

At a press conference for the World Summit on the Information Society in July 2004 Robert Shaw, internet strategy expert with the United Nations' International Telecommunications Union (ITU), spelt this out in blunt terms. 'If we don't work together, we may see millions of people abandoning the Net entirely out of frustration and disgust,' he announced.

The reasons behind this fear are not hard to fathom. It was estimated in May 2004 by email security firm MessageLabs that around two-thirds of all email messages sent on the internet are spam, with tens of billions of them being sent every day[10]. Figures released at the UN 'Spam Summit' suggest the figure could even be as high as three-quarters.

These unwanted messages clog up servers, businesses and home users, and often offend with sexually explicit adverts for porn or absurd claims about how pills can increase a man's penis size. And while 'spammers' (the people sending them) appear to make a living out of their tedious trade, they are also costing world industry some staggering sums of money. The ITU for example suggests that the direct costs of spam worldwide each year could be as high as $25 billion, and that the cost in lost productivity caused by staff having to remove spam from their terminals could reach $100 billion[11].

Given the scale of the problem, one might be forgiven for assuming that there are tens of thousands of people behind the spam scandal who are hard if not impossible to locate in different corners of the globe. In fact, there is a growing consensus that there may be just a few dozen, and certainly no more than around two hundred, key players in spamming, and who are responsible for the majority of this electronic plague.

This is the conclusion of Terry Sullivan, founder of technology company QAQD.com and an expert in anti-spam research. He says, based on detailed 'meta analysis' of available data, that the patterns of spam are 'consistent with a relatively small number of unique sources.' Sullivan says that the numbers fluctuate with time but that, as of the summer of 2004, the analysis indicates that more than 50 per cent of spam comes from no more than 50 to 60 spammers. Indeed, based on his own studies, he personally would go further than that. 'My belief is that most spam comes from roughly 30–40 spammers. But that inference is necessarily tentative.'

Jaron Lanier, mentioned in Chapter 5 and one of the most forward thinking of technology intellectuals, says that given the scale of the damage caused by spammers and the relatively small numbers of spammers involved (see above Box), there should be far greater action taken against them. In historic terms, he believes spamming to be one of the worst forms of business ever devised.

'Lets say if a spammer makes $100 from some spam to sell some silly thing, a sugar pill to enlarge your penis or whatever,' says Lanier. 'This spammer has wasted maybe $10 million dollars or $100 million of distributed time of people just to make that $100. So it's probably the most socially destructive form of wealth creation of all time.'

Lanier also draws an interesting parallel with the fight against terrorism, in which a relatively small number of people can have a massive, disproportionate impact on societies. '[Spammers] are similar to people who have created a huge financial crime against society, for example, defrauded a massive pension fund. It's that kind of crime where everyone has lost something.

'There should be a very serious law enforcement effort to find those people and wipe them out. I mean, they are not rising to the levels of terrorists who are really killing people. But there is a certain similarity in that a small number of people do a great deal of harm, so it's worth putting a lot of effort into finding them.'

Terry Sullivan agrees that the numbers involved could make any anti-spam offensive productive. 'It's easier and more practical to mount a focused forensic effort against, say, 30 spammers than it would be to mount one against 3,000. And "taking out" the most prolific spammers would have an extremely high payback in terms of reducing total spam volume.'

Few people doubt that the unofficial headquarters of world spamming is the United States, or more specifically parts of Florida. Steve Linford, director of non-profit anti-spam organisation Spamhaus[12], and a man dedicated to fighting this social and commercial menace, goes further. 'You could easily say that Boca Raton is the spam capital of the world,' he says.

Linford, who is also an adviser on spam to the European Union, explains why. 'It seems to have started off from its role as a white-collar telecommunications centre. In the US Florida has become the centre for the telemarketing industry, so spam was probably quite natural. Florida also has laws that are attractive to criminals because, unlike other states, criminals can keep the proceeds of their activities rather than having them confiscated.'

Yet while the spammers may be based in the US, most of the spam messages do not in fact originate there, thanks to the power of the internet and of networks. Linford explains how this works.

'The spammers have virtual private networks that run from their houses to the servers that they use in places like Beijing. It might seem innocuous but from that set-up they manage to account for 75 per cent of all the email on the Western internet.'

Soon this figure will be more like 80–85 per cent, he says. And the total number of spam he says is involved is truly staggering. 'At the moment we are blocking 8 billion spam messages a day, which is close to 10,000 a second, though the spammers are sending 30–32 billion messages a day,' says Linford.

'Seven out of ten of the spam email messages you get will be from zombies and seven out of ten of the websites that the emails link to are hosted in China, which is where 70 per cent of all spam comes from.'

Can spam

So why does the world allow so few spammers to continue to wreak such misery on the internet?

In fact, governments and law enforcement agencies have at last begun to start taking some action, both against spam in general and in particular against some of the spam barons; doubtless spurred on by those fears of a general meltdown in consumer confidence. In the United States, which is usually seen as a haven for spammers – especially Florida – there is now a new law on spamming.

The CAN-SPAM Act, which came into force on 1 January 2004, makes it a criminal offence to conceal the true origins of spam mail. However critics point to a major weakness in that it does not outlaw the practice of sending unsolicited junk mail to individuals; surely the core problem of spamming. In effect the new laws have legalised so-called opt-out spamming, to the dismay of many critics.

Nevertheless the Federal Trade Commission (FTC), whose job it is to enforce the new laws, cracked down on two identified large-scale spammers in April 2004, the first of a planned series of targeted assaults on those behind spam[13]. One was against an organisation called Phoenix Avatar from Detroit, the other was against an outfit called Global Web Promotions, run out of Australia and New Zealand. In each case the FTC claimed the firms had breached the new Act. It will remain to be seen first whether the charges will be proven, and second what the overall affect of such charges will have on the rest of the spam 'industry'. Many individual states have also brought in their own anti-spamming legislation. For example in Virginia persistent spammers can have their assets seized plus face up to five years in gaol.

The FTC meanwhile is also using existing consumer legislation against people spamming products – such as penile growth pills – that do not measure up to what they promise.

Over in Europe a European Commission directive on spam has been implemented by members of the European Union. These regulations take a different approach from the laws in the United States; the EU directive does attack unsolicited emails – unlike the US model – but does not criminalise spam. In the United Kingdom for example regulations arising from the Privacy and Electronic Communications Directive – which came into force in December 2003 – are overseen by the Information Commissioner's Office (ICO). Unlike the FTC this body cannot start criminal proceedings against a firm thought to have breached the regulations. Curiously, too, the rules forbidding unsolicited emails apply only to individuals, not business recipients, even though the spamming of business emails can cost industry many millions of pounds. One is entitled to be sceptical as to how effective these rather tepid measures will be against dedicated spammers.

One country that has adopted a tough approach is Australia. Its Spam Act came into force on 10 April 2004 and this not only makes illegal the sending of unsolicited spam, it also backs this up with stiff sanctions. Serious repeat offenders can be liable for financial penalties of up to A$1.1 million a day. Early reports suggest that already the law has begun to reduce the amount of spam within Australia.

Generally, however, by the summer of 2004 the new worldwide assault on spam had shown little signs of reducing the overall amount of unsolicited emails passing around the globe. The experts continue to debate whether, unless spam is dealt with soon, it could spell disaster for the public's love affair with the 'killer application' of the internet – email.

Sullivan, who has studied the issue in detail, is honest about what he thinks the outcome might be. 'I've given up prognosticating about the future of spam – I find myself changing my mind frequently. However, eventually, I think people will ultimately stop or drastically curtail their use of email,' he says.

In fact Sullivan says that email has already lost its once-glittering status as far as many users are concerned. 'One survey done a few years back found that, at the time, people would rather give up the telephone than email. Unfortunately, spam has rendered this once indispensable technology much less useful and usable.'

In a rational world, he says, spammers themselves would consider the implications of what they are doing. 'Metaphorically speaking, "spam is the parasite, email is the host." If the host – email – dies, then the parasite – spam – dies along with it. If I were a spammer, I'd already be really worried that my actions were severely compromising the long-term health of the "host",' he says.

Kings of spam

Unfortunately the identified spammers seem not to be listening. One of the so-called kings of spam is American Alan Ralsky, who lives in Detroit. Ralksy is said to have a mail list of around 150 million email addresses and has an operation using Internet Service Providers – ISPs – in countries all over the world.

Interviewed in the US in December 2004 the 58-year-old admitted he was worried about the implications of the new US laws on spamming. 'Of course I'm worried; you would have to be stupid to try to violate this law,' he told an interviewer from the *New York Times*[14]. But he insisted that the new crackdown would not deter him – and by implication others – from continuing to send 'bulk mail' en masse. 'There is too much money involved. I'm a survivor. And when you are a survivor, you find a way to make it happen.'

Interestingly Ralsky admits to having used a technique that shows the growing similarities between spamming and other forms of crime on the internet; the use of 'proxy' computers.

Earlier we saw how the so-called bot shepherds install robot software on computers to use them for attacks on websites and servers. These compromised machines are called zombie computers. However, using similar technology spammers have also learnt how to take over individual computers, though this time their purpose is not to use those computers to launch DoS attacks but rather to send out endless streams of spam emails. In this context these compromised computers are known as 'proxy' computers' or 'open proxies'.

In his *New York Times* interview Ralsky says: 'I personally hate mailing with proxies. It's rough. But you do what you got to do.'

These compromised computers may not just be sending out spam email either. In some cases they will be taken over to use as servers. Typically some pornographers will use these proxy machines to host their sites. In other words an innocent home computer user could unwittingly be hosting an explicit hard-core porn site.

Mikko Hyppönen, of Finnish-based security firm F-Secure (already mentioned in Chapter 5), says: 'You might have a gentleman surfing away, happily unaware that at same time his home computer is sending out 10,000 spam emails an hour, and that the same computer might have a thousand visitors from all over the world surfing for porn on his computer.'

He adds: 'Home computers have become so fast and so multi-tasking and the network connections so fast with cable etc that it can support all this, and the user might notice nothing different from normal.'

Hyppönen sometimes tracks back the route of spam messages to trace their origin and gets in touch with the owners of compromised machines. One example that we touched on in the introduction has particularly stuck in his mind:

'I remember one gentleman in his 60s from France, who lived in a rural area near Marseilles. Tracing back his computer we could prove that his computer had been sending out millions of spam messages over the past six months, advertising satellite TV de-scramblers and various kinds of medication and cheap loans.

'This gentleman had absolutely no idea. He had bought his first computer six months before and had an ADSL connection and was using it to surf the web and send email around.'

When told about what had happened the man was amazed; though he then realised why some of his emails had never got through to their destination. Hyppönen explains what happens. 'Many ISPs, when they start to see massive amounts of mail coming from one machine, blacklist it. They stop receiving email from that machine to get rid of the spam. But of course the owner of the machine's own messages will get lost too. His emails never bounced; they just never arrived either.'

Steve Linford describes another hapless victim, an elderly lady from Britain. 'She was running a guest house in Scotland and was completely oblivious of the fact that she was sending out 1,000 spam messages a day and was contributing to a net annual cost of $25 billion to the global economy.'

Though new advanced filters are being developed all the time, the use of zombie machines in this way is proving one of the major obstacles to controlling spam, believes Linford.

'At the moment there are around a hundred thousand new machines being infected each week and we are fighting a losing battle because they are out-stripping our ability to take down their networks of bots,' he days.

Spamhaus is also worried about the growing links between spamming and organised crime. 'At the moment there is a collusion between the spammers and the big three Russian spam gangs, all of whom are involved in organised crime,' says Linford. 'Between them and the US gangs they have created an enormous network, but because of the other activities of the Russian gangs they have attracted a lot of attention from the police.

Linford says that perhaps the most obnoxious outfit among these gangs is one called Yambo or Yambo Financials. 'It pretends to operate from the UK from an address in Surrey, which would appear to be a mailing address,' he says. 'Both the Russian spammers and the US spammers are very unpleasant gangsters.' For example, he says, the Russian gang Yambo sends out spam linked to child, animal and incest pornography, while it also runs sites depicting rape. In the US, meanwhile, one leading spammer is a former cocaine trafficker and money launderer, and others have spent time in prison.

Mobile or cell spam

Mikko Hyppönen meanwhile is one of a number of industry experts who warns about a new medium for spam that has already begun to arrive; spam messages on mobile phones. One 'problem' for spammers using mobile phones will be how to avoid paying for the costs of the messages. Unlike emails, SMS or text messages cost money. Hyppönen says the 'solution' for the spammers does not need to be a mobile phone virus to take over someone's phone (even though phone viruses have now been developed, see Chapter 5). Instead spammers could use something as simple as a phone game that mobile users would download free from the internet.

'This might have a hidden function, which is that every morning at, for example 4 am, it starts to send SMS adverts about a product to every single phone number found in the phone book,' says Hyppönen.

'This fixes three problems for the spammer. One, how do you send mobile phone spam anonymously? Two, how do you get the charges moved away from yourself? And three, where do you find the phone numbers to send the adverts to? It is a neat solution. It's not happened yet but . . .'

One bright note in an otherwise gloomy story on spam is that there are signs that porn spam – advertising pornographic websites – is beginning to dwindle. This is perhaps partially explained by new rules in the US from the FTC, which require that the words 'SEXU-ALLY EXPLICIT' be included in the subject line of porn messages. Another explanation is that porn emails simply are not getting the commercial return for spammers that they used to. Instead the growth areas in spam are for pharmaceutical and healthcare products – for example pills claiming to help to reduce weight or increase breast size – and also financially related spam messages. According to a survey by content security firm Clearswift in March 2004[15], porn-related messages accounted for just over 8 per cent of all spam it saw.

Yet if porn has suffered a setback in the spam market, sex still remains a major industry on the internet.

Chapter Eight
Sex and Drugs

Peddlers of pornography have always been expert at exploiting the latest media. Whether it is in the books and postcards of the Victorian era, or the magazines and videos of the 20th century, porn has usually been one of the early adopters of new means of communication.

No one should be surprised, therefore, that pornographers were early users of the internet and that porn is now one of the leading industries on the worldwide web. The figures tell the story. It is estimated that there are around 4.2 million porn websites, more than a tenth of all websites on the internet, and something approaching 400 million web pages containing porn; and the industry is worth billions of dollars every year to the people who run such sites.

A growing problem is that young people are becoming exposed to online pornography at very young ages. A survey in May 2004 by UK-based Email Systems[1] found that children as young as five are receiving porn spam messages by email. Many families now have special filters installed on their computers to ensure their children cannot accidentally stumble across sexual content on the web.

PAEDOPHILIA

But while adult pornography and the exposure to young children of unsuitable images is an area of concern, an even greater menace involving sex and the internet is dominating the headlines: child pornography.

In recent years the problems of paedophilia, especially the taking and swapping of indecent images, have become closely identified with the internet. Barely a month goes by without some headlines in the newspapers and on television and radio about the grim use of the worldwide web made by child abusers swapping appalling images of young children being molested, in photographs, videos and even in live streaming sessions.

But if paedophilia initially started to become identified with the internet in the public minds, a yet more worrying trend is beginning to merge; that the internet itself is becoming synonymous with pae-dophilia and child abuse.

The concern is a real one. The internet is so embedded into so many people's lives now that it rarely becomes a talking point. The use of emails for communications and search engines for hunting down information is so commonplace that people take these activi-ties for granted.

Yet when a new case of online child abuse emerges, the headlines understandably juxtapose paedophilia and the web side by side. This makes us suddenly take notice. Child abuse and the internet; the link begins to forms inside people's mind. The very many extraordinary and beneficial uses of the network of networks are quickly over-looked or forgotten. Instead the connection is there: paedophiles use the internet; paedophiles are a bad thing; the internet is a bad thing. Even though paedophilia pre-dates the technology age, the indelible connection between the two has begun to stick.

This unfortunate equation helps explain why the police and those who help run the internet – Internet Service Providers (ISPs) and major network organisations such as AT&T in the US and BT in the UK – work so hard and so visibly to combat paedophilia on the inter-net. Not only is child abuse illegal and needs to be dealt with in its own terms as one of the worst imaginable crimes (and the prime motivation for police involvement); but the internet is also now inte-gral to the business of Western countries such as the US, UK, France and Germany. Any loss of confidence in the internet through its identification with paedophilia could therefore harm Western economies, another excellent reason for cracking down hard on this particularly unpleasant abuse of modern technology.

One of the assumptions in much of the coverage of the internet and its relationship with paedophilia is that the web has made it easier to take, swap, store and crucially exchange images of abused children; and therefore the internet has unwittingly helped aid the crime.

As more and more images are passed around – and the numbers involved now reach many millions – then the demand increases for new ones, meaning that more and more children get abused to fuel this depraved trade. In the past abusers had to rely on photographic images they processed themselves – taking them to high-street developers was of course unthinkable – or later polaroid images. These had to be moved by postal services, a practice that could always leave a person at risk of discovery; in any case fellow paedophiles were always reluctant to give their real addresses. Meanwhile there was the initial problem of how to contact other like-minded people.

Steve Adams, team leader of the Paedophile Investigation Section of the NHTCU in London, says that the paedophiles are constantly updating their technology, and the police have had to understand this process to help track them down.

'You had people using VHS tapes; to do that you'd physically have to post them. So what we did was to look out for people posting videotapes all over the place.'

The possibilities of the internet and its evolution into the world-wide web appear to have changed all that. 'Now you've got a digital camera that you can buy for £60 or a video camera for £200. You can connect it straight onto your laptop straight onto your computer and within seconds that is in the States, Canada or wherever,' says Adams. 'So you've abused a child and in seconds it becomes valuable.'

Yet there is a counter argument to this assumption that the internet is a paedophile's charter. Yes, the ability to take and communicate images instantaneously and apparently anonymously does make a child abuser's 'work' easier. But it must be remembered that to do all this a paedophile has to make use of a system that stores data; data that as we have seen in earlier chapters is almost impossible to destroy completely, even by the most technically proficient of people. Might not then the internet make it easier to detect and convict paedophiles even as it appears to make their exchange of images easier?

Jaron Lanier, the internet intellectual whom we've met in previous chapters, is not alone in noting these two contradictory tendencies. 'There's a double-edged sword to the internet; on the one hand it enables crimes in a certain sense. On the other hand it makes it harder . . . it makes a lot of crime more visible and more easy to record.'

He continues: 'Every expert on paedophilia I have talked to has said that on the whole the internet has been a tremendous benefit. For while it does enable them [criminals], even more it enables them to be caught. In the past one did not know how many paedophiles there were or how successful they were and now one does. So on balance the situation has now become better.'

Steve Adams at the NHTCU accepts that new technology can make it easier to trap some paedophiles, but he is also aware that the clever and determined offenders make use of technology to hide themselves.

'The internet has made it more freely accessible so therefore more people have been caught because they leave fingerprints. But if you're part of a group, an underground paedophile group, then you are extremely careful; you will use encryption, you will use proxies, you are going to try and protect yourself,' he says.

Adams adds: 'If you want to hide yourself behind anonymity you can do it. There are people out there whom I would like to find, but it's difficult.

'The only time we find them is when they do something stupid.'

The internet intellectual Jaron Lanier, maintains that the arrival of the internet and new technology has, rather than the internet fuelling paedophilia, simply high-lighted for the first time the sheer extent of the number of paedophiles. Nonetheless the figures are quite astounding.

In 2004 the UK telecommunications giant and leading ISP BT set out to block access to websites carrying child porn, at least for its own internet customers[2]. In the first three weeks of operation the firm's Clean Feed system blocked a quarter of a million attempts to view pages containing child porn.

By late August 2004, some 23,000 such attempts were being blocked each day. When one considers the number of different ISPs (around 150) there are in the UK alone, and that the figures include repeated attempts by the same person and even accidental 'attempts', these figures still suggest a remarkable appetite among British users to see child pornography. One can safely assume that the figures for other countries would be no different. The websites to which access was blocked were chosen by experts from the Internet Watch Foundation[3], a UK body formed by ISPs around the country. The organisation itself says that the figures produced by BT for attempts to reach the sites were 'staggering'.

Meanwhile there are thought to be more than one hundred thousand websites around the world offering illegal pornographic images involving children.

Early adopters of technology

The evidence that paedophiles were among the earliest adopters of the new technology is striking. In particular they quickly saw the potential of the internet to further their crimes. For example paedophiles were among the first users of bulletin boards, methods of meeting and exchanging information 'virtually' in the 1980s, the early days in the internet. Bulletin boards may seem a little ancient and old-fashioned by the standards of today's websites and sophisticated chatrooms, but they had one huge advantage; they were and still are immensely secure.

Peter Sommer, a computer forensics expert and academic, describes how it worked. 'At first they were hosted on mainframes and then some very wealthy people started to get hard drives. In the early days of the PC people started to host them on individual PCs that you had to dial in on.'

Sommer explains how using these techniques could shield groups from public gaze. 'The thing about a bulletin board is that it is monitored by the computer owner, who is known as the SYSOP (the system operator), which gives them an element of control.

'Some of them used encryption or non-standard or modified bulletin board software to protect themselves. This would give people a sense of community and the feeling that they were with a group that they were comfortable with, which made them feel normal.'

As the internet and then the worldwide web evolved during the 1990s, so did the ingenuity of paedophile groups in exploiting the advances in technology. They were among the first users of Usenet groups, which were open discussion forums. By dialling a phone number with your computer's modem it would take you to a list of discussion groups; you could simply scroll through until you found what you wanted.

At around the same time systems using Internet Relay Chat (IRC) systems started to emerge. Whereas Usenets rely on email message replies being laid under each other in strings, one after another in linear form, IRC allows people to engage in online typed communications. People could communicate with each other online in real time.

For paedophiles this was a revelation, as it meant that they could communicate freely and speedily; the downside of course was that it also meant that they could be monitored. They soon discovered, however, that they could form direct one-on-one links via the PC or they could direct someone they were interested in talking with to another IRC area they knew to be empty. This would mean they could communicate freely and would simply cease typing if anyone else 'entered' the chat area.

From an early stage, given the uses they could make of new technology, paedophiles who had a good knowledge of computers were naturally highly prized members of the 'gang'.

Elite rings

One early example of new technology being used by paedophiles was by a group known as the Orchid Club[4]. As early as 1996 this international band of paedophiles was using digital cameras to 'broadcast' live abuse of children to other members around the world. It was thought to be the first time investigators had discovered 'real time' online abuse of children.

The arrest in 1996 – and ultimate conviction – of Orchid Club members lead directly to the discovery of another much larger and even more technologically sophisticated paedophile ring: the so-called Wonderland Club.

This elaborately constructed and organised club saw itself as the 'elite' of child paedophile rings and worked on a massive scale. The 'entrance fee' for a new member was to produce 10,000 new – that is, unseen by other members – images of child abuse.

When law enforcement officers behind 'Operation Cathedral' carried out a series of raids worldwide in 1998[5], they made more than 100 arrests in 12 different countries, seized around 750,000 images of abuse and believed that as many as 1,200 children – one a 12-month-old baby – were abused in the making of the images.

The gang had gone to extraordinary lengths to conceal its activities online. It had used encryption to conceal images and even styled its name as 'Wonderland', using a zero instead of a nought to prevent it being found by any searches for its name. Many of the members – who joined by invitation only – were computer literate, some of them working as IT consultants.

Peter Sommer, who was chief technical witness for the defence in the UK, where eight people were charged under Operation Cathedral with conspiracy to distribute pornographic images, recalls how the organisation worked.

'The whole thing was run from the US, where there were two people who were very technically competent,' he says. 'They produced the Trade of Handbook [ie the trade of images], which explained all of the technology required to keep them secret.

'It was like the manuals that you get with software but a lot better, telling them how to use encryption and to move and hide material. It was the discovery of the handbook on someone's computer that tended to prove the conspiracy charge.'

Sommers says that Wonderland members used to spot people who interested them and approach them to become members, providing they could produce the 10,000 new images, at which point they would receive a copy of the handbook. 'The idea that they wanted to put across was that they were an elite. They knew that there was a hoi polloi of paedophiles and they wanted to stress that they were above the common crowd,' he says.

Operation Cathedral and the subsequent smashing of the Wonderland Club marked the first of the very high-profile online paedophile investigations to attract massive publicity, but it has not been the last.

In 2001 Operation Candyman[6] was launched in the United States after an undercover officer discovered the existence of three 'e-groups' connected to paedophilia. E-groups are online forums that use chat, email and file transfer to swap ideas and comments on their chosen subject. In this case the subject was child abuse. One of the groups bore the message: 'This group is for people who love kids. You can post any type of messages you like too or any type of pics and vids you like too. PS. IF WE ALL WORK TOGETHER WE WILL HAVE THE BEST GROUP ON THE NET.'

The e-groups were also linked to paedophile pay sites on which thousands of people worldwide had – astonishingly – used their own credit cards to access child porn. In total the names of around 250,000 people from all parts of the globe were discovered during this huge operation, and US investigators passed on details of names and addresses to colleagues in many other countries. The presence of some 2,000 credit card details and emails relating to people living in the UK then led to the establishment of Operation Ore[7] to investigate the Britons involved; in effect Ore became an offshoot investigation of Candyman. Eventually the Americans handed over 7,000 items of data linked to payment for child abuse porn by Britons.

In fact the trail is almost endless. As each suspect is investigated, the hard drives of their computers tend to reveal the existence of other groups of paedophiles or others who have become interested in trading images. Inevitably, through a lack of police resources, some suspects have escaped prosecution, up until now at any rate, though the police say it remains committed to bringing suspects to court where possible. Of the original 7,000 items the list was reduced to cover 4,000 suspects, of whom around 1,300 have been arrested.

Of those on the original list one was Pete Townshend, the rock star who was eventually given a police caution. Townshend admitted accessing one site with the use of a credit card but said he had been researching paedophilia for a book, believing he had been abused as a child. Meanwhile the ringleader of another child porn ring, Thomas Reedy, a US computer consultant from Texas, was gaoled for a total of 1,335 years in August 2001. The US investigation into Reedy, code-named Operation Avalanche[8], eventually unearthed the fact that he had some 250,000 subscribers around the world and was making around $1.4 million a month. This was telling evidence that paedophilia is not just technologically sophisticated but also big business.

Investigations into online paedophile rings almost invariably throw up new leads into other, previously unknown paedophiles. An example both of this and of the technological know-how of many paedophiles was the case of David Ward, who was gaoled for 19 years at York Crown Court, England, in June 2004, for distributing images of children under the age of five[9]. He was also convicted of the rape of a nine-month-old baby he was babysitting and for then distributing images of the attack, which he had filmed with a digital camera.

The 41-year-old van driver was investigated after a German undercover police officer monitoring the internet for paedophiles came across Ward and passed his details on to the NHTCU in London. Ward had offered to trade images with the undercover policeman. Officers from the unit and from North Yorkshire then carried out a joint investigation into Ward, and he was swiftly arrested.

Following the paedophile David Ward's arrest, his computer was examined; it was then that his technical ability came to light. The paedophile had used two ways of encrypting the images on his machine – images he sent to fellow paedophiles all around the world – many of which could not as a result be viewed.

The NHTCU forensic team, led by Marc Kirby, knew that the files were hidden using encryption software called Magic Folders, but the pirated version Ward had used meant they could not open the software. Instead they enlisted the help of the secretive technicians working for NTAC, the technical section of MI5, to crack the code. This finally – two weeks before his trial – revealed the images of the baby whom Ward had abused while babysitting and then sent around the internet.

Kirby says that finally being able to break open Ward's computer is one of his most memorable moments in the unit so far. 'We could prove he had paedophile pictures, but the key to the case was the identity of one child. Once we got the encryption broken and got pictures of the child, we were able to identify the child with the help of the local police force.'

Had the police not been able to uncover the material involving the baby that Ward had abused, he may well have received a much lesser sentence.

Steve Adams, the NHTCU's team leader on the Paedophile Investigation Section, recalls what else the examination of Ward's computer – which he had used as a file server – revealed.

'We obtained all the logs and all the other files. We then realised that he had a large database; there was 9,500 hits on his server in a matter of about three months. We examined that and we were able to trace 18 people in the UK who had accessed this server, and uploaded and or downloaded quite serious child abuse images.'

All 18 people have since been investigated and at least one person has been gaoled as a result. In August 2004 the NHTCU revealed that as a result of its examination of Ward's computer it had also arrested a computer maintenance technician in Sussex on suspicion of downloading and distributing indecent images of children.

Trojan Defence

One problem for the authorities seeking to prosecute people downloading child pornography is what is known as the Trojan Defence. Put simply the Trojan Defence is when a defendant does not deny that there is pornography on their computer (they cannot, if forensics experts have found it there on the hard drive). Instead the suspect claims that it was downloaded onto their machine by someone else using a Trojan programme. This Trojan software, so the argument runs, turns the defendant's computer into a server hosting websites for child porn without their knowledge.

Defendants have been using this argument even in cases where experts can find no trace of a Trojan programme; the case of the Vanishing Trojan, as Sherlock Holmes might have put it. This defence has proved particularly difficult for the police to deal with, partly because of the lack of technical knowledge among those involved in the judicial system. As a result defence lawyers have been able to present a case to the court that is not technologically credible; that a programme was on the computer and then erased itself without trace.

Alternatively the defence argues that the computer programmes used by the police in all of their investigations are incapable of detecting the Trojan found by the defence team, and that the defence team's system or security expert has found the rogue programme.

Independent forensics experts warn that the law and particular the rules of evidence in such cases need to be tightened, as the current situation in British courts could lead to paedophiles walking free on a technicality.

Professor Neil Barrett, a computer forensics expert who is often called as a prosecution witnesses in such cases, explains their dilemma. 'We don't have an explanation for the Trojan that vanished in much the same way that there is no explanation for the murderer who was in the same room as you and confounded physical laws by vanishing without a trace.'

Meanwhile another expert whom we met in Chapter 7, Andy Blyth of the School of Computing at Glamorgan University, says the Trojan Defence has made prosecuting internet paedophile cases more complex and more expensive. At the moment the law is erring on the side of the paedophile, because the complexity of technical evidence means that some lawyers and the jury may just not understand it.

'We are still in the position where a defence lawyer can turn around and say, "But what if the virus is not found?",' says Blyth. 'We have even been in cases where a defence lawyer has rubbished the competence of a widely used [antivirus] product in court. This is now a very big issue because it is very expensive. We are now seeing the Crown Prosecution Service asking us to restrict our investigations to five or six images; and it is difficult to secure an investigation with five or six images because we are now seeing defences claiming that those images appeared as "pop-ups".'

Pop ups are web pages that automatically appear when you are viewing another page. Experts are thus warning that this style of defence could seriously undermine the prosecution of paedophiles.

Andy Jones, also at Glamorgan's School of Computing, says: 'We're finding that this is the defence of choice for people who are going to court. I think that this is the beginning not just of a paedophile's charter but of a criminal's charter. It's the machine alibi.'

He adds, 'What is noticeable is that this is a software condition that only seems to affect people when they are going to appear in court. Those people who do not come to court tend to notice when their hard discs start to fill up with pornographic images . . .'

Professor Barrett says part of the problem is that the defence team can produce anyone as an 'expert' witness to cast doubt on the prosecution case. 'In trials involving computers anyone can be accepted as an expert witness, which is odd, because if it were a medical case people would be expected to be a doctor or someone of equivalent status.'

What is clearly needed now is for a responsible authority – probably the Department of Constitutional Affairs – to draw up a list of accredited defence and prosecution experts, all certified by a legitimate body such as the British Computer Society (BCS). These would all be experts working within a common discipline and with computer tools that have an acknowledged function.

There should also be a secondary list of respected independent computer experts available who could be cross-examined by both legal teams as to what is and what is not possible within the world of computers. Ideally these would also be recognised by the BCS.

The Trojan Defence became widely used by defendants after a British case in 2003 involving a suspected hacker – who was not linked to any paedophile activity – collapsed.

Aaron Caffrey, aged 19, from Shaftesbury, Dorset, had been accused of hacking into and crashing the computer system of the Port of Houston in Texas. Caffrey argued that the evidence against him was planted on his machine by un-named attackers who used a 'Trojan' attack to gain control of his computer and launch the hack. As there was no trace of a Trojan infection on his PC, the case at Southwark Crown Court turned on whether the jury believed the defence claims that the Trojan theory was possible, or the prosecution case that it was impossible. Caffrey was acquitted.

As a result of the Trojan Defence the police have been forced to make significant changes to the way it conducts its investigations. The police and prosecution services now seek to prove that the accused person was at the computer at the time that the pornography was downloaded, and was in overall control of the machine.

According to officers at the NHTCU, they are confident that the measures they have taken have
'negated' this manoeuvre. Indeed David Ward's defence
team tried unsuccessfully to use the Trojan Defence.
Steve Adams says: 'There's a lot of work involved in it,
but it was negated.'

Staying undetected

Despite the successes of the authorities all over the world in detecting and convicting paedophiles who work online, they are convinced
that there are more cautious and technically aware groups who
never come to light. Unlike the paedophiles who use their credit
cards to buy porn – making them instantly traceable – these criminals go to infinite lengths to protect themselves and their online
identities.

Adams says that each group formulates its own set of guidelines as
to how to stay undetected, and that if it keeps to those it can be hard
to trace.

'I'm sure there are groups out there that are sticking to the rules
and we don't know who they are and they are smiling at us.'

The Trojan and other defences have begun to cause some disquiet
in the United States too.

Parry Aftab is a cyberspace lawyer, as well as an author and inter-
nationally renowned child advocate. She says the Trojan Defence has
been used in the US, though adds that for a number of years there
were no cases brought over pornography because of a challenge
from the Free Speech Coalition, which she says was backed by the
porn industry.

'We're seeing the Trojan Defence and we're seeing the car driving defence, where people are claiming that someone driving past
in their car has downloaded stuff onto their computer via a wireless link.

'Sometimes they are successful – and I don't believe it one whit that they're innocent when they've been able to walk [free] – but it's one of those things that you have to swallow.'

A spokesman for the FBI said it was prepared for suspects adopting this strategy. 'We have dealt with situations of what are called the Trojan Defence and have developed techniques and strategies to deal with that defence – which we are not prepared to go into any details over,' said the spokesman. 'We are confident that we now can deal with this situation.'

DRUGS

In much the same way as with gangs involved in child porn, there are signs that criminals involved in drugs are beginning to exploit the technological capabilities of the internet. The taking and selling of illegal drugs has, as with paedophilia, been around for a great deal longer than the internet. And associations between drug culture and the culture of the internet and computing are not new, of course.

The philosophy that states that access to computers and the internet should be free and unrestricted easily chimes with the libertarian view that drugs should be legalised and available to all. This link was especially strong among the continental European hacking groups of the 1970s and 1980s, groups such as Hack-Tic and the Computer Chaos Club, who readily embraced both philosophies. Even today the police estimates that in about one in ten of arrests of hackers and virus writers it will find drugs among their belongings.

Yet as so often in the story of the internet and computing, where the intellectuals, free-thinkers and radicals have led, the criminals quickly follow, adapting the technology to suit their own needs. And usually they have the money and power to buy in the technological expertise they need.

Andy Blyth of Glamorgan University explains, 'If you think about the employment prospects among organised crime they are massive

– the Cali [drugs] Cartel in Columbia had enough money to build a supercomputer so it went out and bought the best and the people to staff it.

'When it wanted to bug the US Embassy in Columbia it hired ex-people from the National Security Agency (NSA) and set up a state-of-the-art listening station; it was even caught trying to buy a former Russian submarine.'

According to the National Criminal Intelligence Service (NCIS) in the UK there are worrying signs that the drug industry is making use of the internet to talk anonymously to each other, and to place its drugs orders.

'We have a lot of intelligence that the drug industry is now using the ICQ and IRC channels to communicate,' says an NCIS spokesman. 'We are seeing the start of people trying to use it as an ordering mechanism. In terms of supply we do know organised criminals use chatrooms to organise drug supply.'

The team has also discovered that a flourishing internet trade has started in synthetic drugs to avoid national prohibitions. For example, ecstasy variations such as TCI and 5-meo-DMT that are not illegal in the US are being brought by buyers in such countries as the UK, where it is illegal to buy and sell them.

According to Samir Kapuria, director of Strategic Solutions at business security consultants @stake, some criminals are using credit cards and IDs stolen via the internet to buy drugs from sites, and effectively to launder their money into hard cash from subsequent street dealing.

Without giving away too many details of exactly how this system works, Kapuria outlines what such criminals do by using websites whose true purpose is known only to a few.

'One of the things that I have seen would be something like a website where you buy furniture, and everything available has to be paid for by credit card. On the site there would be something like a Louis XVI table advertised. Every time everyone else logged on to buy it, they would be told that the table was not available. But when someone logs in using a particular login ID and password it will become available – except that a table is not delivered to the person who orders it. Instead they will get a kilo of heroin or cocaine.'

It is a perfect illustration of how the 'real' world of crime – in this case the trafficking of illegal drugs – can find new expression in the virtual world of the internet.

CHAPTER NINE
The Future

What does the future hold for cyber crime? One thing we can be sure about is that the world of technology will evolve even faster than it does at present. And we can be certain, too, that the world of cyber crime will change equally quickly and adapt to the new opportunities.

Among the likely growth areas is identity fraud, a crime that is already widely regarded as a serious problem in the United States, but which is still not perceived as a major threat in Western Europe.

Many experts agree that the 'traditional' viruses that are spread by email and attachments may diminish in number and severity. The real threat in this area in the short term is likely to come from worms using networks and file sharing. Longer term the menace will probably come from new hybrids of virus and worms, such as the male/female virus, and the jumping of malware to other platforms such as mobile phones and PDAs. This has already begun.

There are also concerns that viruses that infected older vintage operating systems will gain a new lease of life when developing areas such as Africa start to come online and use older computers and software no longer wanted by the West. Thus there could be two different categories of viruses – the developed world and the developing world viruses – working alongside each other in parallel worlds of cyber space.

One larger-scale fear is that email or possibly the internet itself could be sent crashing to oblivion one day by a determined and skilful attack. We have already seen how in 1988 the Morris Internet Worm unintentionally brought much of the then fledgling internet to a halt.

Also, at 1 pm Pacific Day Time on 21 October 2002 a large part of the backbone of the world's internet began to buckle after a massive cyber attack. The infrastructure of the internet depends on 13 route servers, the locations where the Internet Protocol (IP) addresses are kept. No fewer than nine of these route servers were taken offline in the 2002 incident by what is known as a 'cascading' denial of service attack. In a conventional DoS attack the 'payload' of data traffic is aimed at its target server, which is overwhelmed but then switches to a backup server. In this particular two-day offensive, a sophisticated cascaded DoS attack followed through to the backup server and overwhelmed that one too. According to one of our interviewees, the findings of a secret report into the incident – which sent alarm throughout Western governments – have never been made public. There has been speculation that the attack may either have been by organised crime – perhaps an attack that got out of hand – or may have been the work of a foreign intelligence agency – possibly North Korea, Iraq or Libya. Security around these vital servers has since been massively increased. But the fear is that such an attack could happen again and be even more successful.

There is also a concern that the email system could be brought to a halt by an organised, endless flood of randomly generated emails. Mikko Hyppönen, director of Anti-Virus Research for F-Secure, believes such an attack is more likely than not to happen, and could occur within the next five years.

'The key word is "unfilterable" emails,' he says. 'They would have to be random; if there was anything constant in the emails they could be filtered and probably be handled. But if they could not be filtered there would be a problem.' Hyppönen believes the main question is not when – but who. 'There are lots of guys who would have the skill right now but would not have the motivation.'

Terrorists on the one hand would have the motivation, he maintains, but not the skills. After the events of 11 September 2001 everyone knows what such groups are capable of; thus it would take an exceptionally amoral or greedy hacker group to supply terrorists with the technical ability to carry out such an onslaught.

Hyppönen thinks the most likely culprits could be anarchists and activists from neo-political movements, who may also have the technical skills.

'There are groups who oppose globalisation and capitalism and especially the commercialisation of the internet. They might be motivated to do something like this.'

In any case it seems only a matter of time before terrorists do use the possibilities of the phenomenal computing power available via the internet to launch attacks on Western targets. Professor Neil Barrett, of the Royal Military College of Science, a man with good contacts within the British establishment, has little doubt that this issue needs to be addressed.

'We are now going to have to start seriously considering that terrorists are going to get involved in hacking; that's high up the agenda,' he says. Professor Barrett also believes that to combat cyber crime generally there has to be a fundamental rethink about the operating systems we currently use.

'I think that there will be a complete overhaul of Windows and Unix, which are both toy systems that are currently being used to conduct serious business deals. They were not built for sophisticated users and now the serious business of trying to build security into them will start. I think the result will be that they will be abandoned and instead we will move to the security regimes of the mainframe.'

Indeed throughout this book, Microsoft – who produces Windows – has come under fire for the alleged technical shortcomings of its operating systems and software that allows it to be exploited by criminals, vandals and even potentially terrorists.

One of the most vocal critics is Jaron Lanier (see earlier chapters), who is especially critical of the way he says that Microsoft's email programmes such as Outlook have allowed virus programmes to spread. 'It's amazing that Microsoft is not hauled over the carpet more on this issue,' says Lanier. Emails should not be able to contain embedded programmes, but only text, says Lanier. At a stroke he believes this would stop many virus programmes from spreading.

Microsoft deny that their software is any more vulnerable than those of any other manufacturers. Stuart Okin, chief security advisor for Microsoft UK, says it now has dedicated teams whose main job it is to examine new programmes for any security flaws. But he adds: 'I want to stress that there is no computer platform that is totally secure, because there is always human error and because they are under attack from people who are trying to find a way through.

'None of our competitors have completely secure platforms and we are no more insecure that anyone else. Because of our position we are more attacked than others.'

Okin says that the giant corporation began to look at security very closely around five years ago; till then, he admits, the industry as a whole was 'not that concerned' with security. He adds that it has also had to respond to the demands of customers, for whom security is not necessarily always paramount.

'I can remember finding a vulnerability seven years ago in one of the application security interfaces. When we fixed it, it broke a series of applications that had been developed by other companies. One of our very big customers told us to put the bug back in. They said that the risk to them from not being able to use the application that they wanted was greater than the risk from the security hole.'

Now, says Okin, Microsoft is working closely with governments and the police to fight cyber crime. 'We also work with the banks, who often have larger investigative teams than the police.'

On a wider point Jaron Lanier believes that internet fraud will continue to get worse, despite the ever-greater attempts to secure people's online identities.

His short-term prediction is therefore a gloomy one. 'My inclination has been to believe that we will go through an extended period of chaos over the issue of internet fraud and that at the end of this there will be some very fundamental changes to the way we think about money and transactions.'

Lanier's own idea is that instead of trying to protect the identity of the person, we need to put the emphasis on complete traceability of money. 'What might have to happen is that we move to a less abstract form of money, where you have a global history of each pence, each penny, each rupee.

'If there is a global history of the movement of all currencies everywhere then it becomes impossible to create a fraud for a portion of it. For example, if you are tracing a part penny/rupee from one place to another place and you think, "Actually I am going to pretend that it went there", that would be inconsistent with what the world would remember about the whole global history of that money.' He adds: 'I think that would make fraud almost impossible. And easy to trace.'

Such issues will become increasingly important; as the new century goes on and the convergence of the internet and television proceeds apace, it is inevitable that the number of people using e-commerce will increase. As a result, the number of attacks upon those people using the internet will also rise - a prospect alarming many of those working with the technology, and not just because of any potential public loss of confidence in the system.

What keeps many scientists awake at night is the possibility that someone may inadvertently create a computer virus - or cause an accident by interfering with the technology underlying the internet - that may crash the whole network.

There is also the very real likelihood that a botnet could collapse the world wide web. Given the inter-related nature of the system and the growing dependence on it from all walks of life, such a collapse would inevitably lead to loss of life as well as having huge financial cost.

The prospect of such events has lead some in the technology community to discuss the possibility of having online 'MOTs for computers' in same the way it is now necessary to have an annual check on a car to ensure it is roadworthy.

A related proposal is that users should have a 'computer driving license', whereby all those using technology would be required to pass a test on communication and technology ethics before being allowed to use an internet-enabled computer.

For a senior cyber cop such as Detective Chief Superintendent Len Hynds, head of the National Hi-Tech Crime Unit in the UK, one of the key issues is raising the public awareness of cyber crime; how people are affected by it and how they can prevent it.

'How do you reach out to the people that don't read the security press or the IT press?' he says. 'There's a section of society for whom technology holds no interest whatsoever or a very limited interest. But because of the way our lives are changing, technology touches them as it touches everybody, so we need to find ways of reaching this audience.'

Len Hynds believes that the education of the public should start early. 'In the long term the security issues are things that could be built into training and education in schools.'

And while far from committing himself, Britain's senior cyber cop describes the concept of MOTs for computers and driving license equivalents for computer users as an 'interesting idea'.

Dave Thomas of the FBI's Cyber Division agrees that some of the answers lie in greater public awareness as well as more pro-active moves from industry on computer security. 'The average user has to understand this thing that is the internet and what their computer is and is capable of, and they have got to protect themselves.'

'I think industry has to play its part in making these things more secure,' he adds. Thomas also sees parallels with road safety and the fact that manufacturers were obliged to fit safety belts in cars. 'The need for putting those seat belts in was the enormous number of crashes and of people dying, and so they put in safety features to try and prevent that.'

He points both to the introduction of automatic safety patches for Windows XP and the extra security features of XP's service pack two as signs that industry is listening. Thomas also says that the ISPs need to play a major role too.

'They're the ones that are going to see the bot networks and they're the ones that are going to be able to identify those for us and they're probably going to be the only ones that are going to be able to neutralise those bot networks.'

One encouraging sign for Thomas is the increased co-operation between international law enforcement agencies, without which foreign-based criminals cannot be brought to justice.

'I can track various attacks in various different parts of the world, but I have no powers as a US law enforcement officer to go and do anything about those attacks if that country does not have the technology or the means to do that; then my investigation ends,' he says.

'How far we go really depends on the level of co-operation and diplomacy we have with each individual country. We have outstanding relations with the Brits, we have outstanding relations with the Canadians, with the Australians and many, many, many countries.'

Raising their game

It seems clear that if cyber crime is to be successfully combated in the coming decade, there are three main groups who need to raise their game and take far more responsibility for their part in this battle. These three groups are government, the computer and software industry, and the public – the computer users. Their responsibilities will inevitably overlap.

Governments such as those in the UK have begun to talk a good game when it comes to cyber crime, and could certainly not be accused of ignoring the protection of Britain's national infrastructure from cyber attack. But the message coming out from the UK is a confused one, shared between the Home Office, Cabinet Office and the Department of Trade and Industry.

There has been little attempt to educate the wider public about the risks of cyber crime and a complete lack of imaginative proposals in this area. For example, the dangers of identity theft should be as widely publicised as the risk of having your car stolen or your bag snatched. Where also is the equivalent of the Highway Code for the internet; a Superhighway Code?

More pressure could also be put on computer and software manufacturers to ensure their products are safe and that the issue of security is emphasised to their customers.

Meanwhile the computer and software industry needs to do far more to raise awareness of security issues. When customers buy a new PC or Mac, the retailer and/or manufacturer should ensure that the user is aware of the type of risks involved in using a computer and how to protect against those risks. Public awareness is slowly growing over antivirus software but the recognition by people using broadband that they also need firewalls – arguably more important than AV software – is poor. Meanwhile software manufacturers – and this includes Microsoft – have a duty to produce programmes and operating systems that are safe from cyber attack. Not to do so is a complete failure of responsibility.

Finally, computer users need to wake up to their own responsibility when it comes to digital hygiene. If we all protected ourselves properly with updated AV software and firewalls, then the potential for criminals to use viruses, worms, Trojans and denial of service attacks on others would be greatly reduced. Individual users need to learn that we are all in this together in a digital society, and that the criminal as ever will always exploit the weakest links.

A CYBER MANIFESTO

Arising from the above, the authors modestly propose a Cyber Manifesto in an attempt to improve the Western world's digital hygiene and prevent cyber crime. We propose that:

- Governments need to educate the public better about the dangers of cyber crime, perhaps with a series of high-profile advertising campaigns.
- Computer safety must be taught in schools to all pupils, not just those interested in computer science.

- Governments should devise a minimum safety standard for computers and software and this should be imposed on manufacturers.
- Retailers and manufacturers should be compelled to make security issues far more high profile at the point of sale of both hardware and software.
- Governments and the computer industry should compile a list of do's and don'ts for those using computers and the internet; a 'Superhighway Code'.
- Governments should consider the need for a kind of 'MOT' for computers to ensure they are properly protected, and a driving license equivalent for computer users.
- Individuals need to be reminded that they could potentially be legally liable for negligently failing to protect their own computer if it is taken over by criminals to harm others.
- Manufacturers and retailers need to be reminded that they could potentially be legally liable for failing to make adequate warnings about the dangers of cyber space.
- Countries that refuse to pass laws against cyber crime and that are known to harbour cyber criminals should be named and shamed; the export of new computer technology to such areas could be banned until they fell into line.
- The funding of specialist hi-tech crime police units should be maintained and if necessary increased to match the ever-growing sophistication and resources of organised cyber criminal gangs.

Even adopting the above measures will not, of course, end cyber crime. As we stated right at the start of this book, crime has always been with us and always will, and cyber space is simply the latest medium that crime has exploited. That is the nature of human society. But these measures will hugely help in the fight against cyber crime and the struggle to convince the public that computers and the internet are overwhelmingly beneficial to modern society. Both battles are worth fighting, and both are worth winning.

References

Introduction: A New World of Crime

1. John Leyden, 'Email scammers target Halifax, Nationwide, Citibank', 27 October 2003. For more information see www.theregister.co.uk/2003/10/27/email_scammers_target_halifax_nationwide/.
2. The Office for National Statistics, 2003 e-commerce survey
3. Interactive Media in Retail Group (IMRG), www.imrg.org
4. The Office for National Statistics, monthly bulletin on UK retail sales, 18 November 2004
5. International Security Studies at the University of Pittsburgh, www.gspia.pitt.edu
6. See www.cert.org.
7. Graeme Newman and Ronald V Clarke, *Superhighway Robbery: Preventing E-commerce Crime*, Willan Publishing, 2003
8. Jill Dando Institute of Crime Science, www.jdi.ucl.ac.uk

Chapter 1: The Rise of the Cyber Criminal

1. *Esquire* magazine (US), October 1971
2. A copy of Ron Rosebaum's article can be found on Draper's own website at www.webcrunchers.com/crunch/esq-art.html.
3. Hugo Cornwall, *The Hacker's Handbook*, E A Brown Co, 1985. According to the online dictionary Wikipedia, *The Hacker's Handbook* is 'a legendary book on computer hacking'. Copies can be obtained at www.textfiles.com/etext/MODERN/hhbk.
4. Robert Schifreen, 'Why I broke Philip's password,' *Daily Mail*, 3 May 1988. According to Robert Schifreen they set out to highlight two points, 'Firstly, the incompetence of those people whose job it was to keep hackers like myself away from computers. Second, the total lack of legislation on the subject.'

251

Chapter 2: The Fight Against Cyber Crime

1. Frost & Sullivan, 'Analysis Of The World Antivirus Market,' October 2003. Copies of the report can be obtained from http://www.gii.co.jp/english/fs24997_antivirus_market.html
2. Virus Bulletin, UK-based antivirus organisation and magazine, www.virusbtn.com
3. See www.whatpc.co.uk/news/1125100 and www.computerecono mics.com/article.cfm?id=133
4. See www.infragard.net.
5. National Infrastrucutre Security Co-ordination Centre (NISCC), www.niscc.gov.uk/index.html
6. National Hi-Tech Crime Unit (NHTCU), www.nhtcu.org
7. Central Sponsor for Information Assurance (CSIA), www.knowledge network.gov.uk/CO/KIMSCSIA.nsf
6. Computer Electronic Security Group (CESG), www.cesg.gov.uk

Chapter 3: The Rise of the Cyber Cop

1. Details of the NHTCU's background are available at www.nhtcu.org. The NHTCU made its appearance following the publication of 'Project Trawler' by the National Criminal Intelligence Service. This is no longer available from the NCIS website, but copies are available from www.cyber-rights.org/documents/trawler.htm and www.fipr .org/rip/Project%20Trawler.htm.
2. See www.rmcs.cranfield.ac.uk.
3. The Home Office describes the National Technical Assistance Centre's role on its website, www.homeoffice.gov.uk, as 'to provide technical assistance to UK law enforcement and intelligence agencies in order to assist serious crime investigations and national security activities. This assistance includes access to and delivery of warranted intercept.'
4. The FBI's mission statements on cyber crime can be found at: www.fbi.gov/cyberinvest/cyberhome.htm.

Chapter 4: The Hackers

1. See www.sfgate.com/cgi-bin/article.cgi?file=/gate/archive/2001/12/ 13/commmem.DTL. Additional information can be obtained from www.well.com
2. 'Computer hackers held in KGB spy ring alert,' *Daily Express*, 3 March 1989

3. 'Spycatchers – behind the news,' *Computer Talk*, 28 August 1989
4. 'We are technology's biologists,' Schuuchen Tan, *Media Supplement Daily Trouw*, 4 February 1995. A full copy of the text is available from www.dbai.tuwien.ac.at/marchives/ece/0110.html.
5. The story was always denied by officials, as newspaper reports at the time claimed the attacks had taken place on the MoD's SkyNet system; 'Cyber terrorist strikes,' Steve Morris and Peter Rose, *Daily Mail*, 1 March 1999.

Chapter 5: The Virus Writers

1. CNET News.com, 20 August 2003
2. Virtual reality is a form of computer simulation in which a participant has the illusion of being part of an artificial environment. Lanier was the first to coin the term 'virtual reality' and in the early 1980s founded VPL Research, the first company to sell VR products. Lanier's website can be found at: www.advanced.org/jaron.
3. www.wildlist.org
4. The Risks Digest, 'Yet another virus, The Brain Virus,' *Forum on Risks to the Public in Computers and Related Systems*, Volume 6, Issue 25, 11 February 1988
5. Fred Cohen, 'Experiments with Computer Viruses', University of California, 1984 academic paper
6. Stoll was later to become famous for catching a number of hackers from the Chaos Computer Club who were using computer systems he controlled at the University of California, Berkeley to try and steal military secrets. The hackers used Stoll's computers as a jumping off point into the Arpanet, a combined military and academic system that later mutated into the internet. Stoll's story of how he discovered and trapped the hackers is told in his book *The Cuckoo's Egg: Tracking a Spy Through the Maze of Computer Espionage*, Simon & Schuster Inc, 2000.
7. Michael Wines, 'A Family's Passion for Computers, Gone Sour', *New York Times*, 10 November 1988
8. For an interesting eye-witness report of Morris' sentencing by a fellow student visit www.potifos.com/morris.html.
9. Script viruses are written in script programming languages, such as VBScript and JavaScript. VBScript (Visual Basic Script) and JavaScript viruses make use of Microsoft's Windows Scripting Host to activate

themselves and infect other files. Since Windows Scripting Host is available on Windows 98 and Windows 2000, the viruses can be activated simply by double-clicking the *.vbs or *.js file from Windows Explorer. HTML viruses use the scripts embedded in HTML files to do their damage. These embedded scripts automatically execute the moment the HTML page is viewed from a script-enabled browser. In simple terms the viruses take advantage of extremely basic commands to start themselves. So just clicking on an innocuous looking file will activate them. The html viruses exploit the fact that Windows opens html pages so that they can be looked at, this means that some email programs which automatically open and display messages could be used to infect computers – so simply receiving an email means that your computer became infected.

10. See www.icsalabs.com/html/communities/antivirus/melissa/melissa2a.shtml.

11. See BBC online news report, 2 May 2002:
http://news.bbc.co.uk/1/hi/world/americas/1963371.stm.

12. 26 September 2000. Transcript of online chat can be accessed at:
http://archives.cnn.com/2000/TECH/computing/09/26/guzman.chat.

13. Edited version of Jaschen's *Stern* interview, 17 June 2004, available at www.sophos.com/virusinfo/articles/netskyhero.html.

14. Part of the BBC Wales interview can be found online at:
http://news.bbc.co.uk/1/hi/wales/2680419.stm.

15. *PC Magazine*, 13 July 2004. Can be accessed online at:
http://www.pcmag.com/article2/0,1759,1612207,00.asp.

16. Western Union is a global money transfer and message services company that helps consumers and businesses transfer money or make payments using money orders and other electronic systems. Using it people can quickly and easily transfer money to Western Union Agents in over 190 countries worldwide – the largest network of its kind.

17. 'Virus Writers in the Wild,' Marcia J Wilson, *Computer Cops*, 27 April 2004; provides links to virus-writing websites for those eager to get close up to virus writers. See www.computercops.biz/article5049.html.

Chapter 6: Identity Theft

1. New release, 'ID Analytics Announces Findings from Largest-Ever Research into Identity Fraud with Cooperation of Business Leaders

Across Multiple Industries – Report Details the Sophistication of Identity Crimes, Providing New Insights into the Behaviors of Criminals', about the *National Report on Identity Fraud*, ID Analytics, Inc., San Diego, US, 25 September 2003. See www.idanalytics.com /news_and_events/20030923.html.

2. National Criminal Intelligence Service (NCIS), www.ncis.co.uk

3. Association for Payment Clearing Services (APACS), www.apacs. org.uk

4. Dinah Greek, 'Police net 12 phishing suspects – Eastern Europeans under arrest as Hi-Tech Crime Unit swoops on addresses in London and Kent,' *Computing*, 5 May 2004

5. NHTCU press release, 5 May 2004

6. www.friendsreunited.co.uk

7. www.privacyinternational.org

8. Around 10 per cent of those who receive faxes and 30 per cent of those who receive emails reply to them, according to Tom Craig, the world's leading expert on West African Organised Crime. Those who reply, then become a target market for WAOC who seek to lure them into other frauds. Craig, a former policeman and now a consultant to big business on the criminals' activities, says those that reply to emails do so because it is relatively easy to do so and adds that because of this 419 receive a lot of prank email replies as well as those from potential victims.

Chapter 7: The Bot Herds

1. Considered one of the most authoritative sources for internet data reports on internet data trends. See www.caida.org/home/.

2. For examples of computer giant IBM using networks in this way, for instance, see: http://news.com.com/2100-1001-961902.html and search the web for the use of 'The Grid'.

3. 'Net crime hits gambling sites on Super Bowl Eve', Reuters, 30 January 2004

4. 'Russian internet extortion gang cracked', *New Scientist*, 22 July 2004

5. Comprehensive press release on the attacks issued from US internet performance monitoring organisation 'Keynote', 18 August 2003; seewww.keynote.com/news_events/releases_2003/03august18.html.

6. Nick Nuttall, 'Kosovo infowarfare spreads', http://news.bbc. co.uk/1/hi/sci/tech/308788.stm.

7. Will Sturgeon, 'Disgruntled employee takes down ex-firm's website with spam attack', *Silicon.com*, 13 July 2004

8. Barton Gellman, 'Cyber attacks by Al Quaeda feared', Washington Post, 27 June 2002

9. One of the best sources on this is Michael Young's 'Scada Systems Security', published by the respected *Sans Institute*, 18 February 2004.

10. www.messagelabs.com

11. For more comprehensive information on all the measures now under consideration by the EU and ITU go to www.itu.int /osg/spu/spam/.

12. www.spamhaus.org

13. Roy Mark, 'Feds can spammers under new act', *Internet News*, 29 April 2004

14. *New York Times*, 30 December 2003

15. According to a monthly spam index maintained by California-based content security firm Clearswift, by December 2004 pornography made up just 3 per cent of all spam messages, down from 22 per cent in June 2003. See www.clearswift.com.

Chapter 8: Sex and Drugs

1. The undated press release can be obtained from the Email Systems website at www.emailsystems.com/media/2/20040426-London%20 Schools%20Final.pdf.

2. See for example: www.crime-research.org/news/26.07.2004/508/.

3. Internet Watch Foundation, www.iwf.org.uk

4. Tim Golden, '16 indicted on charges of internet porn', *New York Times*, 17 July 1996. Details of the arrests and sentencing of the Orchid Club members can be found at www.cybercrimelawyer.com /pages/childporno/orchidclub.html.

5. Details of the Orchid Club's expansion into Operation Cathedral can be found at www.msnbc.msn.com/id/3078773/. Further information on the trial and convictions of those involved in Wonderland and the subject of Operation Cathedral can be found on http://news. bbc.co.uk/1/hi/uk/250800.stm and www.archives.cnn.com/2001 /WORLD/europe/UK/02/13/paedophile.police/index.html. For details of Operation Cathedral see Jason Bennetto, 'Seaside clue led to hoards of child porn', *Independent*, 3 September 1998.

6. David Stout, 'Ninety are arrested in inquiry into child sex ring', *New York Times*, 19 March 2002

References

7. The first details of Operation Ore and its relationship to Candyman are released on the BBC website: http://news.bbc.co.uk/2/hi/uk_news/1998515.stm.
8. Details of Operation Avalanche can be found at http://news.bbc.co.uk/2/hi/uk_news/2445065.stm.
9. NHTCU Press statement August 2, 2004 ref 84/04, 'Man arrested for Online-Indecency': 'In June 2004 Ward was sentenced to 19 years imprisonment at York Crown Court having pleaded guilty to the rape of a nine-month-old baby girl, taking indecent photographs of the rape and distribution of over 33,000 indecent images of children.'

INDEX

Index

ABOUT THE AUTHORS

Michael Streeter is an experienced journalist and author who worked in Fleet Street for many years. Among other roles, he was Whitehall editor at the *Daily Mirror*, legal affairs correspondent on the *Independent* and editor of the *Scottish Daily Express*. Now freelance, he has written a number of books including ones on the history of witchcraft and on the origins and nature of hypnosis.

Peter Warren is a freelance television and print journalist, specialising in investigations, who has worked for BBC2, *The Sunday Times, Observer, Sunday Express* and *Scotland on Sunday* and is an expert on computer security issues.